DEFEND YOUR WEALTH

DEFEND YOUR WEALTH

PROTECTING YOUR ASSETS IN
AN INCREASINGLY VOLATILE WORLD

DANIEL A. PRISCIOTTA
FOREWORD BY ROBERT T. SLEE

PRISCO PUBLISHING
RAMSEY, NJ

Published by
Prisco Publishing
Ramsey, NJ

Publisher's Cataloging-in-Publication Data
Prisciotta, Daniel A.

    Defend your wealth : protecting your assets in an increasingly volatile world / Daniel A. Prisciotta. – Ramsey, NJ : Prisco Pub., 2011.

    p. ; cm.

    ISBN13: 978-0-9846422-0-5

    1. Finance, Personal. 2. Inheritance and succession. 3. Estate planning. I. Title.

    HG179.P75 2011
    332.02401—dc22   2011905728

FIRST EDITION

Project coordination by Jenkins Group, Inc.
www.BookPublishing.com

Interior design by Brooke Camfield

Printed in the United States of America
15 14 13 12 11 • 5 4 3 2 1

DEDICATION

To my sweetheart, Teresa, and our wonderful children,
Michelle and Danny, who bring so much joy into our lives—
you make me a very lucky man.

Contents

SECTION II: DEFEND YOUR FAMILY WEALTH

SECTION III: DEFEND YOUR BUSINESS WEALTH

FOREWORD

By Robert T. Slee

As a person who has owned a number of businesses, I've learned that building wealth is easier than protecting it. I suspect that most successful people feel this way, particularly nowadays. Wealth preservation is currently a sophisticated and timely subject that requires effort and vigilance.

If you're like me, you've been uncertain about how to defend your wealth through wealth preservation planning. Talking with the professionals who claim to be experts in this industry can be unsettling. You get the feeling that they are working for themselves and not for you or your wealth.

Fortunately, this book is one of the most straightforward, most realistic, and easiest to read road maps that you'll find. If you haven't gotten around to taking action because you're just "too busy" running and growing your company, your career, or your portfolio, you are not alone. If you've already done some work in this area, however, you probably suspect that you really should be doing more about protecting your wealth and passing it on to your family in an era when the threats to your wealth are growing.

The time and energy invested in fully understanding your vision, values, and goals for the future, along with proper data gathering and analysis, are more urgent than ever before. The time is now to make critical decisions to reach your specific wealth preservation goals and safeguard all that is important to you, your business, and your family.

Owning assets has never been riskier, and the more you have, the bigger the bull's-eye you are wearing. If you believe that building wealth entitles you to decide how to keep it, *Defend Your Wealth* is a must-read. I have known Dan Prisciotta for many years and have shared dozens of high-net-worth clients with him during that time. They would all agree with me: Dan is a master in this field.

Reading this book is a great way to take the first step on the road toward defending your wealth, achieving financial security, and making a significant difference in the lives of the people you care about most.

Robert T. Slee is founder of MidasNation, a worldwide community that helps business owners dramatically increase the value of their companies. He authored *Private Capital Markets*, *Midas Managers*, and *Midas Marketing*.

ACKNOWLEDGMENTS

I want to acknowledge those who have contributed significantly to this labor of love. We are all passionate about what we do, and the goal of this book truly is to showcase our "deliverables." The coauthors and contributors to *Defend Your Wealth* work with me daily to keep a promise made to our clients to protect their wealth from myriad threats.

I would like to thank my coauthors who have written parts of this book and deserve much credit.

When it comes to understanding and believing in a holistic, comprehensive planning process as described in chapter 2, "The Value of a Planning Process," no one in the industry can hold a candle to Russ Jones, executive director of Sagemark Private Wealth Services (SPWS), affiliated with Lincoln Financial Advisors. Russ's enthusiasm, storytelling abilities, and passion are an inspiration to all members of this elite group throughout the United States. His partner, Doug Richmond, also provided valuable input for our chapter on wealth preservation. I have been involved with Russ, Doug, Bill Wright, and Leslie Marinaro since the founding of SPWS and have proudly participated in its mission to meet the needs of advisors and our high-net-worth clients. Kevin Cox, a leading authority and creative mind in the area of wealth preservation, also reviewed and provided valuable input.

Results are of paramount importance to our firm and our clientele. Mark Gould and Mark Jordan, cofounders of VERCOR Advisors, a leading middle-market investment bank, collaborated with our Equity Strategies Group and recently achieved an (almost) impossible price for the sale of one of our client's businesses. This story is captured in the case study in chapter 6, entitled "Exit Planning: Maximize the Sale of Your Business."

Greg Klipstein, JD, LLM created many of the analytical tools used in the Prescott family case study. His dedication to this effort and client engagements over the years has contributed greatly to our firm's success and the insights in this book.

Bob Teichart has been a mentor and coach from my early days in management at Sagemark, right up to establishing my own planning practice. Bob knows how to keep me on track to serve my clients better. He has recently written an excellent book on coaching and was eager to share his experiences.

Thanks to Mark Sheer, also a coach and author, who painstakingly read every page of the book and made excellent suggestions. Mark has the amazing ability to keep our clients' (and the readers') visions, values, and goals top of mind. He has also taught me the importance of working as a team with the best legal and accounting minds for the benefit of our clients.

Bob Gaida reviewed this book through a variety of lenses. Bob was a successful leader of one of the largest accounting firms in the world. He is now a business consultant who has become a client of mine and, most important, a friend and mentor.

Bob Appel, MBA, JD, LLM, a National Design attorney within our firm, generously gave of his time to review chapter 3, "Wealth Preservation Strategies," and chapter 5, "Building, Protecting, and Transferring Your Business." Bob has been instrumental throughout my career in providing excellent advice and creative case design support for our clients.

Nasser Ali, CFA, CFPR, CRPCR, AAMS, CMFC, our director of planning, reviewed chapter 1, "Threats in an Uncertain World," and provided valuable insight.

I am also grateful to Allan Bell, JD, LLM, chair of the Trust & Estates Practice Group and partner with the law firm of Sills Cummis & Gross PC. Allan has been selected by his peers for inclusion in Best Lawyers in America 2010. He reviewed our section on defending your family wealth and shared his insight and practical experience in counseling high-net-worth families.

Michael Nolan, president of Nolan Financial Group, contributed important content on nonqualified deferred compensation for owners and key executives to our section dealing with planning for the closely held business owner or the family business owner. Mike is considered an expert in this area, and we have successfully collaborated on several client engagements.

Mike Greece provided expert editorial guidance and helped make this book even more relevant and timely for you, the reader.

Finally, I want to thank and acknowledge my dedicated operations manager, Lori Chakonis, for her tireless efforts in organizing all of the materials that went into this book. Amazingly, she also managed to keep our practice humming while I focused on writing.

The writing of *Defend Your Wealth* was indeed a team effort, and I hope you, the reader, benefit from our efforts to help you defend and preserve the wealth you have worked so hard to create.

—Dan Prisciotta

You can find more information at **http://www.danprisciottaspws.com** and **http://www.equitystrategiesgroup.com** and may also sign up to receive our complementary newsletters.

Disclaimer/ Disclosure

This publication is designed to provide information about the subject matter covered. It is sold with the understanding that while the author is a financial advisor and registered representative, he, his firm, and the publisher are not engaged by the reader to render legal, accounting, or other professional service. The purpose of this book is to educate. Neither the author, nor Sagemark Private Wealth Services, nor Lincoln Financial Advisors, nor Equity Strategies Group, nor Daniel A. Prisciotta shall have any liability or responsibility to any person or entity with respect to any loss or damage caused, or alleged to be caused, directly or indirectly by the information contained in this book.

If you do not wish to be bound by the above, you may return this book to the publisher for a full refund.

Any discussion pertaining to taxes in this communication (including attachments) may be part of a promotion or marketing effort. As provided for in government regulations, advice (if any) related to federal taxes that is contained in this communication (including attachments) is not intended or written to be used, and cannot be used, for the purpose of avoiding penalties under the Internal Revenue Code. Individuals should seek advice on the basis of their own particular circumstances from an independent tax advisor.

Securities offered through Lincoln Financial Advisors Corporation, a broker/dealer. Equity Strategies Group is the marketing name used to reflect specialized planning strategies and techniques. Investment advisory services offered through Sagemark Consulting, a division of Lincoln Financial Advisors Corporation, a registered investment advisor. Insurance offered through Lincoln affiliates and other fine companies.

SECTION I

DEFEND YOUR PERSONAL WEALTH

CHAPTER ONE

THREATS IN AN UNCERTAIN WORLD

by Dan Prisciotta

T oday, the wealthy in America are under attack. The current economic crisis has caused many people, especially the affluent, to reevaluate the security of their personal, family, and business wealth. Many are troubled by the volatility of the global economy; a health-care crisis; and threats of inflation, deflation, and political unrest. Unemployment and foreclosures are at record highs, and our national debt is mounting by the trillions of dollars as the result of rampant government spending.

Potential threats to your wealth can be broken down into several categories, including:

1. A tsunami of changing income, capital gains, estate, and generational transfer taxes converging to confiscate your wealth. A new tax law was recently passed that provides clarity for only the next two years. The ultimate fate of tax rates and exemptions has been deferred to the end of 2012, when the new law expires.

2. An onslaught of potential "creditors and predators" standing ready to strike at any time

3. Unprecedented systemic failure and institutional financial mismanagement, creating a backdrop of fear that can strike at the heart of your personal wealth

These threats combine to assault your

- Personal wealth

- Family wealth

- Business wealth

A comprehensive plan of action to defend your wealth is now more urgent than ever.

THE TAX MAN COMETH

The only certainty in the new tax law is that uncertainty and anxiety over future tax rates will return in two years when the Bush-era tax cut extensions lapse. The new law merely postpones the day of reckoning and pushes the debate into the midst of the 2012 presidential race. If consensus is not reached, the new tax amendments will again "sunset" and revert to pre-2002 estate, gift, and GST law. We hope that such draconian increases in taxes will not occur, but no one can predict exactly what will happen.

Record federal budget deficits ($14 trillion and growing; $45,000 per U.S. citizen), long-term high unemployment, and the resulting demands on the government for benefits and resources (at both state and federal levels) can drive taxes to higher levels and may come in many forms.

Expirations

- Tax cuts that previously lowered marginal income tax rates and provided lower rates on dividends and capital gains on the sale of stocks, bonds, businesses, real estate, etc., have been extended for only two more years. They expire on December 31, 2012.

Surcharges

♦ As debate continues on how to fund health-care reform, in 2013, an additional 3.8% Medicare surcharge tax may be assessed on your income from dividends, interest, rents, and capital gains. Couples with adjusted gross incomes over $250,000 (the high net worth) will be especially hard-hit. Will the new tax law also increase the ordinary Medicare tax by 0.9%? Depending on which state you live in, adding another 5%–10% for state income taxes could bring total income taxes to 50%!

Estate Tax Redux

♦ The single largest threat to preserving your family wealth—the estate tax is back! It disappeared for 2010. Now, the tax will kick in for estates worth more than $5 million ($10 million for married couples). That's right: add up the value of your home, portfolio, retirement plan and IRA, business, and everything else you own. If the pile is bigger than $5 million (or $10 million for married couples), Uncle Sam takes upward of 35% if your death occurs in 2011 or 2012. The law sunsets on December 31, 2012. Beyond that, the estate tax crystal ball is unclear. Since most of us do not plan to check out in the next two years, long-term planning is essential.

On December 17, 2010, President Obama signed the **Tax Relief, Unemployment Insurance Reauthorization, and Job Creation Act of 2010 (the Tax Relief Act of 2010).**

This new multibillion-dollar tax cut has tremendous impact on high-net-worth families and opens up an immediate and unprecedented two-year window of opportunity for planning.

Some highlights of the new law are:

♦ The estate tax was retroactively reinstated to January 1, 2010. For those who died in 2010 only, their executor has a choice of either paying the estate tax or electing to have carryover basis rules apply. Most high-net-worth estates will likely make this election.

♦ **For 2010, 2011, and 2012, a $5 million** exemption per person ($10 million for a married couple) is granted for estate and GST taxes (indexed for inflation in 2012). Many feared the return of a $1 million exemption and a 55% tax rate, so passage of this law is excellent news.

- **For 2011 and 2012, the gift tax exemption increases to $5 million** per person ($10 million per couple).

> *The new tax cut— opens up an immediate and unprecedented opportunity for planning.*

- There is a **35%** top tax rate on transfers over the exemption limits.

What an opportunity! In the recent past, lifetime transfers were limited to $1 million per taxpayer ($2 million per couple) before a gift, estate, or GST tax of up to 45% was triggered. For 2011 and 2012 only, it is possible to transfer $10 million of private company stock (or any other asset, i.e., marketable securities, real estate, personal-use assets, etc.) completely free of taxes during your lifetime or upon death. Furthermore, the actual amount transferred can be increased exponentially over time once valuation discounts and advanced planning techniques are used, resulting in massive tax savings. Structured properly, these family assets can also be protected from creditors and predators over multiple generations.

Will everyone be in a position to take advantage of the generosity provided by the new tax law before it expires on December 31, 2012? Absolutely not! Careful planning and financial modeling are necessary to determine whether your financial independence is secure *prior* to engaging in gift giving or other lifetime transfer techniques. For those who can afford to transfer significant amounts of assets during their lifetimes, particularly over the next two years, the tax savings are enormous. For those who have already engaged in sophisticated estate preservation planning, now is the time to revisit those plans to take advantage of this limited opportunity to do more. Confiscatory taxes are already attacking your family wealth. There are numerous timely strategies to minimize the future tax bite, and many will be shared with you throughout this book.

A BULL'S-EYE ON YOUR BACK

More and more, high-net-worth families are becoming targets of public-sector passion for wealth redistribution, as well as private-sector predatory behavior such as lawsuits, divorce proceedings, and even extortion. As a result, successful people increasingly feel as though they have a bull's-eye on their backs.

Today, high-net-worth individuals have more liability lawsuit risks than at any other time in history. If your net worth exceeds the liability limits provided by your insurance carrier, all of your wealth can be exposed. The typical umbrella liability policy won't protect you. Ensuring that you have proper coverage to protect your wealth from lawsuits and legal defense fees can be the simplest and most effective first step toward asset protection. Additional threats include employment practice liability, worker's compensation, or board member or family trustee issues, just to name a few. Asset protection is the process of using legally acceptable methods to ensure that your wealth is not unjustly taken from you. Wealth preservation planning offers an effective way to discourage lawsuits and structure assets to provide legal shelter from potential litigation, as well as taxes.

HOW BIG ARE THE STORM SIGNALS?

Continuous economic turmoil is unthinkable but has become a reality. The stock and real estate markets shudder. Our great nation is bankrupt. The Federal Reserve and the U.S. government have been tap-dancing to prevent a systemic collapse. Stimulus plans and the corollary deployment of cash have had little long-term benefits. The national unemployment rate was 9.4% as of December 31, 2010, and many fear that this is a very conservative estimate. The fact is that as of this writing, 14.5 million Americans are out of work, with another 8.9 million working only on a part-time basis, according to the Department of Labor.

As business activity sinks further, more government intervention into the private sector could occur. Could this trigger massive flight from the U.S. dollar and force the Fed into heavy monetization of unwanted U.S. Treasury debt? If this plays out, it could lead to hyperinflation or skyrocketing interest rates. The U.S. economy is in the longest and deepest economic contraction since the Great Depression, with no near-term stability or recovery in the forecast. Financial markets, industries, and specific businesses are experiencing increasing uncertainty.

Institutional financial mismanagement is widespread. This causes a lack of trust in the financial system of bond dealers, bankers, and broker-age houses, who acted without restraint; scams perpetrated by con artists such as Bernie Madoff and others; and the "too-big-to-fail" institutions. Fed Chairman Ben Bernanke warned in February of 2008 that as many as 150 banks would fail over the upcoming three years. Per the FDIC, 321 banks failed from March of 2008 to December 31, 2010.

The integrity of many financial institutions and advisors has been called into question. In 2008, the Dow Jones Industrial Average plummeted from 13,000 to 8,500. Why? Fear! Panic causes investors to pull out of the stock market and invest in cash equivalents and treasuries. Yields fell below 1%. We even had negative returns for a while. People paid the U.S. Treasury to stash money in the "safe" government mattress. Fear was higher at that point than it was right after 9/11. Shell-shocked investors remained in cash and watched as the S&P gained 20.6% over the last four months of 2010. People have been so badly burned by poor advice in the stock market and real estate that they don't know whom to listen to anymore. Emotions are taking over, lots of money sits on the sidelines, and people are searching for answers.

The World Around Us

Increasingly, we seem to be experiencing natural disasters such as floods, earthquakes, fires, hurricanes, and shifting climates. In our man-made world, we have seen an unprecedented wave of financial skulduggery, shaky infrastructure, environmental issues, oil spills, wars, immigration problems, and ongoing displays of humankind's inhumanity to others. People are increasingly worried about a significant "Black Swan"–type event, for example, a disruptive cyber attack, bombs, crippled financial markets, declaration of national bankruptcy by a significant country, political subdivision, class or age warfare issues, and the global effects of shifts in political power throughout the world. Any of these events can increase risk, uncertainty, and loss of financial security.

Public issues do become your business because they threaten your personal, family, and business wealth and well-being, and they impact long-term financial survival. We constantly hear, "Am I OK? Is my family OK? Will the world around me ever be OK again? Do I have enough? What is enough?"

WHAT YOU CAN CONTROL

With the constant threats of increased taxes, a shifting political climate and economic meltdown, keeping your guard up is more important than ever. How do you defend yourself while at the same time manage your business and investments, spend time with your family, and have a life?

If so many things are out of control, you now actively need to defend your wealth. This book will focus on helping you control the things you can while keeping your eyes open to adjust for developing changes. Clearly, high-net-worth families will always have ways to use the tax code and legal system to protect their wealth. But with the new threat environment already in place, people need to exert more energy to preserve freedom, independence, security, peace of mind, stability, and the integrity of their financial affairs. Consider the myriad of risks and exposures; identify the minefields and think about how to steer around them or defuse them before they blow up. Unfortunately, many people see the threats and don't act. The goal of this book is to encourage action through a holistic, cross-disciplinary approach.

This book is organized into three sections:

I. Defend Your Personal Wealth

II. Defend Your Family Wealth

III. Defend Your Business Wealth

DEFEND YOUR PERSONAL WEALTH

"Am I OK?"

"Will all of these threats to my wealth cause me to run out of money, give up my lifestyle, or become dependent on others?"

This is the question we hear day in and day out, at all income and net worth levels. "Are my investments OK? How do I know for sure?" Do you really know what your rate of return on investments was for the past 12 months or year to date? REAL return (less inflation) is even worse. For the time period of 2001–2010, the S&P 500 gained 1.4% per year (before taxes). Inflation has risen by 2.3% per year. Most people are actually walking backward! What have you done to offset these negative real rates of return? Have you ever discussed it with a trusted advisor? What about the increasing costs associated with long-term health care and their effect on your assets?

Don't get discouraged or overwhelmed. You can plan and prepare. Personal wealth protection fits into a holistic wealth preservation plan. It starts with an inventory of available resources compared to your expenses or lifestyle needs. It continues with identifying the gap between what has been done and what should be done going forward to defend your wealth.

Obviously, your income tax liability greatly impacts your personal wealth. The Tax Relief Act of 2010 temporarily extends the top income tax bracket of 35% for an additional two years. Lower capital gains and dividend tax rates have also been extended. Let the good times roll. Perhaps now is the time to consider income tax strategies to accelerate income into years of lower tax rates and defer expenses into higher-tax years when they become more valuable. Prior to taking action, your long-term comprehensive plan must be analyzed.

DEFEND YOUR FAMILY WEALTH

"Is My Family OK?"

Numerous threats to your family wealth include:

- A neglected, out-of-date wealth preservation plan and estate documents. A plan more than three years old should receive a comprehensive review. Inappropriate or outdated wills, trusts, powers of attorney, and health-care proxies can do more harm than you realize.

- Children who are uninformed, inexperienced, and unprepared to handle large sums of money. Unfortunately, divorce and drug or alcohol problems are on the rise.

- Creditors your children (and grandchildren) may face, including siblings, divorcing and disgruntled spouses, bankruptcy, contract, or tort (malpractice, slips and falls, automobile accidents, etc.)

- Dying too soon or living too long. A shortened or extended life expectancy can jeopardize family wealth distribution.

- The wrong fiduciaries and a lack of proper successors or trust protectors. These unfortunate conditions place assets at risk.

- Not adjusting your plans for births, deaths, adoptions, special health needs, or other family changes

- Lack of liquidity to pay estate taxes. This can result in the forced sale of your most valuable family assets, such as a business or income-producing real estate. Even if your estate is liquid (has cash or short-tem investments on hand), the liquidity you stockpile is itself subject to taxes. The answer is to create a tax-exclusive stash of liquidity.

Another often unrealized threat to your wealth is the lack of frequent attention to your life insurance policies. More than $1 trillion of life insurance is now owned in trusts in the United States—not a static buy-and-hold asset. The industry and policies have changed dramatically over the years. Since the financial markets collapsed, wealthy families have been reexamining their investment portfolios and searching for answers. They expect up-to-date analysis and recommendations for changes. You should expect no less from your life insurance portfolio and the advisors and trustees who

> *Another often unrealized threat to your wealth is the lack of frequent attention to your life insurance policies.*

manage it. Trustees have a fiduciary duty to make changes to trust-owned life insurance, just as you would expect to make changes to an investment portfolio held in trust. Yet most trustees (whether professionals, such as accountants or lawyers) or your family members often do little more than glance at a statement and pay the premium when it comes due. Such indifference could cost your family millions.

Life insurance policies are complex and are impacted by many of the same external forces that affect your investments, i.e., decreasing interest and dividend rates, lack of stock market performance (if a variable policy), and financial challenges insurance companies themselves face. Add to this:

- Longer life expectancies and declining mortality changes

- Absence of no-lapse guarantees

- Medical underwriting anomalies

- Life settlement and viatical sales

- New regulations for split-dollar insurance taxation and administration

- Vanishing premiums that don't vanish

- Repricing of policies

Are you sure that your policies are performing as well as they should be? How would you know? Are they structured and paid for correctly? Are your insurance policies alleviating your estate tax problem or exacerbating it? With the recent increase in the estate tax exemption, many people are wondering whether they should continue to maintain existing life insurance policies acquired to pay taxes. Now that some estates have fallen below the taxable threshold, should they continue to pay premiums? Should policies be cancelled, reduced, sold, or kept in force in anticipation of future tax increases?

Ordinarily, a thorough policy review should be conducted at least once every three years to protect you, your trustees, and your beneficiaries. With all of the tax turbulence and changes in the insurance marketplace, a thorough review is now a necessity.

DEFEND YOUR BUSINESS WEALTH

"Is My Business OK? It Is the Primary Source of My Wealth!"
Here are other reasons to stay vigilant:

What would happen to your business if your partner or coshareholder met an untimely death? Do you have a shareholders' agreement (aka a buy-sell agreement)? Is it up to date? Does the price reflect today's valuation? Unless your agreement has been reviewed in the past 12–18 months, it may pose a serious threat to you, your business, and your family. Is the agreement properly funded to give it teeth and make it operative? Without proper funding, the burden of additional debt assumed by you, your partner(s), or the business could be crushing.

Similarly, what will happen if the banks call in loans and mortgages that you have signed for and guaranteed personally? An infusion of cash at a critical point in time (such as the death of the borrower or guarantor) can make the difference between business survival and business failure. How do you attract, retain, and reward key employees? Everyone offers the typical package of 401(k) plans, medical benefits, dental insurance, etc. An employer can make a difference by offering special incentive programs to reward long-term retention. This can be an excellent alternative to giving up equity or cash now. These nonequity performance packages can also be designed creatively to align with corporate growth goals and increased revenues and profitability. The better the employee performs, the bigger the payoff will be in the end. These programs can also serve as a sort of "golden handcuffs," in that if the employee leaves before an agreed-upon time frame, benefits will be reduced or forfeited.

A recent McKinsey study stated that less than 30% of family businesses survive into the third generation of family ownership.

> *A recent McKinsey study stated that less than 30% of family businesses survive into the third generation of family ownership.*

Many factors threaten your business wealth, including:

- Not knowing the value of your business for different purposes, i.e., collateral, estate and gift taxes, future sale, etc. Planning is difficult if you don't know what it's worth.

- Lack of a business succession plan. Who will lead your business after your retirement, disability, or death?

- Operational issues. Who will run your company in your absence? Will key employees stay or go? Issues of compensation, governance, dealing with inactive siblings, etc., need to be addressed.

- Lack of a buy-sell agreement, the wrong agreement, or one that is underfunded and can't become operative without potentially disrupting or even bankrupting the business with debt.

- The financial and legal structure of stock transfers to children. Consider the emotional impact on parents, as well as children, throughout the transfer process.

- Tax planning to mitigate income, capital gains, and gift and estate taxes

- Creation of liquidity to pay remaining unavoidable taxes due at death and avoid forced liquidation of the business.

- Corporate taxes, a constant treat that hits businesses especially hard these days. Increasing income taxes directly affect your bottom line and ability to create (or just maintain) jobs, provide employee benefits, satisfy lenders, perform R&D, compete effectively, and maintain your lifestyle.

- Increased regulation, compliance requirements, and bureaucratic red tape

- Insufficient capital

- Lack of an exit strategy to get maximum value and minimize taxes

- Employee benefit packages that fall out of compliance or become prohibitively expensive or ineffective

- Lawsuits

"But I've Had it All Done!"

We caution you not to fall into the proverbial "I've had it all done" mind-set. In more than 25 years of practice, I have never met a client whose wealth defense could not be meaningfully improved or updated in some way. Our clients have found that the difference between merely having their planning work done versus having it done as well as possible can literally mean hundreds of thousands or millions of dollars in additional wealth protected or taxes saved. No single advisor has a monopoly on all of the good ideas. Even if he or she does, by the time he or she figures it all out, the rules change again. For example, our real estate clients are experts in the real estate industry, our manufacturing clients know everything there is to know in their niche, etc. They don't know, nor do they want to know, wealth preservation to the depth of detail that we know and live every day. It's truly a team effort. Proper planning requires working in concert with experts and advisors, such as your CPA and attorney, to provide a truly coordinated effort to keep you out of harm's way.

Stay in Bounds

We've found that our clients want solutions that are advanced and cutting edge but not into the gray area that could get them into trouble, i.e., IRS audits, penalties, or worse. Certain red flags such as the requirement for you to sign a "hold harmless" or nondisclosure agreement to learn about a black-box tax strategy are out of bounds. The number of IRS audits has risen. Those with incomes of $1 million or more experienced the largest increase in IRS audits in 2010; 8.36% of all tax returns were audited, up from 6.42% in the prior year. That's one out of every 12 tax returns filed. It is more important than ever to plan properly and comply with the law.

We will not cover tax avoidance, offshore strategies, or anything bordering on unethical. The arcane world of asset protection trusts is full of hazards, as well as opportunities. Choose the wrong foreign asset protection trust and you could wind up in jail. Certain domestic trusts could make you a test case for the U.S. Supreme Court. Certain trusts set up to avoid creditors, after it is too late, may be viewed as a conspiracy to commit fraud. The strategies in this book are clear, legal, and well tested. Pros and cons will be addressed. At the end of the day, implementation decisions are always yours.

My coauthors and I urge you to become educated, using tools such as *Defend Your Wealth*. An informed client is always the best client. This book is not intended to give you an exhaustive technical dissertation but rather a practical familiarity of the issues and concepts, along with a comfort level to ask your advisor the right questions to help you make proactively sound decisions.

CHAPTER TWO

THE VALUE OF A PLANNING PROCESS

By Dan Prisciotta and Russ Jones

S*o, our world is more complex and perilous today than ever. This creates uncertainty and poses challenges to your financial future. How do you make it all clear and understandable? How do you better prepare yourself for important decisions that will preserve, grow, and transfer the assets you have worked a lifetime to achieve?*

It's all about following a process that anticipates and helps you see the solutions clearly. You are the center of the process. Your advisors are your advocates and defenders. Ultimately, your success is measured by the creation and implementation of a personalized wealth preservation plan through a process that helps maximize the probability of attaining your vision, values, and goals.

Congratulations! The very fact that you are reading this book implies two very important things: first, having a comprehensive, holistic, well-thought-out plan to defend your wealth is important to you and your family and, second, you have already achieved—or are on your way toward accomplishing—a financial component of the American Dream and have wealth to defend.

By "American Dream" we mean that you likely started with very little and have through sheer will, hard work, intelligence, and perseverance (and maybe a little luck) managed to accumulate significant net worth. For that you are to be truly congratulated. However, you may or may not be aware that you are currently being pursued by a ravenous and relentless horde of people (described earlier) wanting to take away a significant part (their "fair share") of your financial success. They have, up until now, been only a grumbling partner or a somewhat nagging problem, largely unseen (except for the April 15 and quarterly tax payments and the occasional legal shot across the bow).

That said, one must understand that not to plan for these potential adversities and protect oneself is tantamount to inviting them in. A holistic, comprehensive, and sustainable wealth preservation plan is what will minimize the likelihood that they will triumph.

We all remember the old adage "Failing to plan is a plan to fail." In this chapter, we will look at the many advantages to having a well-thought-out and well-executed wealth preservation plan, what a well-orchestrated planning process looks like, and, conversely, the dramatic consequences of failing to have a comprehensive and holistic plan.

WHO ARE THE "HIGH NET WORTH"?

This book is written for high-net-worth individuals (and those who plan to be) and their families. Our definition of "high net worth" is more than $10 million. This includes the value of your real estate, savings and investments, retirement plans, business interests, and personal effects (less liabilities, such as mortgages). As our clients' net worths approach and exceed $100 million, their issues become even more complex and perilous. Some estimates identify more than 700,000 high-net-worth families in the United States, representing more than $61 trillion in assets. This represents a mind-boggling account receivable for the IRS in terms of income, capital gains, gift, estate, and generation transfer taxes.

Some feel uncomfortable with the terms "high net worth," "affluent," or "wealthy." Some don't feel it, citing that they don't consider themselves to be high net worth. This is often because their definition of wealth is felt in comparison to others they befriend or associate with who display greater wealth. Fancy cars, jewelry, and mansions are not necessarily signs of real wealth. Many of the clients we work with are "invisible": understated, conservative, and unapparent. Yes, they live extremely well and take excellent care of themselves and their families, but they are not overly conspicuous about their wealth and spending habits. We have discovered that those who lavishly display wealth often don't have it—at least not for very long.

Years ago when speaking at educational workshops, I described categories of "spenders" and "savers." I would ask the audience members which category they thought they fell into, and almost all of them raised their hands as savers—which makes perfect sense. The spenders were not in attendance! Excessive spenders earn enough money to support their lifestyles but fail to accumulate much wealth for their retirement and, ultimately, to pass on assets to their children, grandchildren, and charities of their choice. They do not create a legacy to pass on. They are consuming it now and, by their actions, don't care about planning for the future.

Another interesting aspect discovered over the years is that many high-net-worth people don't *feel* wealthy because of restricted cash flow. From time to time, some people feel that they are cash poor but balance sheet rich. Their wealth is often tied up in closely held business interests, real estate holdings, non-dividend-paying stocks, or other assets that don't pay a very high current income all of the time. On paper, they have a high net worth and live comfortably, but they don't feel as though they have sufficient cash flow, liquidity, or high spending habits. They don't see themselves appearing on TV shows such as yesterday's *Lifestyles of the Rich and Famous* or today's MTV *Cribs* or the Wealth TV network. Still others have the cash flow, but their beliefs about money and their upbringing (Depression-era or children of Depression-era parents) have not programmed them to spend extravagantly. Good for them!

If you don't derive satisfaction from keeping up with the Joneses, then don't. If you are the Joneses, then maybe it's time to review your spending habits relative to your long-term goals to make sure that they are attainable.

We are certainly not passing judgment on how people choose to spend their money. In fact, it is just the opposite. A person's lifestyle and legacy goals are specific to that person. Each person has a vision of his or her ideal future. Our job is to help you obtain it by crystallizing your goals and analyzing your current assets, resources, and income compared to your expenses and then providing feedback and guidance on how best to accomplish your vision and defend against erosion of those goals. Most of our clients are extremely good at earning money and excelling in their careers or businesses. However, they are not often stewards of their own wealth. Furthermore, they find focusing on things such as tax management, estate preservation, and business succession difficult because they are so immersed in their careers or running their businesses day to day.

Our job, as advisors, is to take the burden of planning off of your shoulders and put it on ours. Together, we can address and resolve all of your pressing wealth preservation issues. We will discuss this process, in much more detail, throughout the book.

How Did the High Net Worth Become That Way?

Did they inherit their millions? Did they come from blue-collar beginnings? Wall Street, Main Street . . . how did they get there? The answers vary and may surprise you.

One might say that many of the highly successful people in this country are heroes. Most of our clients made their wealth as entrepreneurs: starting or growing a business, managing a company, or running a financial institution. They are remarkable people who took an idea and turned it into a business or investment that after 20, 30, or 40 years of hard work made them wealthy. Along the way, they brought jobs, energy, innovation, and prosperity to those around them. They often deferred gratification as they toiled and built up their net worth. They don't typically own personal helicopters or Leer jets. Their rise to high-net-worth status was not always linear. Often, there were setbacks and doubts along the way that required perseverance and courage and often called for taking risks and course corrections. But they stayed at it until they became successful. Most are captains of industry who excelled in fields such as:

- Manufacturing
- Technology

- Real estate

- Energy

- Finance, including investment banking, private equity, hedge funds, and Wall Street executives

- Publishing and media

- Sales and marketing

- Food services

- Retail

- Health care

- Government contractors

- Aerospace and defense

- Life sciences

Some were born in the United States, and others were immigrants. Some had formal education with postgraduate degrees from top universities, and others were dropouts with street smarts. Some inherited wealth. Most started out with nothing. Some are in long-term first marriages. Others are in second or third marriages, with children along the way.

Does luck play a role? Timing? Certainly they help, but more often it's vision and hard work over an extended period of time and mastery of their craft. These people are often very competitive and share love and passion for their work, children, grandchildren, and often extended families, as well as charitable causes.

A Fully Integrated Planning Process

Michael Gerber, in his classic business book *The E-Myth Revisited*, suggests that in order to be as successful as possible and to then have that success be repeatable,

> *All worthwhile ventures must have a system, process, procedure, and "how-to" manual.*

all worthwhile ventures must have a **system, process, procedure, and "how-to" manual** (S, P, P, HTM). His reasoning is quite elegant:

- Having a S, P, P, HTM increases the likelihood of success for that venture.

- It allows that venture to be replicated by more than just one person or group and in more than one location.

- The outcome provides a greatly enhanced sense of confidence in your plan working and thereby accomplishing your goals.

The bottom line is that having a S, P, P, HTM allows you, your business, and your family to know what you are intending to do, how you are intending to do it, and why—before you do it.

In this regard, having a S, P, P, HTM is much like running a play in football.

Why do professional football players (and let's focus on the offensive side of the ball for a moment) spend so much time scripting plays, practicing those plays, working out, focusing on the opponents' defensive alignments, watching films, etc.? In short, it is because if they don't, they will likely lose the game. The defense does the same things. They practice defensive schemes, work out, script plays, and create a climate for winning and achieving success.

In many ways, this is the same situation that high-net-worth individuals face in their financial lives. If the high-net-worth individuals don't build a game plan (script plays for different scenarios) and practice those plays (keep the plays up to date and fresh), the opposing team—the IRS, creditors, business competitors, etc.—will beat them silly. In other words, whether we admit it or not, planning, or less than adequate planning, has consequences, often severe.

Conversely, most people (myself included) would rather endure a trip to the dentist without Novocain than embark on a plan of this scope and magnitude. It often requires us to think about unpleasant things. It will cost money to have a plan created and implemented. It will need to be maintained and updated. It involves areas we are, for the most part, not well versed in: taxes, estate documents, retirement planning, business succession plans, concerns about our children and grandchildren, and on and on.

To make matters worse, who wants to discuss a plan concerning your own death? Disability? Long-term care? How short you may fall of reaching financial independence? Who will run and/or is capable of running your business when you are not around? These topics are not on most folks' top 10 list—that's for sure.

How about reviewing all of the investment missteps we have made? We train ourselves to have selective memory and remember the great trades, not the ones that burned us. What about issues concerning our children's decision-making abilities? What we might be owed from (or owe to) a prior marriage? How about the amount of taxes we would owe if we were to die today or 10, 20, or 30 years from now? How about the fears we have regarding our businesses, either doing extremely well or faltering? How about the who, how, and when of someone taking over and running our businesses? Should it be our children? Our partners' children? Our key employees? Where will they get the money to buy us out? Will we ultimately have to buy ourselves out by paying them (one way or another) to buy us out? What alternatives do we have?

Who can you even talk to about these issues? Your spouse? While your spouse is probably closest to you in many ways and trusted, he or she may not be sufficiently familiar with these kinds of issues and decisions. Your partner? He or she may be too close, involved, or threatened by this sort of discussion. Your neighbor? The answer is probably no to all of the above.

Ultimately, all of these concerns and obstacles to maintaining your wealth underscore the extent of the need for comprehensive and holistic planning. Said another way, even though we can list dozens of reasons to avoid doing this sort of planning, the avoidance doesn't change the urgent and pressing need. Avoidance will only worsen the outcome and could lead to more financial pain and loss.

The System, Process, Procedure, and "How-to" Manual of Building Your Plan

A comprehensive, holistic plan involves, well, being comprehensive and holistic—meaning your wealth preservation plan should cover *at the very least*:

- Estate preservation and documents
- Asset protection
- Business succession or exit planning
- Income taxes
- Financial independence/retirement
- Philanthropy
- Risk Management and insurance
- Investment planning
- Lifetime gifting
- Multigenerational legacy planning

It should also address any and all threats to your personal wealth. To mention just a few:

- Taxes, such as income, capital gains, alternative minimum, gift, estate, generational transfer
- Divorce (yours and your heirs')
- Liability concerns
- Creditor issues
- Financial mismanagement
- Illness or disability
- Premature or just plain "mature" death

- Property and casualty claims; absent proper coverage, your entire net worth could be left exposed

- Economic shifts, such as inflation, stock market crashes, lower/ higher interest rates

- If you own a business, your plan should address succession issues, retention of key personnel, valuation, and effects of contingencies such as death, disability, and retirement

- Inflation and potential loss of purchasing power

- Long-term support of family members: parents in need of long-term care or children who can't find jobs after graduation in need of financial support (more prevalent than ever)

- Rising health-care costs

- Lack of investment performance

- Improper asset allocation for your stage of life, risk tolerance, and need for income or growth

Specifically, each of the above items should be viewed from the perspective of you and your family and your family's family; i.e., a plan should consider each of the following groups: spouse, children/stepchildren (generation 2), grandchildren (generation 3), and beyond (generation(s) 4, 5, 6, 7, etc.). Siblings, nieces, nephews, cousins, parents, grandparents, and additional significant others, as defined by you, should also be considered.

DEFEND YOUR WEALTH: FOUR-STEP PROCESS

Step 1—**Discovery**: Discover what you want to achieve with your wealth (and business).

- Your vision, values, and goals

- Time frames for achievement

- Assets/liabilities

- Income/expenses

Step 2—**Document audit**: Assess your current wealth defense, i.e., what you have done so far to protect your wealth. Identify threats, such as estate taxes, income taxes, marketability of your business, asset protection, premature death, disability, etc. Audit the following documents:

- Wills and trusts

- Tax returns (personal and business)

- Investment statements

- Insurance policies and statements

- Business financial statements (balance sheets, profit and loss statements)

- Business benefits programs, etc.

Step 3—**Brainstorming**: Evaluate your alternatives and discuss pros and cons of each strategy to defend your wealth.

- Creation of your financial independence model

- Business succession/exit plan

- Wealth preservation strategies

Step 4—**Action plan**: Implement your selected action items.

- Prioritize

- Assign action items to your advisors (and yourself) to implement

- Impose a time frame to get things done

- Follow up and monitor as internal and external changes occur

THE FAMILY LEGACY PYRAMID: "ARE WE OK?"

The key issues to defending your wealth are highlighted in the pyramid on the next page. Starting with a solid foundation is always a wise first step.

Our experience in working with thousands of very high-net-worth families during the past 25-plus years has led to the conclusion that in all family plans, the single most important objective is to make sure that the people desiring to create a plan (you and your spouse/significant other) are OK (as we show on the pyramid, "Are we OK?").

> *The single most important objective is to make sure that the people desiring to create a plan are OK.*

Our experience is that exactly zero families say that they are willing to plan for successive generations and large community charitable gifts until the creators of the plan know that their personal wealth is protected and they feel OK, however that is defined in their minds. This usually means making sure that you (or you and your spouse, if married) won't (1) run out of money, (2) lose the lifestyle you have worked so hard to create, (3) or wind up dependant on your children or the government for support. Even wealthy people live in a state of fear over this.

Family Legacy Pyramid

Will you be able to give back to the community or the charities?

Is our Community OK?

Charitable Desires
- Civic
- Religious
- Community Groups

Once you and your spouse are "OK," what does it mean for your family to be "OK?"

Is our Family OK?

Estate Planning	Estate/Asset Protection	Business Succession
• Multi Generational	• D,L,C, Fin. Mgmt., F.E.T.	Exit Planning
	• Distribution provisions	529 Planning
	• Dynasty concerns – Bene. Prep. GSTT	

You've succeeded in so many ways. But you may still wonder, "How much do we need to protect our lifestyle?"

Are We OK?

Retirement Income	Estate Planning	Spousal Income Needs
• Income Dist.	• Federal and State Taxes	Property and Casualty
• NQDC	**Asset Preservation**	Sickness and Injury
	• Investment ROR • Inflation	Income Tax
	• Life Expectancy • Std of Living	Long Term Care
	• D,L,C, Fin. Mgmt. • Risk Tolerance	

Legend:

Dist = Distribution	C = Creditors
NQDC = Non-Qualified Deferred Compensation	Fin. Mgmt. = Financial Mis-Management
ROR = Rate of Return	Std = Standard
D = Divorce	F.E.T. = Federal Estate Tax
L = Liabilities	Bene. = Beneficiary
	GSTT = Generation Skipping Transfer Tax

A quick example: Several years ago we worked with a large beverage distributor in the Pacific Northwest. The owner was on his third marriage and his wife on her second. Their combined net worth was in excess of $35 million, and their annual pretax income was approximately $2.4 million. They were both extremely concerned about the estate tax their family would have to pay after the second of the two of them passed away. To make the estate tax issue even worse, they were only 60 and 62 years old. Their concern was that their estate, over the next 25–30 years of their life expectancy, would grow to about $150 million (at 7% growth—their estimate, not ours), with a corresponding estate tax of approximately $75 million. Said yet another way, how do you think they felt about owing the IRS, over the next 25–30 years, an amount twice that of their current net worth?

We ultimately helped them create a wealth preservation plan by employing a process that, over time, would reduce their current and future estate tax liability by more than $40 million. It all looked great until we jointly discovered that their combined and ongoing standard-of-living expenses were in excess of $2.1 million per year, net of all taxes. In other words, they were spending more than they were taking in! It matters not what size your estate is or how much you earn per year IF you are spending more than you take in. You will eventually either run out of money or significantly reduce your net worth. In this couple's case, they needed approximately $3.6 million before income taxes to support the $2.1 million spendable income needs they had. Unchecked, this would have (we recalculated their projections and worked together with this couple to modify many parts of their plan) led to the two of them running out of money by their late 80s—not anywhere near their idea of being OK or achieving financial independence. Their wealth was at serious risk.

We use the above example to suggest that most people are not willing to look at planning strategies that benefit other family members, charitable groups, and other possible beneficiaries until they know for certain that they are OK first. One client used these words to describe it: "I'll be damned if I'm going to work another 10 years [he was 68] so my kids can each get an additional $3 million!" The moral to this part of the book is that ALL plans must start with the creators of the plan being OK with their personal wealth before moving up to the middle or top layers of the family legacy pyramid on the previous page.

One final point on the idea of "Are we OK?" is the notion of buffers or shock absorbers for the creators of the plan. We have reviewed countless preexisting plans that assumed optimistic outcomes and failed to recognize the possible threats. For example, a plan was prepared by a national wire house that assumed the following: (a) a 3% inflation rate, (b) both husband and wife would pass away at their exact actuarial life expectancy, (c) their investments would grow at a constant 7.8% net after income taxes through life expectancy, and (d) they would reduce their current standard of living to 60% of what they currently spend after they retire. Their conclusion was that they would be OK on the basis of those assumptions and they would have a $1 million buffer at age 87. In our opinion, there are no shock absorbers in the above assumptions. Everything must play out exactly as planned or this couple will be living together—but under a bridge and in a cardboard box. Their plan did not consider the threats and fell tragically short of defending their personal wealth.

- What if inflation is 4.5%? If this were to occur, this couple would NOT have the $1 million surplus, and they would run out of money completely by age 74—hardly OK!

- What if one of them lives to age 100 rather than just to normal life expectancy? What are they supposed to do for income for the last 15 or so years of life?

- What if they need 80% of their preretirement income (not 60%) each year due to inflation, a medical problem, or disability?

- What if, as in the past 10 years in the United States, the real return, after inflation, on their portfolio was not only less than 7.8% net but close to 0—and, when adjusted for taxes, was actually a LOSS?

- Consider what income tax rates may be when the current 35% top income tax rate and 15% capital gains and dividend tax rates expire on December 31, 2012. With raging political and financial pressures, can the Bush-era tax cuts remain indefinitely?

Can we all agree that making sure that we are OK, with room to spare after considering numerous threats, is a good place to begin our planning process?

WHAT ARE THE COMPONENTS OF A WEALTH PRESERVATION PLAN?

A comprehensive wealth preservation plan encompasses five critical areas of planning, and to ignore any one of these areas could be disastrous.

I. Financial Independence

Taxes, living expenses, inflation, death. That's about as much as most people can predict about their future. But what if you could get a realistic early perspective on the ability of your income and assets to help meet your long-term needs and objectives? What if you could analyze a variety of what-if scenarios to prepare for various contingencies the future might hold? You can stack the deck in your favor, and you don't need a crystal ball to do it. What's needed is a financial independence planning model that gives you the power to chart your own future financial course. Without it, your plans for the future are not plans at all—they're nothing more than guesswork.

A **comprehensive financial independence model** can help:

1. Project your annual cash flow (income and expenses) alongside your assumed asset growth over the full length of your life expectancy and beyond

2. Estimate the size of your net worth each year, as well as your savings, your investments, and your transferable estate

3. Assess the long-term impact of taxes, inflation, and each of the financial strategies you are now using or planning to use

4. Consider and quantify the impact of potential threats to achieving your financial independence

Financial modeling of this nature can help you project and control your financial future and help you decide whether the course you are following today is prudent or even adequate. How does the strategy you just implemented or are now considering compare with other available options? What might happen if circumstances change (such as higher taxes, higher inflation, extended life expectancy, or lower returns on your investment, as in our previous example)? The answers might change your mind about the way you've prepared for the future; you might create or re-create your wealth preservation plan.

A forecast of the next 20, 30, or more years is critical to your financial well-being. On a year-by-year basis, it is important to project your income from the following sources:

- Salary

- Bonus

- Profits (from S corps, partnerships, LLCs, etc.)

- Investments (interest, dividends, capital gains)

- Gifts/inheritances

- Retirement plan distributions

- Trust distributions

- Other income sources

These income sources should then be compared to your living expenses. Frequently, the most significant expense is the income tax. Are you doing all you can to minimize the cut that goes to your silent partner, Uncle Sam? In addition to income taxes, consider your personal living expenses, which include:

- Mortgage payments

- Real estate taxes

- Food

- Clothing

- Auto payments

- Insurance (homeowner's, auto, life, health, etc.)

- Contributions to retirement plans

- Gifts

- Travel/vacations

- etc.

In the next chapter, we will take a look at a sample **financial independence model** prepared for John and Mary Prescott as part of this comprehensive wealth preservation plan. It was prepared on the basis of the data gathered throughout several collaborative discovery meetings and a review of the Prescotts' existing financial situation.

The Objective of Your Plan

Many Americans, even those with high net worth, are concerned about their financial independence when facing 20, 30, or even 40 years in retirement, particularly with current and expected stock market volatility, inflation, and taxes that can significantly erode purchasing power and personal wealth.

The objective of your plan is to provide a financial profile that will help to structure and monitor your financial resources (income and assets) to meet your financial objectives most effectively—personal, business, and family—particularly with the economic forces now in play.

You've worked hard over many years, taken risks, persevered, and succeeded. As a result, you have accumulated significant assets (even after paying income taxes). These assets are generally grouped into six broad areas:

1. **Business assets** - These include any businesses you own an interest in, such as C or S corps, partnerships, sole proprietorships, and LLCs.

2. **Real estate assets** - These include your personal residence(s) and vacation and/or rental real estate.

3. **Savings and investments** - These include all types of savings/ checking accounts, money markets, CDs, stocks, bonds, ETFs, mutual funds, hedge funds, etc.

4. **Qualified plans and IRAs** - These include all types of qualified retirement plans, such as pensions, profit-sharing plans, 401(k)s, 403(b)s, SEP, Keoghs, IRAs, etc.

5. **Life insurance** - Consider all policies on your life (and your spouse's life) owned personally or by a business or trust.

6. **Personal property** - This includes automobiles, jewelry, furs, collections, and any other personal-use items.

These assets accumulated over the course of your lifetime will ultimately be distributed to your heirs through different methods, such as titling, trusts, beneficiary designations, and your will.

While you most likely have competent advisors, such as an accountant, an attorney, a stock broker, and an insurance agent, have you ever wondered whether your finances are arranged and planned for as well as possible? If new techniques are out there, how do you find out about them? Are changes on the horizon that you need to be prepared for and react accordingly? When was the last time all of your advisors (CPA, attorney, and investment and insurance profes-

When was the last time all of your advisors sat down together in a conference room for half a day to focus on your situation?

sionals) sat down *together* in a conference room for half a day to focus on your situation? Most people I speak with laugh when I pose this question—because it's never happened! Many express a desire to find that one trusted advisor who can coordinate, lead the charge, and act as a catalyst to help implement their plan. No one advisor can replace all of these profession-als (nor is it advisable to do so). However, the need for cross-disciplinary collaboration with an overall knowledge of how these interrelated areas impact your financial independence plan is imperative. Lack of coordina-tion can cost you hundreds of thousands and possibly millions of dollars over your lifetime and the lifetimes of your heirs. The problem we often uncover is that people have different plans for distributing their assets, set up at different times, often with different advisors—resulting in a lack of coordination.

The Process

The financial independence planning process involves a series of discovery meetings in which you share, in detail, financial and personal information about your values and your future vision of what you want to accomplish with your life's work. Questions follow a well-thought-out and ever-deepening sequence; these are not random questions fired out in an interrogation or "let's fill out this questionnaire" fashion. Ideally, both spouses should be present during all meetings. On a select basis, adult children, parents, business partners, and other advisors should participate. Meticulous records of these data-gathering sessions should be kept and documented for future reference and a reminder of decisions made. Decisions can always be changed, but it is helpful to recall the thought process and value judgments that went into past decisions as modifications are contemplated. All of this will result in the creation of a customized plan to help you reach your goals and defend your wealth.

Implementation

While development of your written plan is an essential first step toward the achievement of your financial objectives, timely implementation of the specific strategies you choose is paramount. The analytical planning process identifies problems, opportunities, and strategies; it does not produce results. Effective implementation (deployment of the plan) allows you to realize the full benefits of the financial planning that you have undertaken.

Your plan is not worth the paper it is written on unless and until *you actually implement it*. One of the most important roles an advisor can play is that of a catalyst to make this happen. Once you make implementation decisions, empower your advisor to carry them out.

> *Your plan is not worth the paper it is written on unless and until you actually implement it.*

Annual Review and Update

Planning is not a one-time event, especially in these turbulent times. To ensure that your plan remains current and accurately reflects changes in personal circumstance, tax laws, investment results, and economic threats, you will need to review, monitor, and update your plan on an annual basis.

Amazingly, one year since you reviewed your plan can become two, five, or 10. I met recently with a high-net-worth individual who had not reviewed his will and trusts for 26 years! You must update your plan to keep current with the constant changes in the world around you.

When does a plan become stale? Most advisors agree that a plan is stale after just two years. Using this standard, probably 80%–90% of high-net-worth families have stale, out-of-date plans.

II. Business Succession Planning

More than 90% of the roughly 23 million businesses in the United States have some form of family ownership. Yet, family business experts concur that less than one-third of these family businesses will survive into the second generation, and only about 12% will still be viable into the third generation. The reasons are varied but include family conflict, failure to design a proper succession plan, and federal estate taxes. To avoid a similar fate, you need a current plan to achieve your objectives.

To Keep or Sell Your Business? That Is the Question

Keep: If you decide to keep the business for your family, how will you pay estate costs, provide income for your spouse, and equalize the distribution between your heirs if some are active in the business and some are not? Will you transfer it during your lifetime or upon your passing? How will you structure and value your business?

Sell: If you decide to sell your business, how will you maximize value and minimize taxes? To whom will you sell? When? On what terms?

There are three major steps to business succession planning:

1. Select and adequately develop the next generation of management, regardless of whether you plan to sell or keep the business in the

family. This involves training and proper design of executive compensation to retain and reward key leaders.

2. Decide when and how to transfer your business.

3. Minimize the impact of taxes so that your family, your company, and your employees are not at risk.

If you plan to transition ownership of the business to your family, you need to decide how you will pay estate settlement costs, provide income for your spouse, and equalize distributions. If you have a buy-sell agreement in place already, it should be reviewed to ensure that it doesn't cause significant inequity between the owners' families. If you don't have an agreement, you may want to consider one that allows you to maintain control over the business, buy out your partners under various scenarios, and enjoy built-in flexibility.

Executive Compensation Planning

Even if your business is running smoothly, you will remain competitive only if you can attract, retain, and reward the highest level of talent in your industry. One way to do so is to implement a custom-designed executive compensation program. Selectivity and flexibility are the hallmarks of this type of plan. For instance, you might want to consider offering high-performing key executives some type of ownership in the business (actual or phantom stock) or providing a way to make up for retirement benefits lost as a result of qualified retirement plan limitations.

Business succession planning is also not a static, one-time event but an ongoing process that, over time, can provide you with the ability to accomplish your goals.

III. Exit Planning: M&A/Investment Banking

This component applies to business owners who do not choose to keep the business in their family and do not have business partners to buy them out (or all partners are in agreement to sell). If you are considering a sale to outsiders, you are not alone—more than 12 million owners of privately held businesses (mostly baby boomers) are approaching a point in their lives when they need to develop a plan for their successful exit. For most business owners, this is a once-in-a-lifetime event and one of the most important decisions they will ever make. The key is to make sure that you fully understand and evaluate all of your exit options, including:

- Sale of 100% of your business

- Equity recapitalization (sale of a portion of your business)

- Mergers and acquisitions

- Raising capital for growth and expansion prior to exit

- Management buyouts

- Employee stock ownership plans (ESOPs)

IV. Risk Management/Estate Preservation Insurance

Risk management deals with many of the involuntary circumstances that can occur on the way to financial independence. As the old saying goes, "You plan your life—then life happens!" Even with a comprehensive wealth preservation plan, things can go wrong (for you and for your spouse, children, parents, business partners, and key employees) that are beyond your control, such as:

- Premature death

- Accident or illness

- Permanent disability

- Need for long-term care as you age

- Property and casualty losses

- Imposition of draconian taxes (gift, estate, generation-skipping, income, and capital gains taxes)

Many of these contingencies can be planned for in advance. You hope that these things don't happen, but if or when they do, at least your plan will not fall into ruin. Risk can be mitigated and often shifted to a third party, such as an insurance company. In some cases, proper legal documents can help spell out what should happen if one of these unfortunate events occurs.

Insurance provides the "teeth" and financial wherewithal to carry out the provisions of various contingency plans effectively, such as:

- Buy-sell agreements

- Key person and nonqualified deferred compensation plans

- Trusts created to support your spouse and children

- Tax payment/liquidity plans and others

V. Estate Preservation

Estate preservation is the process of protecting and planning for the disposition of your assets. Does your current planning take full advantage of all of the tax credits, exemptions, and deductions provided by the Internal Revenue Code? What have you done to mitigate the impact of future estate growth on estate taxes and settlement costs? Estate preservation includes asset protection, which deals with keeping your family's assets safe from potential claims of creditors and predators. These may include potential divorce, litigation, malpractice, bankruptcy, and false claims.

The goals of estate preservation are to provide for your financial security while you're alive and to maximize your estate for your family and any charities you favor following your death. Estate taxes will significantly impact the wealth you have accumulated unless you employ proper and on-going planning. A well-designed estate preservation plan can help create and conserve assets during your life. In addition, effective planning can minimize estate taxes and deliver an orderly distribution of assets that helps meet your family wealth objectives.

To fully leverage estate preservation opportunities and develop strategies to achieve your distribution objectives, consider:

- **Will and trust design strategies** - Review your legal documents to uncover whether they're up to date and what types of trusts are in place.

- **Property ownership alternatives** - By titling your assets appropriately, you can avoid unnecessary taxation or probate exposure. Coordinate the three methods of estate distributions,

(1) beneficiary designation, (2) joint titling, and (3) separately owned assets, ensuring that your primary and contingent beneficiaries are coordinated with your existing will and trust documents.

- **Qualified retirement plan distribution** - Avoid the significant drain that income and estate taxes can have on your qualified retirement plans at death, and take advantage of available strategies to minimize these costs.

- **Estate tax reduction techniques** - It's critical to determine your current estate tax liability and implement steps that will minimize estate settlement costs. These steps may include implementation of a variety of strategies to mitigate the impact of future estate growth and how to hedge the uncertainty of future estate tax legislation.

- **Family gifting strategies** - You may avoid a significant tax penalty if you restructure or reposition your assets during your life rather than waiting until your death. Further, you may want to consider strategies that would allow you to make gifts to your family but retain certain control over your assets. The Tax Relief Act of 2010 creates time-sensitive planning opportunities to shift substantial wealth in 2011 and 2012.

- **Life insurance analysis** - The arrangement of your current life insurance may be causing unnecessary taxation within your estate. You need to determine your requirements for estate liquidity— both now and in the future—and you may want to consider using discounts or leverage to pay estate settlement costs.

- **Charitable planning** - If philanthropy is important to you, you should coordinate your lifetime giving with additional charitable planning at death. Explore alternatives to leverage the tax advantages of charitable giving for you and your family.

We will expand on these concepts and more in chapter 3, "Wealth Preservation Strategies."

What Does it All Mean? Examples

We have now covered the process and components of a comprehensive wealth preservation plan. We suspect that many readers will conclude that they already have addressed some, perhaps even many, of the aspects of a plan. We also suspect (in fact, we know from experience) that some readers may think that their plan is some percentage of the way there—70%, 80%, or even 90%. This might be correct. However, the truth is that "the devil is in the details" when it comes to defending your wealth, just as in any other field of endeavor. Specifically, it's not just what you think you understand that matters. You may find that the old axioms of "I don't know what I don't know" and "I didn't see that coming" are what will hurt you the most.

Earlier in this chapter, we used the analogy of a football team creating plays and practicing in preparation for game time. Let's take a look at several examples where a lack of pregame preparation or "I don't know what I don't know–itis" resulted in creating a losing situation. We will focus on estate preservation and business succession planning examples for now and use actual case examples. Please keep in mind that each of these examples concerns very high-net-worth families ($25–$50 million and above). That said, each example pertains to nearly all families with a net worth starting at $10 million.

In the next few scenarios, notice the significant consequences involved in "not knowing what you don't know can hurt you." Without exception, the items in question involve between two sentences and three paragraphs in a person's legal (estate or business) documents. In these little details the devil lies in wait. These items can often result in severe and irreversible consequences for your family. They can beat your family silly financially, emotionally, and relationally. What is the reason (or reasons) for the documents or plan being sub par? They are as varied as we are but fundamentally more similar than dissimilar and often the result of the following thinking:

- "I thought everything was taken care of."

- "I've had it all done."

- "These things wouldn't affect me."

- "I/we are somehow immune or the tax rules didn't apply to my/our specific situation."

- "My attorney or accountant has handled it all."

- "I just finished going through all of this planning work; I'm sure it's fine."

- "Who cares what happens? I'll be dead and gone."

- "I'm too busy or distracted. I'll get to it later."

- "I hate this stuff."

- "My situation is unique."

- "The tax laws keep changing . . . let's wait and see what happens next."

The consequences could care less about your reasons, just as not keeping your cholesterol levels in check will not make the consequences of a heart attack less severe.

On the following pages are several examples of specific troublesome provisions we routinely encounter when reviewing the preexisting plans and estate documents of high-net-worth families.

Specific troublesome provision 1: Mandatory distribution of all income to the surviving spouse from the family trust (after the death of one spouse)

We estimate this pattern to be true in more than 80% of **ALL** high-net-worth cases. Howie and Judith have amassed a $10 million estate. Upon Howie's death in 2009, his estate plan (will and trust) left $3.5 million to a family trust (this was the maximum amount that the federal government permitted a person to transfer at death without imposition of estate taxes in 2009). The balance of $6.5 million went into Judith's marital trust for her exclusive benefit. At Howie's death, no estate taxes were due. Judith needed about $200,000 a year to maintain her standard of living. She was 60 years old, with about a 25–30-year life expectancy.

Let's assume that after Howie's death, Judith and her investment advisor think they can earn a 5% net after-tax return on her money. In other words, she will earn 5% on the $6.5 million in her marital trust ($325,000) and 5% on the $3.5 million in the family trust ($175,000). If Judith needs $200,000 per year to live on and her marital trust provides $325,000 a year in interest, she obviously is well provided for and has a considerable cushion to fall back on should the need arise (or if the economy takes a turn for the worse or she lives to age 105, etc.).

The question then becomes, what happens to all of the income produced by the family trust? The trust **requires** that the income, in this case $175,000 per year, be distributed to Judith. If we assume that Judith doesn't want or need the income, she will reinvest and accumulate it in her taxable estate each year until she passes away, possibly 30 years from now.

The problem is that the estate document requires distribution of $175,000 per year for 30 years **OUT** of the estate **TAX-EXEMPT** family trust and *forces it* into an estate-**TAXABLE** marital trust. Where else in life, or economics, does it make sense to exchange a *tax-exempt* status for a *taxable* one? Nowhere!

You might think, "OK, so how bad can that be? Judith [or my spouse] has an additional $175,000 she doesn't need. That doesn't sound like the end of the world." Let's look at the financial impact of this. How much will $175,000 growing at 5% for 30 years inside the (estate-taxable) marital trust be worth at the time of Judith's passing? Answer: **$12.275 million**. The estimated federal estate tax due on that amount is approximately **$4.3 million** under current 2011 estate tax law. This tax loss is the result of one sentence in a 40-page will and trust document that 80% of the high-net-worth families in America have. What a waste! Those dollars could have gone to children or grandchildren, charitable groups, community groups, or other family members, but instead the choice became **irrevocable** the day Howie died. Now it will go to the U.S. Treasury, where it will be used to pay the interest on our federal debt for approximately six hours or perhaps to build 50 feet of the new exit off the freeway. The heart of what took 40 years to build and grow spent to support the interest on our debt for a matter of hours—talk about throwing good money after bad or throwing money into a black hole. Final reminder here: once Howie died in this scenario, this disastrous outcome became *unavoidable.*

Specific troublesome provision 2: Predetermined and irrevocable distribution dates of all assets to children and/or grandchildren from the will and trust

This provision is in approximately 80%–90% of all documents we review in the high-net-worth marketplace. George and Phyllis had a $20 million net worth. They decided while they are both still alive to transfer $10 million of their assets into a trust for their children and distribute it to them at ages 30 (one-third of the balance), 33 (half of the balance), and 35 (the remaining balance). George and Phyllis have five children. Two of their children (Herbie and Tim) took their share ($2 million each) at age 35 and started a business. The business grew to be worth $92 million over the next 11 years (actual case facts). Therefore, $46 million is the value for each child. One day, Herbie shows up in the office of his brother Tim and says:

"After years of trying, Sarah and I are giving up the ghost and getting divorced. Her attorney says she wants half of everything: half the value of the house, our stocks and bonds, my retirement plan, my income, this business—everything. Damn it, Tim ... I don't even have a prenuptial agreement!"

"Herbie, we don't have $23 million to give her. Hell, we can't even borrow $5 million from the bank to buy XYZ company we've been wanting to buy. We certainly aren't going to be able to borrow that much to give to her. What are we going to do?"

Observations

a) This happens every day, even with prenuptial agreements, and (b) this was **completely avoidable** with good planning and proper documents that George and Phyllis could have created.

Do you want to know how this story ended? Sarah wound up getting 100% of the house ($1 million), the stock and bond accounts ($4 million), the savings account ($1 million), the vacation home ($1.2 million), and a note from Herbie for another $9 million payable over the next 10 years. Herbie is renting a townhouse now and has essentially no discretionary income. He and Tim are hoping to sell the business over the next three years.

This could have played out much differently. Had George and Phyllis simply gifted the assets into trusts for the benefit of (FBO) each child, without specific ages of mandatory distribution, the assets would not have been subject to the ramifications of divorce, liability, or creditors. Specifically, the trusts established for the lifetime of Herbie and Tim would have been the owners of the business, and when Sarah filed for divorce, or some other type of lawsuit was filed against any of the five children, **the assets in the trust would *not* have been subject to these claims.**

Yet, the assets in each child's trust would have been for his or her exclusive use and enjoyment. A child's trust assets could have been used to pay for a grandchild's education, a vacation home, unforeseen and catastrophic medical expenses, long-term-care expenses, or the purchase of a primary residence—virtually any reasonable expenditure for the benefit of that child.

What a tragic ending for two brothers who had achieved the American Dream with their business. Failure to notice the risks around them had severe consequences. Once again, a slight modification to the document would have had a meaningful change in the trajectory of the family's business and avoided a huge and negative impact downrange.

Specific troublesome issue 3: No limited power of appointment given to the surviving spouse. In plain terms, this provision in a person's will and trust permits the surviving spouse to amend and adjust the dollar amounts (or the percent to be distributed) to children and/or grandchildren. It provides the survivor a "second bite at the apple" and the ability to react if family circumstances change.

Most wills and trusts (our estimate: 70% plus) don't allow a surviving spouse the ability to appoint or distribute the trust assets differently from what the original creator of the trust put into the document. Again, at first blush this sounds perfectly reasonable. The creator of the trust (the husband, in this case) says, for example, that he wants all of his assets to pass to his spouse and then to his five children, so that each will receive 20% of the assets from his trust after his surviving spouse passes away. What could possibly be wrong with that?

Let's use another real-life example and look at a couple of possible outcomes. Bruce and Marie were happily married for 40 years, with five children ranging from 25 to 35 years of age. Bruce passed away and left his assets to Marie. Five years after Bruce passed away, one of the five children developed a drug and alcohol dependency problem. If Marie were to die that day, each child would receive his or her 20% inheritance **outright**. Would Bruce and Marie have considered a 20% outright distribution to each child the best possible outcome in that scenario? Would anyone willingly give a drug- or alcohol-dependent child millions of dollars of cash in a moment such as this?

Without being too melodramatic, this provision (which becomes irrevocable when either Bruce or Marie dies) could unintentionally lead to the death of their child! Suppose for a moment that Bruce left Marie with the **power** to change that 20% allocation to whatever she saw fit at any time after he passed. She might have changed the document to leave the 20% share to the troubled child *in trust*, with a special trustee to oversee the distributions and management of those monies. She might have changed the 20% to 5% or 10% for the troubled child. She might have left this 5%–10% in trust or left it outright to a grandchild instead. Marie might have decided to have these monies used for a drug and alcohol rehab program or instead go to a charity of her choice.

In a scenario like this, ignorance is not bliss. Instead, it is a potentially deadly, albeit unintended, consequence.

Let's take another look at a more positive use of the limited power of appointment given to a surviving spouse. Suppose one of the children has a special-needs child (or grandchild) that will need a lifetime of care and special education. Might Marie (or Bruce) make a provision in the will and trust to permit the surviving spouse to leave a bit more to that branch of the family with the special-needs child? Maybe it's a flat additional dollar amount ($250,000) or perhaps an additional percentage of the estate, say, 30% instead of 20%. If both Bruce and Marie were still alive, might they have at the very least considered this?

In either case, the surviving spouse would most likely be the person best able (and most trusted) to make decisions like the ones outlined above. The alternative is that a document created by someone who may have died 20 years earlier controls, providing absolutely no flexibility to the surviving spouse. Distributions to family members whose facts and circumstances in life may have changed in dramatic and unforeseeable ways since the document was drafted are left without any flexibility and potentially catastrophic consequences.

Risk Management: Property and Casualty Examples

Another common occurrence is a lack of coordination around one's property and casualty (P&C) insurance. At first blush, this seems a rather mundane topic of insignificant consequence. From an asset protection and risk management standpoint, nothing is further from the truth. Two brief true stories dramatically illustrate the potential consequences to any family that downplays the potentially devastating outcomes.

WYOMING RANCH EXAMPLE

The first involves a $100-million-net-worth family that owns a 2,000-plus-acre ranch in Wyoming. The family operates the ranch as a "gentleman farmer" might. They visit from time to time, go there for vacations and holidays, and let friends use the home whenever they aren't there. They also use the property as a working ranch with several hundred head of cattle. They have several "out" buildings and eight ranch hands that work the property. The ranch hands live in the bunkhouse, as the ranch is some 40 miles from the nearest town.

Imagine for a moment what a Friday night at the bunkhouse after a long week of fence mending, riding, and roping looks like. The boys all get together for a bit of R & R, they knock a few back . . . one says something that offends another, they push and shove, and one falls out of a second-floor window of the bunkhouse. But unlike the cowboys on the old Wild West TV shows, this cowboy breaks his back in two spots and his hip in another. He becomes a paraplegic.

The family had all of the usual P&C and liability insurance on the family's retreat home (14,000 square feet), all of the ranch vehicles had insurance, and even the guesthouse was insured—but the bunkhouse was not. The family wealth creator had a $3 million umbrella policy and decided to self-insure any amount above that. The amount above that was an additional $6 million. It doesn't much matter what one's net worth is; a $6 million hit is going to leave a mark and is likely not to be forgotten quickly.

The real message here is twofold. First, did the family need the insurance, or could they afford to self-insure? Truly, they could afford and ultimately did pay the expense, and they were still OK in the end. The bigger question was, should they have considered insurance? Obviously, in hindsight, they should have. This is the essence of risk management. An axiom frequently used to capture this situation is as follows: "Liquidity is a problem only if you don't have it, and then it's a matter of economics." In this situation, a few thousand dollars (liquidity) spent to shift a potential $6 million cost makes for compelling economics. By the way, this applies to any insurance one considers, such as car, fire, life, long-term-care, etc.

A thought to chew on: forget the label (insurance) and instead consider, with calculator in hand, the economics. We'll revisit this concept later in a subsequent chapter.

DALLAS SANDWICH TRUCK EXAMPLE

In this instance, a successful business owner thought he, too, had his P&C insurance completely taken care of. In fact, he had done a much more thorough job than most people. That said, the difference between having the work done—in any area of planning or life—and having it done as well as it can be done is substantial. In his case, it was $8 million worth.

This client, like many, had his son working in the business with him. This son had two prior run-ins with the law regarding drinking and driving, resulting in two DUI convictions. This particular night, he was headed home at 4:30 in the morning (as an aside, almost nothing good can happen while driving home at 4:30 in the morning). He had been drinking (though not heavily) and ran into the back of a sandwich truck preparing to go on its rounds to various work sites around town. The operator of the truck had been preparing and provisioning the truck. Tragically, he lost both of his legs and sued for damages and physical suffering. The son had been driving the company car, and while the company carried insurance on the car, the insurance didn't cover the car for someone who had a prior history and/or conviction for driving while under the influence. In this case, the business (owned by the father) had to come up with $8 million out of its own pocket.

BUSINESS SUCCESSION EXAMPLE

A business founder/owner (with no spouse or children) died and left his business and all of his other assets ($110 million combined) to his brother, who had diabetes severe enough to require use of a dialysis machine twice a month. He had a six-month life expectancy and was divorced. The surviving brother disclaimed one-third of the assets to his three children, who, in his own words (please do not take offense) he described as "one who is a pothead, one who is married to a spouse who loves to spend money, and one who just got out of mechanic's school."

Note: To "disclaim" an asset means to pass it to another person(s) or entity (trust) as if you had died before the deceased. In this case, instead of one-third of the assets going to the brother, they would bypass him and go outright (free of trust) to his three children equally.

With only those facts, can you imagine a favorable outcome? The accountant and attorney of the deceased brother introduced us to this situation. While we had worked with these other advisors before, we were new to this family situation. It gets better (actually worse).

We were asked to assist the diabetic brother and his children with a wealth preservation and distribution plan. The objectives were to protect the children from:

1. Themselves (financial mismanagement)

2. Divorcing spouses

3. Creditors

4. Potential liabilities for the third of the assets given outright (disclaimed above)

A second set of objectives dealt with the disposition of the remaining two-thirds of the deceased brother's estate—specifically, to keep the business up and running. The company employed more than 200 employees, all of whom depended upon the business flourishing in order to support themselves and their families. In other words, what was the immediate business succession plan now that the founder was gone? Equally important, how could we possibly keep the doors open, with the surviving brother having a fairly short life expectancy himself, AND address the estate taxes to be paid upon both the deceased brother's estate (about $45 million— note that all estate taxes are due and payable within nine months of the date of death and must be paid in cash) and the surviving brother's estate? The total estate tax payment issue became even worse when the surviving brother passed away. In other words, another $15 million would be due when the surviving brother died!

ESTATE TAX NIGHTMARE

Imagine for a moment how your business might be affected. Assume, like most high-net-worth business owners, that your business represents between 60% and 90% of your net worth. Further assume that your business is worth $25 million of your $32 million net worth. Your estate taxes will be approximately $8 million. If your heirs needed to come up with $8 million to pay your estate taxes AND your estate didn't have the liquidity to do so BUT is **required** by the IRS to pay this amount, in cash, within nine months, how would your family pay it? Essentially, they have only two, maybe three, alternatives. First, they would likely liquidate all liquid and semiliquid assets (cash, CDs, marketable securities, etc.). For argument's sake, let's say that you have $3 million in cash and marketable securities (exclusive of your qualified retirement plan assets). Your family still needs another $5 million. The choices are (1) borrow the money or (2) liquidate the business at a "fire sale" price.

Let's look at borrowing. First, in today's lending environment, healthy businesses with strong balance sheets and management teams (owner/CEO alive and well) are having an extremely difficult time getting financing. But, let's assume that we find a bank willing to loan money to a business where the majority shareholder/CEO has recently died. We've gone from difficult to nearly impossible to get a loan—but, still, let's assume that we can. What will the terms likely be? Let's assume $5 million at 9% for 10 years. That's principal and interest of $760,000 PER YEAR. Assume that this business (your business) nets 5% of gross sales to the bottom line each year. Can a business worth $25 million **increase** its sales by $15.2 million the first year after the majority shareholder/CEO dies, just to pay the estate tax obligation? This might represent an increase in gross sales of more than 20% that first year—maintained for 10 years—to break even! Is this reasonable? Is it even possible? Is this the *best* plan the collective wisdom of a team of advisors can come up with?

Before we get back to our case history, I mentioned a fire sale above. Some thoughts regarding a sale after the majority shareholder/CEO has died: As much as this is a difficult time for the family and the business, I can assure you that no one is going to pay fair-market value for a business that was likely dependent on that majority shareholder/CEO and is likely faltering without him or her present. One would hope to get 50 cents on the dollar in a situation like this but may end up with only 25–35 cents on the dollar.

Where does this leave the family and the business? The majority shareholder/CEO is gone, all of the liquid cash reserves and readily marketable securities are depleted, and the business is strapped with a quite possibly unsustainable debt. Hardly ideal. As you can see, the problems begin to cascade one on top of another. The owner is gone; no liquidity is left (it's all been paid to the U.S. Treasury); the debt service exceeds the income the owner was likely drawing (and only the interest expense is income tax deductible); and the surviving spouse or children running the business need income, have none, and have no assets that are easily converted into cash. In addition, competitors are aggressively grabbing customers, employees, and market share; the bank has its loan covenant committee knocking on everyone's door; and on and on. Again, the consequences outlined here could care less that the owner and the current team of advisors couldn't find the time or were too busy or "hated this stuff," etc. The consequences are amoral—they just are—and the owner, his or her spouse, their family, the hundreds of employees, and the community all suffer.

That said, as it turns out, we were not able to help the family in the above scenario as we had hoped. We were brought into the situation too late. About two weeks into our engagement, the diabetic brother passed away. The family's attorney sold the business at a fire sale for 20 cents on the dollar. All of the net assets were distributed outright to the children and thereby exposed to all of the risks inherent in outright ownership of assets, i.e., no asset protection from divorce, liability, creditors, financial mismanagement, federal estate taxes, and generation-skipping taxes. The employees were, for the most part, let go. The community suffered, the employees suffered, the families of those employees suffered, the family of the founder suffered, and the business suffered. Only the U.S. Treasury made out well, with more than $60 million in revenue collected over a two-year period of time.

CHAPTER SUMMARY

The starting point for creating a plan to defend your wealth is a four-step process:

1. Discovery

2. Document audit

3. Brainstorming

4. Action plan

Consider the family legacy pyramid and answer the questions: Are we OK? Is our family OK? Is our community OK? Under any reasonably foreseeable circumstance, will you run out of money, lose the lifestyle you have worked your entire life to achieve, or become dependent on others? Testing to make sure this won't happen is of paramount importance. Do not progress to the next step (i.e., transfer of assets to your family, trusts, charitable planning, etc.) until you are absolutely certain of your financial independence. How do you become certain? The best way is to run the numbers. Guesswork or gut feeling won't cut it. Engage a financial professional to help you create a series of financial independence models to analyze your assets, liabilities, income, and expenses to determine whether you will be OK. Don't forget to build in shock absorbers or buffers in the form of different assumptions for inflation, rates of return, taxation, and life expectancy. Factor in all of the threats to your wealth, and defend yourself from loss of financial independence. Consider the unpleasantries of disability, premature death, lawsuits, creditors, and other contingencies discussed in the previous chapter.

Don't confuse having the ingredients or components of a plan in place as having a comprehensive plan. What you don't know *can* hurt you. A wealth preservation plan utilizing a comprehensive planning process reduces the likelihood of coordination gaps that drastically and negatively affect you, your family, your business, and your community. A fully integrated plan includes a system, process, procedure, and how-to manual that covers all of the bases or areas of planning, such as financial independence, business succession/exit plans, risk management/estate preservation insurance, and estate preservation strategies.

Working with an experienced professional who (1) is an extremely well-informed specialist; (2) is capable as a communicator and relationship manager; and (3) brings a wealth of knowledge, wisdom, and experience to the process exponentially increases the likelihood of a holistic, client-centered plan being not only recommended but also implemented.

Implementation of your action plan provides the defense necessary to protect your wealth and your family. Gather all of your important financial documents and have them audited. Your comprehensive plan should be in writing and updated regularly (every two or three years or more frequently if changes occur). With the sweeping tax law changes and recent economic events, now is the ideal time for a thorough review.

Start the discovery step by asking yourself the questions at the end of this section.

THE VALUE OF A PLANNING PROCESS

Questions—"Am I OK?"

☐ What are your major life goals (retirement, travel, career, and leisure goals)?

☐ Have you prepared some type of forecasting tool, such as a financial independence model, to prepare for the future? When was it last updated to reflect recent changes in the markets? Consider changes to your:

- Assets (growth and income assumptions)
- Liabilities (interest rate and terms)
- Sources of income
- Uses of income
- Income taxes (current and future)
- Inflation assumptions
- Specific objectives, i.e., cost of children's education, long-term care of parents, etc.

☐ Financial independence means different things to different people; how do you define it?
- For you
- For your spouse
- For your children

☐ Have you followed a comprehensive, holistic process to defend your personal wealth, or is it piecemeal, fragmented, and lacking coordination?

☐ Is your plan in writing?

☐ When was it last updated?

☐ Does your plan address and answer all of the threats to your personal wealth, including:
- Financial independence?
- Income tax reduction?
- Retirement planning?
- Disability (the effects of sickness or injury)?
- Long-term care?
- Defensive investment strategies?
- Extended life expectancy and the need for your investments to last longer?
- Inflation and loss of purchasing power?
- Property and casualty exposure?
- Financial support needs of family members who depend on you?

☐ What are your greatest fears concerning achievement and maintenance of your financial independence?

☐ Where do you plan to be financially in five years?

☐ What are your three major financial priorities? Why?

☐ When do you plan to accomplish these priorities? How?

- ☐ What's keeping you up at night? Any financial concerns or opportunities (anything goes here)?

- ☐ How have your overall financial needs changed as a result of recent economic turmoil?
    a. Time horizon: When will you need to start spending your investments and savings?
    b. How have your current or future income needs changed?
    c. Has your tolerance for risk changed?

- ☐ What is going on with you and your family? List recent and expected significant events or changes in situation for you, your spouse, children, parents, grandchildren, and others.

- ☐ If you and your spouse were no longer here and looking over the shoulder of your heirs, what are some of the things they might be doing or experiencing that would make you smile or bring a tear to your eye?

- ☐ Have any significant financial events occurred or are they likely to occur soon? A significant inheritance? A sale of a home, business, or major asset? A job change?

- ☐ What are your planned sources for retirement income? Have you stress-tested them to make sure you won't outlive them? (Have you assumed different assumptions for inflation, tax rates, rates of return, and life expectancy?)

- ☐ What techniques are you using to help reduce your income tax exposure?

- ☐ How have you planned to pay for the cost of long-term care for yourself, your spouse, or other family members?

- ☐ When did you last review your property and casualty and liability policies?

SECTION II

DEFEND YOUR FAMILY WEALTH

CHAPTER THREE

WEALTH
PRESERVATION
STRATEGIES

By Dan Prisciotta

T
he estate tax is back along with its companion, the generation-skipping transfer tax (GST). They represent the largest threat to your family wealth.

Taxes increasingly threaten your family wealth. The new estate tax regime is temporary and is scheduled to sunset on December 31, 2012. It is entirely possible that rates and exemptions may change and that various estate preservation techniques available today may be restricted or eliminated in the future.

No wonder holding onto your wealth is more challenging than ever. With businesses not fully recovered from the Great Recession and portfolios and real estate in flux, what should you do to defend your family wealth?

> *Holding onto your wealth is more challenging then ever.*

Some have called it the "death tax" and have fought hard for permanent repeal, saying it is a form of double taxation for people who have already paid a lifetime of taxes. For most of American history, inheritance taxes were imposed on the wealthiest citizens only as a temporary measure in

59

times of war. By the early twentieth century, as the Industrial Revolution led to a growing gap between rich and poor, leading figures such as President Theodore Roosevelt and steel baron and philanthropist Andrew Carnegie began promoting estate taxes as a way to diffuse the concentration of wealth they considered a threat to democracy. These days, Congress views estate and gift taxes as lucrative revenue sources. According to the latest data available, the U.S. Treasury collected more than $25 billion in estate taxes in 2008. We caution you not to become complacent about the threat of estate taxes on your wealth because of a two-year relief period. Your life expectancy (and your spouse's) may be another 20, 30, or 40 years. Who knows what tax rates and exemptions will be in place at that time. Consider the steps our country may need to take in order to address a $14 trillion growing deficit and other fiscal woes. It is estimated that enactment of the Tax Relief Act of 2010 will cost the U.S. Treasury more than $68 billion.

Overview of Key Tax Rates

Provision	2011	2012	2013
1. Income Tax	35%	35%	39.6%
2. Top Rate for Investment Income			
Long-term capital gains	15%	15%	20.0%
Qualified dividends	15%	15%	39.6%
3. Gift & Estate Tax			
Maximum rate	35%	35%	55%
Exemption	$5 million	$5 million	$1 million
4. Generation-Skipping Tax (GST)			
Maximum rate	35%	35%	55%
Exemption	$5 million	$5 million	$1,340,000

A GOLDEN OPPORTUNITY

The Tax Relief Act of 2010 creates an unprecedented opportunity for lifetime wealth transfer. The law sets the gift, estate, and GST tax exemption at $5 million per person ($10 million per couple) for 2011 and 2012. The increase in the gift tax exemption

> *The next two years will bring about a bonanza of activity to avoid future taxation.*

to $5 million means that you have a two-year window to transfer assets out of your taxable estate such that all future appreciation escapes estate and GST taxation. The new law omits all of the restrictions included in previous bills, such as:

- Limitations on grantor-retained annuity trust (GRAT) terms

- Restrictions on discounts for family-held entities

- Uniformity of basis for estate and income tax purposes

This is all great news, especially in a low-interest-rate environment with generally lower asset values. It is the perfect storm for estate preservation planning! The world may change drastically after the sunset on December 31, 2012, when the estate, gift, and GST provisions revert to the onerous 2001 rules. The next two years will bring about a bonanza of activity to avoid future taxation.

The threat of excessive taxation on your family wealth can arise from the lack of outdated or improper planning. Estate, gift, and generation transfer taxes can be significantly reduced or avoided entirely if you know what you are doing. However, wealth preservation can be complex and ever changing. It requires careful attention to details; is developed through a deep understanding of your vision, values, and goals; and involves a comprehensive analysis of all of your estate documents and planning work you have done up to this point. A financial independence model is necessary to assess your current financial situation and to evaluate alternative strategies. This process can best be illustrated through a case study.

CASE STUDY -
THE JOHN AND MARY PRESCOTT FAMILY

To illustrate what a comprehensive, holistic wealth preservation plan looks like, we have created the John and Mary Prescott family plan. After following the planning process described, beginning with (1) an initial "concept" interview to understand the Prescotts' vision, values, and goals for the future and (2) gathering comprehensive data (including copies of existing documents), we were able to construct the following financial independence model for the Prescott family. It reflects the family's current situation through the following models:

1. Family Member Report

2. Personal Balance Sheet

3. Life Insurance Summary

4. Financial Independence Model Snapshot—shows year-by-year:
   a. Asset growth
   b. Annual income sources
   c. Annual income uses
   d. Discretionary income
   e. Total net worth
   f. Estate distribution

5. Cash Flow/Asset Accumulation Summary

6. Estate Tax Liquidity Analysis

7. Qualified Retirement Plan Analysis

Seen in a high-level overview, the Prescott family has the following assets that will ultimately pass down to their children and grandchildren, subject to multiple layers of taxation (rates effective for 2011 and 2012).

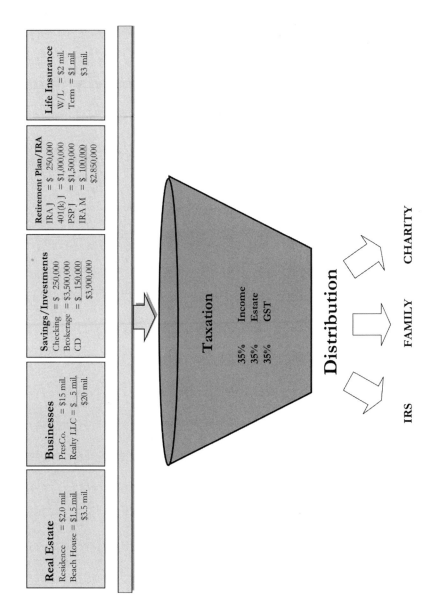

THE PRESCOTT FAMILY
Family Member Report

Name	Relationship	Date of Birth	Age
John Prescott	Client	03/15/1945	65
Mary Prescott	Spouse	12/24/1945	65

James	Son	02/17/1973	37
June	Daughter-in-law	10/23/1974	36
Robert	Grandchild	05/16/2002	8

Mark	Son	07/12/1975	35
Lynne	Daughter-in-law	11/04/1976	34
Casey	Grandchild	12/02/2004	6
Anne	Grandchild	01/24/2006	4

Judy	Daughter	08/15/1978	32

THE PRESCOTT FAMILY
Personal Balance Sheet

Assets Owned by John	Value	Debt	Net Value
Checking	$ 250,000	-0-	$ 250,000
IRA	250,000	-0-	250,000
PresCo (S corporation; 100%)	15,000,000	-0-	15,000,000
PresCo Realty, LLC	5,000,000	-0-	5,000,000
PresCo 401(k) plan	1,000,000	-0-	1,000,000
PresCo profit-sharing plan	1,500,000	-0-	1,500,000
Subtotal	**$23,000,000**	**-0-**	**$23,000,000**
Assets Owned by Mary			
IRA	100,000	-0-	100,000
Subtotal	**100,000**	**-0-**	**100,000**
Jointly Owned Assets (ROS)			
Residence	2,000,000	-0-	2,000,000
Beach house	1,500,000	(250,000)	1,250,000
Brokerage account	3,500,000	-0-	3,500,000
CD	150,000	-0-	150,000
Subtotal	7,150,000	-0-	6,900,000
Totals	**$30,250,000**	**$(250,000)**	**$30,000,000**

THE PRESCOTT FAMILY
Life Insurance Summary

Policy Description	Policy Information	Annual Premium	Death Benefit	Cash Value
XYZ Mutual Whole-Life Issued: 5/01/98	Insured: John Owner: John Beneficiary: Mary	$ 58,000	$2,000,000	$250,000
Term Insurance Company (20 yr) Issued: 4/01/94	Insured: John Owner: John Beneficiary: Mary	$ 2,050	$1,000,000	-0-
Totals		**$ 60,050**	**$3,000,000**	**$250,000**

Observations

What observations can be made regarding John and Mary's current situation? On the basis of extensive data gathering and several hours spent with both John and Mary, we learned the following about their family vision, values, and goals.

Background

- The Prescotts are a close family. Their two sons and daughter live nearby. Sons Jim and Mark are successful businessmen and married with children (three grandchildren so far, whom John and Mary adore). Their daughter, Judy, was married but is now divorced. She is a successful pediatrician. Judy is engaged to be married again by the end of this year.

- John owns PresCo, a successful manufacturing and distribution business. He plans to sell it in five years and retire at age 70. His children are not active in the business and therefore have no desire to succeed him. His management team cannot afford to buy him out, so he plans to sell to outsiders. Over the years, various competitors have approached John with inquiries (not real offers) to acquire his business. He has never felt comfortable divulging confidential information. He has never sold a business and realizes that he will need professional representation to obtain maximum value, terms, and tax advice.

- The 30 years spent building and running PresCo have taken a bit of a toll on John's health, but, thankfully, his high blood pressure and cholesterol are now well controlled by medication. Mary is in excellent health, and together they enjoy golf, tennis, and traveling. They plan to do more in retirement.

- The three most important things John and Mary said they can teach their children in life are:
  1. "Family comes first" - They value family time, holidays, vacations at their beach house, and supporting one another through life's trials and tribulations.
  2. Education - All three of their children have been college educated, and Judy also graduated from medical school. They want their grandchildren to receive the finest education possible, including postgraduate studies if they choose.
  3. Charity - John and Mary have taught their children to give back to society and support causes and charities they are passionate about.

- John's parents are deceased. Mary's mother is now approaching 85 years old and may soon rely on them for financial support. No inheritance is anticipated.

- If John were to pass away, Mary would like to stay in their current home, where they have lived for more than 30 years and raised their family. They enjoy their community. They absolutely want to keep the beach house in the family for future generations to enjoy.

- The Prescotts are concerned about potential threats to their net worth and their family.
  - Excessive taxation on their income, their portfolio, and the future sale of their family business. They are aware of the

estate tax but don't know how much they will owe or how their family will pay it.

- Inflation and loss of purchasing power
- Making sure that their wills and trusts pass their assets in accordance with their wishes and protect their heirs (outright distributions) from potential future creditors and predators
- Other dangers to their business and personal assets, to be uncovered during the process, of which the Prescotts were previously unaware

- The Prescotts have serious questions about the impact of the recently signed Tax Relief Act of 2010. They want to know how to take advantage of it to transfer and protect wealth. They realize that there is only a two-year window for certain strategies and wish to maximize opportunities.

Net Worth/Cash Flow Snapshot

This component of the financial independence model built for the Prescott family shows their:

- Assets
- Annual income sources
- Annual income uses
- Discretionary income (excess/shortage)
- Total net worth
- Estate distribution

We have shown only three years in our example. Typically, the model is run for 20 or 30 years or more.

Financial Independence Model—Snapshot

Assets (end-of-year values)	Age 65 2011	Age 66 2012	Age 67 2013
Cumulative discretionary account	-	207,650	418,683
Cash	400,000	400,000	400,000
U.S. large cap	3,500,000	3,748,500	4,014,644
Qualified retirement plans	2,899,000	3,124,880	3,364,313
Net Investable Assets	6,799,000	7,481,030	8,197,640
Residence	2,000,000	2,040,000	2,080,800
Beach house	1,272,126	1,314,194	1,357,586
Net personal use assets	3,272,126	3,354,194	3,438,386
PresCo	15,000,000	15,000,000	15,000,000
PresCo Realty	5,000,000	5,000,000	5,000,000
Net business assets	20,000,000	20,000,000	20,000,000
Net assets	30,071,126	30,835,224	31,636,026
Annual Income Sources			
Earned income—John	400,000	412,000	424,360
Investment income	80,750	91,408	102,539
Qualified plan income	-	-	-
Social Security	42,228	43,495	44,799
PresCo earnings	250,000	250,000	250,000
PresCo Realty earnings	350,000	350,000	350,000
Total Income Sources	1,122,978	1,146,903	1,171,698
Annual Income Uses			
Living expenses	(350,000)	(360,500)	(371,315)
Taxes	(461,087)	(471,129)	(481,559)
Gifts	-	-	-
Mortgages	(25,741)	(25,741)	(25,741)
Insurance premiums	(58,000)	(58,000)	(58,000)
Retirement plan contributions	(20,500)	(20,500)	(20,500)
Total Income Uses	(915,328)	(935,870)	(957,115)
Discretionary income	207,650	211,033	214,583
Total Net Worth	30,278,776	31,046,257	31,850,609
Estate Distribution			
Life insurance in estate	3,000,000	3,000,000	3,000,000
Total estate	33,278,776	34,046,257	34,850,609
Estate settlement costs	(13,959,145)	(14,428,045)	(19,991,924)
Net estate after taxes	19,319,631	19,618,212	14,858,685
Trust proceeds	-	-	-
Net to family	19,319,631	19,618,212	14,858,685
Percent shrinkage	42%	42%	57%

Cash Flow/Asset Accumulation Summary Report

For the Prescott family, the following model shows the next 15 years of financial activity (again condensed here; typically projected for 20–30-plus years):

Cash Flow/Asset Accumulation Summary

Year	CASH FLOW		ASSETS					Total Estate	ESTATE	
	Annual Surplus/ Deficit	Cumulative Surplus/ Deficit	Personal Assets	Investable Assets	Business Assets	Qualified Plans	Life Insurance (in estate)		Estate Settlement Costs	Net to Heirs
2011	207,650	-	3,522,126	3,650,000	20,000,000	2,899,000	3,000,000	33,278,776	(13,959,145)	19,319,631
2012	211,033	207,650	3,604,194	3,898,500	20,000,000	3,124,880	3,000,000	34,046,257	(14,428,045)	19,618,212
2013	214,583	418,683	3,688,386	4,164,644	20,000,000	3,364,313	3,000,000	34,850,609	(19,991,924)	14,858,685
2014	218,334	633,266	3,774,774	4,449,684	20,000,000	3,618,112	3,000,000	35,694,170	(20,515,776)	15,178,394
2015	10,824,992	851,600	3,863,432	4,754,962	5,000,000	3,747,166	2,000,000	31,042,152	(17,913,966)	13,128,186
2016	14,301	11,676,592	3,954,438	5,081,914	5,000,000	3,822,110	2,000,000	31,549,355	(18,213,801)	13,335,554
2017	10,887	11,690,893	4,047,873	5,432,080	5,000,000	3,893,177	2,000,000	32,074,910	(18,523,228)	13,551,682
2018	7,580	11,701,780	4,143,823	5,807,108	5,000,000	3,959,692	2,000,000	32,619,983	(18,842,777)	13,777,206
2019	4,392	11,709,360	4,242,377	6,208,763	5,000,000	4,020,917	2,000,000	33,185,809	(19,173,003)	14,012,806
2020	1,361	11,713,752	4,343,628	6,638,935	5,000,000	4,076,051	2,000,000	33,773,727	(19,514,520)	14,259,207
2021	(1,516)	11,715,113	4,447,674	7,099,649	5,000,000	4,124,223	2,000,000	34,385,143	(19,867,947)	14,517,196
2022	(4,685)	11,713,597	4,554,616	7,593,074	5,000,000	4,165,465	2,000,000	35,022,067	(20,234,425)	14,787,642
2023	(7,162)	11,708,912	4,664,561	8,121,532	5,000,000	4,197,886	2,000,000	35,685,729	(20,614,293)	15,071,436
2024	(9,991)	11,701,750	4,777,622	8,687,511	5,000,000	4,221,556	2,000,000	36,378,448	(21,008,881)	15,369,567
2025	13,106	11,691,759	4,868,174	9,293,674	5,000,000	4,235,564	2,000,000	37,102,277	(21,419,376)	15,682,901

Financial Threats and Observations

1. **Balance sheet** - John and Mary have achieved the American Dream and more! Their combined net worth is $30 million and growing. They started with nothing when they married 38 years ago. PresCo was responsible for creating most of their wealth and represents two-thirds of their net worth today.

2. **Cash flow** - As a result of John's salary and K-1 distributions from the business and real estate in excess of $1.1 million per year, plus perks, the Prescotts have plenty of excess cash flow or discretionary income. Even though only one model is shown here, alternative models were run to "stress-test" the Prescotts' financial independence under different rates of inflation and return assumptions. Their personal living expenses are $350,000 per year and growing with inflation. After they pay income taxes, their discretionary income is still more than $200,000 per year. Aside from birthdays, holidays, and other special events, John and Mary have not made formal recurring gifts to their children or grandchildren. Note: At age 70, when John is projected to sell PresCo, their discretionary income jumps more than $10 million in that year (2015).

3. **Estate settlement costs (ESCs)** - Federal estate taxes, state inheritance taxes, and the cost of probate and administration will take the largest chunk out of their estates—which is why minimizing ESCs is a primary concern. Total taxes and other costs if John and Mary passed away this year are **$13,959,145**. They have a serious liquidity shortfall. Assets will need to be sold in order to pay taxes—possibly PresCo and real estate.

4. **Wills** - The Prescotts have simple wills created in 1990. Not only are these wills outdated and tax inefficient but also they provide absolutely no asset protection for future generations.

5. **Assets pass outright to their children** after John and Mary pass away. No opportunity for multigeneration tax planning or asset protection exists.

6. **Life insurance** - $3 million in coverage is owned by John and is therefore includible in their taxable estate; 35% of their insurance proceeds will be lost to unnecessary taxation.

7. **Asset titling** - John and Mary's asset titling is currently improper; only $100,000 is in Mary's name. In fact, since the money is an IRA with John as primary beneficiary, it does not even pass under Mary's will. The Tax Relief Act of 2010 provides for "portability" between spouses of the maximum estate tax exemption. Generally, portability would allow John to take advantage of Mary's unused exception amount if she dies without using it completely and John dies prior to 2013. It would be available to John only if an election is made on a timely filed estate tax return. Reliance should not be placed on portability. This is merely a default for those who do not plan in advance. Problems arise if a surviving spouse remarries. Further, all postmortem appreciation of assets will be taxed. Proper asset titling, i.e., $5 million of assets in each spouse's name, is preferable to maximize tax savings and creditor protection.

8. **Qualified plans taxation** - Their 401(k)s, profit-sharing plan, and IRAs totaling $2.85 million will be devastated through double taxation. The combined income taxes and estate taxes due at death on these plans are $1,645,875 in 2011!

Objectives

- John has spent the past 30 years growing his business and, along with Mary, raising their children to appreciate hard work and an "attitude of gratitude." He would like to pass on not only assets to his grandchildren but also the same work ethic and family values his children have.

- John and Mary would like to ensure that Mary's lifestyle is secure if John dies prematurely and the business loses value.

- John and Mary despise estate taxes because they threaten the pool of legacy assets available for their children and grandchildren. They would like to pay no more in taxes than they have to and would like to shelter their children and grandchildren from the same tax challenges. They want to preserve and optimize their hard-earned assets.

◆ Because of Judy's past divorce, John and Mary are adamant about wanting to protect and keep Prescott family assets inside the Prescott family only.

◆ The Prescotts realize that a complete review of all of their estate documents and risk management program, i.e., life, disability, health, and P&C insurance, is necessary because no one has taken an objective, comprehensive look at them in many years. John and Mary do not want to be exposed to any unpleasant surprises or potential losses.

◆ Finally, John and Mary like the idea of charity but have no idea how to create something with lasting meaning. They are looking for ways to make the world a better place. However, they do not want to benefit charity at the expense of their family goals.

What is surprising is that John and Mary have long-term advisors in place, such as their accountant and attorney, and felt that their financial affairs were in pretty good shape. However, their estate preservation plan is another matter. They have not heard from their insurance agent since he sold them their policies in the mid-1990s. Their other advisors are extremely competent and have provided excellent guidance over the years, but John and Mary had been so focused on raising their family, running the business, and all of the other day-to-day activities that they neglected to pay attention to their over-all wealth preservation plan. They did not clarify and prioritize their goals because they thought they would get to it some day. Well, that day has come.

Let's take a step back and look at some global planning issues, and then we will relate how they specifically threaten the Prescott family wealth.

WHAT IS ESTATE PRESERVATION?

Estate preservation is the process of prearranging your financial matters for the benefit of your family or other beneficiaries of choice, both during your lifetime and after death. Estate preservation considers both tax planning and wealth distribution planning. Our four-step approach toward our high-net-worth clients is to:

1. Understand what they want to accomplish (that is, their objectives) during the **discovery process**

2. Educate them regarding what is already in place (that is, an **audit of their current documents,** the manner in which assets will pass under those documents, and the tax impact of their choices)

3. **Brainstorm** and illustrate options

4. Implement appropriate solutions through an **action plan**

"My Attorney Wrote a Will for My Spouse and Me— Our Estate Preservation Plan Is Done"

Is a will an estate preservation plan? How about a revocable living trust, power of attorney, or life insurance policy/trust to pay estate taxes?

The answer is that these are all *ingredients* of estate preservation. An effective plan is personal to you. It should not be boilerplate or the same as your neighbor's or the past 10 people who saw the same attorney you did. Once it's done,

> *These are all* **ingredients** *of estate preservation.*

can you put it in a drawer and forget about it? Not on your life! Estate preservation plans change constantly as a result of internal (family, net worth, new objectives) and external (tax laws, economic conditions, etc.) forces. For instance, the Prescotts' plan may have been adequate 20 years ago when it was created, but today, it falls drastically short of accomplishing their goals.

What Should an Estate Preservation Plan Do?

It will help accomplish your objectives in the following areas:

- Provide for your surviving spouse and other family members in the event of your demise.

- Provide that assets will be managed properly if you become disabled or incompetent.

- Distribute your assets in accordance with your wishes after you (and your spouse) are gone.

- Protect assets from predators and creditors (yours and those your children and grandchildren may someday face).

- Maximize use of all applicable Internal Revenue Code deductions, exclusions, and tax credits.

- Make sure that your family pays the absolute minimum amount of income, gift, estate, and generation-skipping taxes.

- Ensure that your charitable intentions are met.

- Provide for an equitable distribution of assets among your children (note: equitable does not necessarily mean equivalent dollar value, just a distribution plan that meets your definition of "fair").

- Objectively review your existing legal documents, such as wills, trusts, powers of attorney, living wills, health-care directives, prenuptial agreements, divorce decrees, etc.

- Review the ownership and beneficiary designation of life insurance policies and qualified retirement plans to minimize tax consequences and make sure they flow to whom you want, when you want, and in the proper amounts.

- Develop a prearranged plan for the management and expenses associated with long-term care.

- Create an exit strategy to monetize your business across all contingencies:
  - Lifetime sale
  - Family succession
  - Death
  - Disability

An estate preservation plan should be customized to meet any special needs you or your family may have and should anticipate both the good things and the bad things that could happen in the future.

WHY ISN'T PROPER ESTATE PRESERVATION ALWAYS DONE?

Since virtually everyone agrees that he or she ought to have a personalized holistic estate preservation plan, why is it that many people fall short? After reviewing literally thousands of plans over the past 25 years, we have found that most contain serious shortcomings. These can often be categorized as acts of omission, i.e., failure to address the important issues. Sometimes, the problems are minor and will result only in some unnecessary expense or delay for future heirs. More often, the mistakes are severe and will cost unnecessary millions in estate taxes that could have been easily avoided, or they may even cause assets to pass to unintended heirs.

Part of the problem is obvious: estate preservation, on some level, requires us to accept the fact that we're going to die. Most of us don't start our day with the thought that we could be dead tonight so we need to get our affairs in order. Wealth transfer will

> *Estate preservation, on some level, requires us to accept the fact that we're going to die.*

take place with or without your input. Successful wealth transfer planning, however, is a lifelong endeavor. Estate preservation and confiscatory taxes always seem to be the "problems" that can wait until the day's (or month's or year's) more pressing problems are addressed.

A less obvious part of the problem is advisor selection. Either people confuse higher costs with decreasing value and hire discount advisors to address this highly specialized area of their affairs or they keep the same advisor and plan that they've had for the past 20 or 30 years out of loyalty.

Even with sophisticated advisors in place, the client may not be ready to do proper planning. Some plans never become a reality. Some high-net-worth individuals feel that the estate plan recommended by previous advisors did not deal with their specific goals, objectives, and desires or was too complicated for them to understand, which caused them to become uneasy about implementation. They get derailed before documents are drafted and the trusts, LLCs, and other structures are even created. Many times we have clients come to us with documents that are unsigned and therefore ineffective. Furthermore, advisors don't always follow through. They are not immune to becoming discouraged by their clients' procrastination. They send a letter or place phone calls to clients and then move on. For some advisors, once clients pay their bills, seeing the plans come to fruition loses its urgency. Obviously, this is unacceptable for you and your family.

In our experience, virtually all patriarchs and matriarchs care deeply about the impact their actions will have on their families and legacies both during their lives and after they are gone. So why not resolve these issues during life through proper planning? The financial and personal lives of high-net-worth individuals tend to be very complex, and family dynamics can sometimes be intensified when money is brought into the equation.

Understanding what lifetime actions an individual is willing to undertake to secure his or her estate preservation objectives is paramount. For some, fear of the unknown or a desire to avoid conflict leads to inaction. For others, a desire to retain complete control of everything during life results in less than optimal planning. For many—and maybe most—not understanding the incredible positive impact planning can have on the people or institutions they care most about leads them to accept less than perfect methods and continued procrastination.

WHY GET A SECOND OPINION?
THE VALUE OF A FRESH LOOK!

Roughly 90% of the clients we are introduced to already have some level of planning in place. Regardless of all the good work they may have done in the past with their advisors, our clients find it to be extremely worthwhile to take a fresh look at estate preservation. Consider it a second opinion as seen through another set of eyes. The biggest mistake we see is the lack of periodic review or document audit. This should occur every few years or annually in the case of a complex, dynamic estate. Those periodic reviews can uncover potential threats, coordination gaps, and opportunities that allow for implementation of new strategies to control taxes and better assure that your assets will pass in the most efficient and protected manner.

Further, the decisions you and your spouse made years ago when documents were originally created probably do not reflect your thinking and circumstances today, on the basis of all of the financial turmoil, tax, and economic changes you have experienced of late. With passage of the Tax Relief Act of 2010 and the unprecedented planning opportunities it creates, all plans should be reviewed now.

> *With passage of the Tax Relief Act of 2010 and the unprecedented planning opportunities it creates, all plans should be reviewed now.*

Ask Yourself...

Can you describe, in simple terms, how your estate documents work? Do they contain any special distribution provisions relative to your family and their needs? Are the documents boilerplate or custom to meet your needs? Do you know who gets exactly what, when, and how? Do your children (and/or grandchildren) receive assets outright or under the protection of a trust? How do your testamentary trusts (created under your will upon death) or living trusts operate? Do beneficiaries receive an income stream for a certain number of years? Who decides how much they will get?

Will your children (and grandchildren) receive multimillion-dollar outright distributions before they are ready to invest wisely? Are assets protected from your heirs' predators and creditors? Have you done everything you possibly can to reduce the bite the IRS will take? While estate preservation is typically not a conversation starter at a cocktail party, do you wonder from time to time whether your planning is done as well as it absolutely can be, particularly in light of the ever-changing environment? Does this uncertainty keep you (or your spouse) up at night?

By the way, none of these questions are meant to disparage your attorney or accountant or the other professional advisors who helped craft your present estate plan. Ultimately, the responsibility for implementing and monitoring a proper plan is yours alone. What was done several years ago (and it's amazing how several years quickly become a decade or more) may have been state-of-the-art planning at that time. However, since this is not typically a top-of-mind area, you may be startled by how quickly your once current documents fade away into obsolescence.

Worse still, the IRS and the tax court system do not do a very good job of updating American taxpayers to alert them that their documents have fallen out of date, have become tax inefficient, or can potentially subject their assets to creditors they or inheriting family members may face. Again, it is up to you periodically to review and update your estate plan as the tax laws change and as your family needs change. Consider births and the adoption of children; new grandchildren; divorces; marriages; the passing on of beneficiaries, trustees, and guardians; and the multitude of other outside factors that could impact you and your family wealth.

So What Could Go Wrong?

Estate Settlement Costs

Estate taxes are the single largest threat to the transfer of wealth in this country. You work your entire life to earn a buck. You lose roughly 40 cents to various income taxes (federal and state), leaving 60 cents out of every

> *Estate taxes are the single largest threat to the transfer of wealth in this country.*

$1 to live on and invest. The 60 cents will manifest itself in savings, investments, and business or real estate assets that are taxed again at a minimum of 35% upon your death. This is the ultimate in double taxation.

If we look at your estate in its entirety (100%), you actually own and control the disposition of 65% of your assets. The U.S. Treasury has a "lien" on 35% above the exemptions, and it is waiting patiently to collect it. In fact, it hopes that you continue to work hard to grow your assets so that its share increases proportionately. After 2012, it is likely that the estate tax rate and exemption amount will change again. No one knows whether the tax will return to the 55% rate, as scheduled.

Most high-net-worth individuals are not aware of the dollar amount of the estate taxes that will be levied upon their estates after their demise— nor are they aware that the IRS demands cash payment of these taxes, generally within nine months of death! A forced sale of your most valuable assets or highest-income-producing property or the loss of control of a family business will result from not enough cash at the right time. Worse still, forced sales—because they yield pennies on the dollar to pay the full-priced tax bill—only compound the impact of failing to address one's estate preservation needs.

Upon the passing of John and Mary (assuming that both deaths occurred in 2011), total estate taxes and other settlement costs (probate, valuation, administration) will be **$13,959,145**.

Like most people, the Prescotts did not realize that the tax bill would be so high. Further, they had not considered which assets their family would be forced to liquidate in order to pay the tax bill. We can't help but wonder how many children have sat down nine months after the passing of their parents to write a check—the biggest check ever—to the U.S. Treasury. We wonder whether they ask, "Did our parents do all they could to help reduce the size of this check?" We also can't help but wonder what further loss in value was incurred as a result of poor timing, i.e., the forced liquidation of a stock portfolio, real estate, or closely held family business during a down market, and how, with just a little bit of planning and liquidity, much of this pain and financial loss could have been avoided.

Estate Tax Liquidity Analysis

Estate Settlement Costs (ESC)	$13,959,145
Assets to be sold/liquidated:	
Checking account	< 250,000>
IRA—John	< 250,000>
PresCo 401(k) plan	< 1,000,000>
PresCo profit-sharing plan	< 1,500,000>
IRA—Mary	< 100,000>
Brokerage account	< 3,500,000>
CD	< 150,000>
Less: Total	**≤ 6,750,000>**
Remaining ESC	**$ 7,209,145**

Which assets to sell now?

PresCo	$15,000,000
PresCo Realty	5,000,000
Residence	2,000,000
Beach house	1,500,000

Proper planning will enable you to calculate your estate taxes today and into the future, on the basis of conservative estimates and projections. More importantly, the process will educate you on all of the relevant strategies you may choose to implement to reduce estate taxes—and in some cases avoid them entirely. If we consider a 35% estate tax, the investment of time in estate preservation can help prevent the past 20 or 30 years of hard work and estate growth from going up in smoke. Moreover, it assures that assets pass to those you care about most.

Your Estate Can Go in Three Directions

A discussion of estate preservation often starts with a simple diagram that shows that your estate assets can go in one of three directions:

1. The IRS

2. Your family

3. Your charities of choice

Let's suppose that the estate tax is voluntary. What percentage of your assets would you choose to allocate to each of these three potential recipients?

- IRS ___%

- Your family ___%

- Charity ___%

The Estate Tax Is Voluntary

Obviously, just about everyone chooses some combination of family and charity. No one ever chooses to leave his or her assets to the IRS. This kind of "patriotism" is often inefficient and its effects unknown. We sometimes refer to the concepts of "voluntary" vs. "involuntary" philanthropy. Voluntary philanthropy proactively directs resources toward causes that are meaningful to the donor and society at large. Involuntary philanthropy is the confiscation of assets by taxation. In fact, developing a "zero estate tax" plan is entirely possible by integrating charitable giving strategies to reduce your taxable estate below the $5 million taxable threshold ($10 million for married couples in 2011 and 2012) and leaving the rest to charity. So, you see, the estate tax is voluntary.

A Brief Review of Federal Transfer Tax History

The year 2010 was an incredible year in the history of estate taxes in our country. For one year, the estate tax did not exist! The family of George M. Steinbrenner and many others who died in 2010 benefited from Congress's failure to impose a tax.

Most people believed that Congress would take action before the end of 2009 to prevent the temporary repeal in 2010 (the "sunset") by either introducing a new transfer tax regime or keeping the 2009 exemptions of $3.5 million and tax rates of 45% into 2010. However, the fight over health care and other political and economic issues diverted Congress's attention. Therefore, repeal took place in 2010 and shocked the advisory community. After a year filled with confusion and anxiety for families and advisors, Congress finally acted. President Obama signed the Tax Relief Act of 2010 on December 17 of that year.

Unfortunately, the estate tax is back. As a consequence, your plan needs to deal with this. The estate tax exemption for 2011 and 2012 is $5 million per taxpayer, and the top estate and generation-skipping transfer (GST) tax rate is 35%. Estate, gift, and GST taxes are unlikely ever to be repealed permanently, due in large part to budgetary concerns at both the federal and state levels and the surprising support of the super-affluent. Even Warren Buffett is a very vocal and visible supporter of estate taxes.

The most probable outcome for the federal estate tax after December 31, 2012, is, ultimately, some type of reform, not repeal. The Tax Relief Act of 2010 will "sunset," and we will revert to the higher-taxing pre-2001 estate, gift, and GST law unless a new compromise can be reached. Therefore, your estate preservation plan must address future estate, gift, and GST taxes and their tremendous impacts.

State Death Taxes
Bear in mind that state-level estate or inheritance taxes are expected to remain at current levels (or go higher), especially as states lose revenue from other sources and face major financial crises. The states have not increased their exemptions to the $5 million federal level. For example, the exemption in New Jersey is only $675,000; in New York, it's $1 million. So while an estate may pass free of federal estate taxes, state death taxes can be substantial. State death taxes remain deductible on federal estate tax returns. However, the newly enacted 35% federal estate tax rate effectively increases the cost of dying as a resident of a high-taxing state, such as New York or New Jersey. You now have greater incentive to establish domicile in a state that does not impose state death taxes, such as Florida, New Hampshire, and Virginia. Careful analysis is needed to determine how to minimize, defer, or provide for payment of state death taxes in your state of residence and *all* states in which you own property.

WEALTH DISTRIBUTION PLANNING

The wealthy often have reasons that extend beyond just tax planning to review and revise their wills and trusts. Your estate documents, such as wills and trusts, along with asset titling, beneficiary designations and other instruments control the distribution of your wealth. John and Mary Prescott had created simple wills more than 20 years ago. They are insufficient, given current events, their objectives, and the size of their net worth.

Simple Wills
Surprisingly, we frequently come across high-net-worth individuals, such as John and Mary, who still have simple, or "I Love You," wills with their spouse. In other words, each spouse leaves everything he or she owns directly to the other, and upon the death of the second spouse, the estate is passed on to the couple's children, often outright in a lump-sum inheritance.

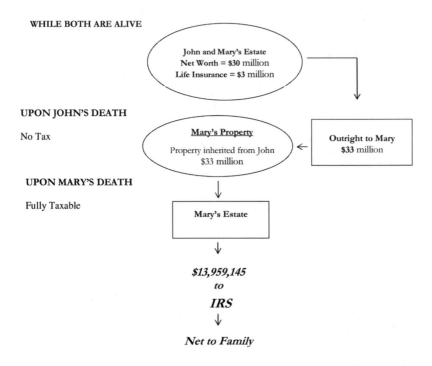

While this may appear to be perfectly acceptable on the surface, as all assets are transferred to Mary upon John's passing, it poses a host of tax, distribution, and asset protection threats.

- Assets pass outright to surviving spouse
  - No asset protection
  - No protection in the event of a second marriage
  - No assurance that assets will pass to your children
  - No ability to have professional asset management assistance from a trustee

The Tax Relief Act of 2010 creates the concept of portability. This means that a decedent's surviving spouse will be able to add the unused $5 million exemption amount to his or her own exemption amount. However, portability is neither a panacea nor a substitute for proper estate preservation planning. Portability sunsets on December 31, 2012. It's a bad bet to rely on it if you and your spouse plan to live beyond 2012. Instead, proactive trust planning is desirable. In addition to the substantial non-tax benefits associated with trusts, including asset management and asset protection, opting for trust planning in lieu of portability by default can produce major tax benefits. Under the new portability rules, the deceased spouse's unused estate tax exemption is effectively frozen. Alternatively, if a deceased spouse has used the exemption by creating a "credit shelter" trust for the benefit of the surviving spouse, *all* appreciation of the trust's assets during the survivor's lifetime will escape taxation at the survivor's death. Furthermore, portability does not apply to the GST exemption for assets passing to grandchildren. Therefore, for families wishing to ensure tax savings and asset protection over multiple generations, proper trust planning remains an essential component of estate preservation planning. Finally, portability doesn't apply to state death tax exemptions. Thus, for residents of New York and New Jersey and many other states that impose an estate tax, trusts are needed to secure state death tax benefits. Careful planning is necessary to save taxes, preserve flexibility, and defend your family wealth for future generations.

Other problems associated with simple wills that threaten your family wealth include:

- Assets subsequently pass outright to children
  - Exposure to their potential creditors and predators
  - Inclusion of assets in children's taxable estates before passing to grandchildren

Joint Assets

Another common estate preservation threat is the misuse of jointly titled assets. Most married couples tend to acquire assets in joint name, typically as joint tenants with rights of survivorship, or JTWROS. John and Mary have $6.9 million in assets titled as JTWROS. Commonly, the personal residence, vacation home, bank account, CDs, brokerage accounts, and other assets are jointly titled between married spouses. Would you be surprised to learn that joint titling bypasses the tax efficiencies and asset protection created by your wills? The reason is that JTWROS assets (just like assets under a simple will) pass to the surviving joint tenant and do not pass through your will or testamentary trust. In fact, it is often said that the will is the *weakest* document. Joint titling and beneficiary designations will *override* whatever your will and testamentary trust may say. As previously mentioned, John and Mary each have the ability to shelter $5 million in assets from estate and GST taxes. However, they are able to take full advantage of this only to the extent that their assets are structured and titled properly. With jointly titled assets, they will not be able to take full advantage of both estate tax exemptions. In order to use both exemptions and maintain flexibility, they need to have sufficient assets titled in each name separately, along with the proper wills that direct $5 million of the first person to die's assets to a family trust. The problem is that if that person does not have enough assets controllable by his or her will, the trust will not be fully funded. John has plenty of assets in his sole name ($23 million); however, Mary does not have any assets in her name (other than her $100,000 IRA, which does not qualify, as it passes by beneficiary designation, not through her will). Therefore, her $5 million credit could be wasted, resulting in potentially $1,750,000 (at 35% estate tax rate) of completely unnecessary taxes if she predeceases John.

Life Insurance Ownership and Beneficiary Pitfalls

Much confusion surrounds the proper ownership and beneficiary arrangement of life insurance policies. In all my years, I have never seen the IRS named as a beneficiary of a life insurance policy on an application. However, this is exactly what

> *I have never seen the IRS named as a beneficiary.*

happens every day as a result of lack of proper planning. Again, the tendency with married couples is often to name their spouse as the beneficiary of a life insurance policy. John and Mary are no exception. Mary is the beneficiary of the $3 million life insurance policies on John's life. John is the owner of his policies. This is the way most insurance is written in the United States today and has been since the beginning of the insurance industry. When it comes to planning for high-net-worth individuals, this arrangement is entirely unacceptable because this type of life insurance ownership and beneficiary designation inadvertently makes the IRS the beneficiary of more than half of the insurance proceeds upon the passing of the surviving spouse. I am sure that's not what John and Mary had in mind.

Most people are shocked by this discovery because they believe that life insurance is tax free. In fact, it is *income tax free* under the Internal Revenue Code. However, when the insured (or spouse) owns the policy, it becomes includible in his or her taxable estate. This tax problem also applies if the policy is owned by a corporation or another entity controlled by the insured.

The Prescotts, in essence, are paying premiums for $3 million of life insurance coverage but are receiving only $2 million of net proceeds. No client I've ever met is OK with paying one and a half times the premium amount he or she should for life insurance.

Why is this wasteful tax problem so common? It can be due to any number of reasons. People care about their spouses and want to fix the problem as quickly and simply as possible, so they just buy the insurance. Furthermore, many people either don't know about the tax problem (nor does their insurance agent) or don't care enough about the impact to take the time and additional steps to defend against it.

Some other consequences of incorrect life insurance ownership include:

- Children could potentially be disinherited. What if John dies and Mary remarries? Through no fault of her own, Mary may create another simple will (or title her savings and investment accounts into which the proceeds are deposited in joint name) with her second husband. As a result, if Mary dies before her new husband, assets pass to him and then under **his** will to whomever he designates (possibly not John's children and grandchildren).

- Children or grandchildren (at age 18 or 21) could inherit unnecessarily taxed life insurance proceeds in a lump sum.

- Assets are not protected from the surviving spouse's creditors and, ultimately, children's creditors and potential divorce.

- Professional asset management of proceeds is lacking for the family

Qualified Retirement Plan Taxation

Another area of major concern for high-net-worth individuals is the taxation of their qualified retirement plans and IRAs at death. People establish qualified retirement plans such as pensions, profit sharing, 401(k)s, 403(b)s, and IRAs to provide for their future retirement income and to defer income taxes

> *Qualified retirement plans and IRAs may well be the best place to accumulate wealth while you are alive, but they may be the absolute worst place to own assets when you die.*

as long as possible. These are admirable goals. However, the IRS levies a significant penalty for keeping money in such plans for too long and deferring distributions (which deprives the IRS income tax revenue) and attempting to use these vehicles as a way to pass on wealth to children and grandchildren. Most people wait until required minimum distributions are necessary at age 70 1/2 before taking money out of their plans. Because of the substantial value of assets held in John's and Mary's qualified retirement plans and IRAs, they will trigger significant taxation upon death—both income and estate taxes. These qualified retirement plans and IRAs may well be the best place to accumulate wealth while you are alive, but they may be the absolute worst place to own assets when you die.

Let's examine the Prescott family example. When the survivor of John and Mary dies, the first tax that applies to their $2.85 million retirement plans as they pass to their children is the federal estate tax. If we assume that they are in the 35% marginal estate tax bracket, estate taxes attributed to their retirement plans would be $997,500. Second is the income tax. At a 35% marginal income tax bracket, the income tax on a lump-sum payout would be another $648,375. The bottom line is a total tax bill of $1,645,875, resulting in a loss of 58% of their plan assets. That leaves only $1,204,125 of the original $2.85 million for their children. Imposition of state-level income and inheritance taxes makes matters worse. Once again, taxes threaten and divert wealth intended for the family and transfer it to the IRS and state tax collectors instead.

Qualified Retirement Plan Analysis

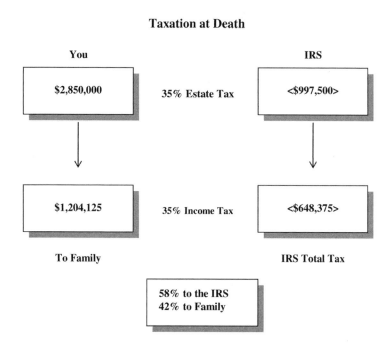

Taxation at Death

You		IRS
$2,850,000	35% Estate Tax	<$997,500>
$1,204,125	35% Income Tax	<$648,375>
To Family		IRS Total Tax

58% to the IRS
42% to Family

Some clients ask, "What if my children don't take a lump-sum distribution and 'stretch' my qualified plan and IRA over their lifetimes after I'm gone?" First, this is possible only if enough "other" cash is available to pay transfer taxes at death. If that luxury of estate liquidity does not exist, then the children will be forced to take a lump-sum distribution from the qualified plan/IRA itself to pay the estate tax due. Moreover, deferring withdrawals from qualified plans saves *overall* income taxes only if income tax rates decrease over time. Otherwise, deferring income taxes on qualified plans (by stretching out distributions) often serves to *increase* the amount ultimately paid to the IRS.

Leaving Assets Outright to Children

We commonly review the will or trust of high-net-worth individuals and find that these instruments are designed to leave assets outright to their children once they attain specified ages (age 30 or 35 is common). This is the case with John and Mary. Twenty years ago when John and Mary created their wills, their children were minors and their net worth was much less. The thought of estate distribution probably seemed so distant. Now that their estate is as large as it is and their children are adults and they have grandchildren, this is clearly no longer an advisable plan. In any event, John and Mary are unaware that they have chosen to leave assets to their children in such an unprotected manner.

Assets left to children *outright* will be subject to:

♦ The potential claims of a divorcing spouse

♦ The potential claims of children's creditors (lawsuits, auto liabilities, malpractice, bankruptcy, etc.)

♦ Gift taxes, should they try to give away the assets they have inherited to your current or future grandchildren while living

♦ Estate taxes when assets are left to the next generation (i.e., grandchildren)

So, for every $1 million left to children outright, it is subject to $350,000 in estate taxes. The remaining $650,000 will be subject to estate taxes again when the children try to pass those assets on to their children. At a 35% marginal rate, the $650,000 gets hit with another 35% tax, equal to $227,500. Thus, the original $1 million inheritance generates $577,500 for the government (57.75%) and $422,500 (42.25%) for grandchildren (not including growth). This is not the way to defend family wealth—it is the antithesis.

Estate Preservation Strategies

Once you have your arms around your current situation and determine how it may fall short of achieving your goals, the time has come to design a plan to defend your wealth that makes sense for you and your family on the basis of your objectives, values, and preferences.

There are many transfer tax and estate preservation strategies and options, some of which just about everyone ought to put in place and others that, while important to some of our clients, may not be applicable to others. They are too numerous to cover in this book. We have selected a few of the most effective and universally appropriate ones.

We have organized chosen strategies on the following wealth preservation planning pyramid (another pyramid!). We will explain various potential recommendations in accordance with the following levels of planning:

1. **Fundamental** - Ensure that your cash flow needs are satisfied to maintain your preferred standard of living (preparation of a comprehensive financial independence model will help determine whether you are on track). Creation of up-to-date core estate documents is necessary. Proper asset titling, beneficiary designations, and ownership of existing life insurance policies are essential.

   You would be amazed by the number of high-net-worth families who, unfortunately, have not executed even the fundamental level of proper planning or have not kept current.

2. **Basic** - This involves simple lifetime planning to reduce your taxable estate through annual exclusion gifts, either outright to family members or into estate-tax-exempt trusts.

3. **Intermediate** - This utilizes your $5 million lifetime gift tax exemption proactively to reduce future estate taxes and protect assets inside various trusts.

4. **Advanced** - This focuses on managing estate tax liability by utilization of remainder interest transactions and creative financing tools for the acquisition of estate liquidity insurance.

   Also, consider techniques that provide leverage through various discounting techniques that allow you to transfer a dollar of value for less than 100 cents. These discounts are created through the use of:
   ♦ Valuation discounts, such as minority interest, lack of marketability, or lack of voting control

- Time value of money
- Life insurance (ratio of premiums paid to death benefits provided creates leverage)

5. **Charitable planning** - For those who choose to aspire to this level of planning, it focuses on optimal charitable planning through the use of trusts and foundations.

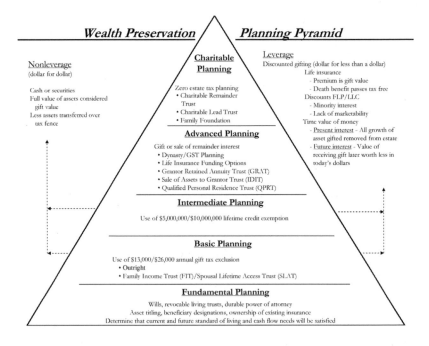

FUNDAMENTAL PLANNING

Cash Flow Analysis

Our Financial Independence Model (FIM) shows that John and Mary are projected to be OK. They have substantial excess cash flow, or discretionary income, to maintain their standard of living, even under a variety of assumptions. Their annual discretionary income is in excess of $200,000 per year. After John sells his business in five years, their cumulative discretionary income account is projected to be more than $15 million, even after income and capital gains taxes are paid.

Therefore, the Prescotts are excellent candidates for all levels of planning, i.e., fundamental, basic, intermediate, and certain advanced and charitable strategies.

Fundamental Estate Distribution Documents
A/B Testamentary Trust Will with QTIP

A/B testamentary trust plans require the execution of a will or revocable living trust, which, at death, optimizes tax exemptions by dividing the deceased spouse's probate assets into two portions: a credit shelter trust and a marital part.

The credit shelter trust is funded with the amount that can pass free of federal transfer taxes at both spouses' deaths, currently $5 million for 2011 and 2012. The trust is held for the benefit of the entire family. Often, we recommend that our clients consider keeping the credit shelter trust in continuing trust and use discretionary (not mandatory) distributions of trust assets to give their family access to these family assets while providing asset protection and management assistance.

The marital part is funded with the balance of the deceased spouse's probate estate. The marital part is held for the ***exclusive*** benefit of the surviving spouse, who ***must*** receive all trust income. We often recommend that our clients keep the balance of the marital part in a marital trust, or QTIP, in continuing trust for the surviving spouse and use discretionary (not mandatory) distributions or trust principal to provide for the surviving spouse. Assets passed down through the marital, or QTIP, trust are subject to estate taxes when the surviving spouse dies. On the following page, you will see a flow diagram showing how an A/B testamentary trust will work for the Prescott family.

A/B Testamentary Will and QTIP Trust

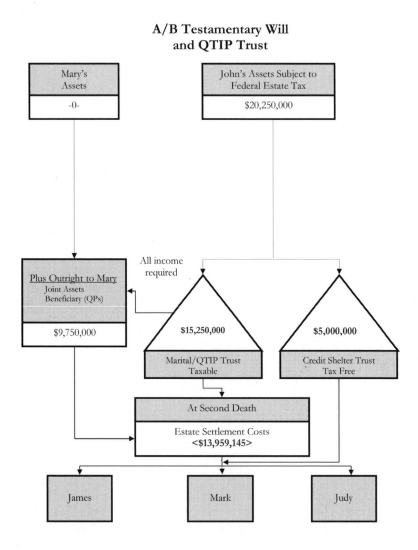

Asset Titling

Because no one can predict which spouse will die first, to best optimize each spouse's credit, we advise retitling enough assets into each spouse's individual name to provide for the optimum use of unified credit and generation-skipping exemptions available to each at death. Jointly titled assets will not work for this purpose. For 2011, $5 million should be retitled into Mary's separate name.

We also recommend that the following additional estate preservation documents be created (or updated) to protect you and your wealth.

Durable Power of Attorney

- In the event that either you or your spouse should become incompetent, the management of your property would experience a significant break. Simple matters such as cashing checks, signing tax returns, endorsing insurance policies, etc., could not be conducted without petitioning a court to appoint a guardian for the incapacitated spouse's affairs. A guardianship proceeding can be very time-consuming, bothersome, and expensive for your family. A durable power of attorney is a document that provides an informal and inexpensive alternative to a guardianship by appointing an agent to manage the incapacitated principal's assets during incapacity. Typically, a spouse or an adult child is appointed. A durable power of attorney can provide your family with the ability to plan for taxes even if you are unable to do so.

Living Wills

- A living will is a document that lets your family members and doctors know what type of care you do or do not want if you become terminally ill or permanently unconscious. It allows you to direct your doctor and hospital to refrain from using certain life-sustaining medical treatment, such as respirators and feeding tubes. A living will may also allow you to instruct that certain treatment be undertaken, such as medication to ease pain.

- Importantly, the administration of the directions contained in a living will necessarily calls for a judgment on the part of someone as to when death is imminent, with no hope of recovery. Usually, this will be your doctor or attending physician, who will most likely want to discuss the decision with a designated close relative who shall be named in the living will.

Also consider a HIPAA release and authorization. Under today's stringent privacy rules, this permits family members to receive your medical records and other health information on your behalf if you become incapacitated.

BASIC PLANNING

Annual Exclusion Gifts

An individual donor can annually give up to $13,000 to any other individual free of transfer tax liability (of course, the receipt of the gift is not taxable income for the donee). This $13,000 can be combined (or split) with a gift from the donor's spouse to the same donee, to double the amount transferred to $26,000 per year. The donor and spouse may make annual exclusion gifts to any number of donees during a given tax year.

Let's look again at the Prescott family. John and Mary have three children, two children-in-law, and three grandchildren, for a total of eight possible donees/beneficiaries. In 2011, John and Mary can make split gifts to each family member or a trust for their benefit, resulting in a gift-tax-exempt transfer of **$26,000 × 8** beneficiaries = **$208,000** each and every year.

Let's start with the idea of making gifts to reduce the size of the taxable estate. This can best be explained with the "tax fence" concept.

Referring to the diagram below, we see that the assets on the left side of the tax fence are includible in the Prescotts' estate and are subject to estate taxes. Assets on the right side of the fence in a vehicle, such as the Prescott family income trust, will pass tax free to family members. Assets can be transferred from the left side to the right side of the fence by making gifts and taking advantage of the annual gift tax exclusions and lifetime exemptions.

Prescott Family Example

TAX FENCE CONCEPT

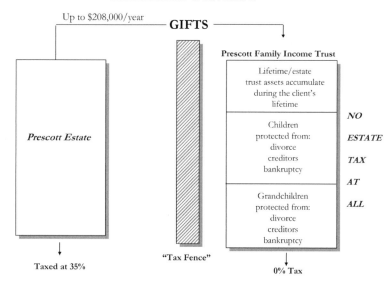

Bottom line: *Every dollar you throw over the fence puts an additional 35 cents in your heirs' pockets and provides multigenerational asset protection.*

The tax fence concept also reminds me of the "left pocket/right pocket" story. Let's suppose that all of the money in your left pocket was taxed at 35%, while the money kept in your right pocket was tax free. What would you do? You would remove all of the money from your left pocket and stuff it into your right pocket! While oversimplifying, I am trying to make a point. The IRS taxes the assets you leave behind inside of your taxable estate to pass down to your family through your (and your spouse's) wills and revocable trusts on the left side of the fence. The assets you transfer over the tax fence into an estate-tax-exempt family income trust are completely free of estate taxes and, if properly structured, generation-skipping taxes. This is an excellent way to defend your family wealth.

So why doesn't everyone do it?

Two reasons:

1. **Gift tax exposure.** If you carefully navigate and utilize available gift tax annual exclusions and lifetime exemptions, this should not be a problem. Utilize your:
   a. $13,000/$26,000 annual exclusion gifts
   b. $5 million/$10 million lifetime exemption gifts (in 2011 and 2012)

   Arguably, paying gift taxes while you are alive is mathematically superior to paying estate taxes after you (and your spouse) are gone. Walk before you run; exhaust all tax-free strategies before considering payment of gift taxes.

2. **Affordability.** Again, remember "Are we OK?" No one wants to impoverish himself or herself (or even come close) in order to minimize future estate tax exposure. Therefore, you need to create and analyze your financial independence models (before and *after* contemplated gifts, to make sure that you and your spouse will continue to be OK).

Once you and your advisors ascertain that you will not inadvertently create gift tax liability or compromise your financial independence, the long-term economics and benefits of a gifting program are staggering.

See the following spreadsheet for the economics of gifting based on the Prescotts' ability to make annual $208,000 gifts to a tax-exempt trust. Note that in 30 years, the trust will hold $9,273,221 (column 5) for the family (completely free of gift, estate, and generation-skipping taxes) rather than $6,027,594 (column 4).

The Economics of Gifting
For John and Mary Prescott

Assumptions:

Annual gift	$208,000
Pretax rate of return	7.00%
Income tax rate	40.00%
Estate tax rate	35.00%

Year	Annual Gift (1)	Balance Forward (2)	After-Tax Earnings (3)	Investment Balance Left to Family	
				In Taxable Estate (4)	Out of Estate (5)
2011	$208,000	$208,000	$8,736	$140,878	$216,736
2012	208,000	424,736	17,839	287,674	442,575
2013	208,000	650,575	27,324	440,634	677,899
2014	208,000	885,899	37,208	600,019	923,107
2015	208,000	1,131,107	47,506	766,099	1,178,613
2016	208,000	1,386,613	58,238	939,153	1,444,851
2017	208,000	1,652,851	69,420	1,119,476	1,722,271
2018	208,000	1,930,271	81,071	1,307,372	2,011,342
2019	208,000	2,219,342	93,212	1,503,160	2,312,555
2020	208,000	2,520,555	105,863	1,707,172	2,626,418
2021	208,000	2,834,418	119,046	1,919,751	2,953,463
2022	208,000	3,161,463	132,781	2,141,259	3,294,245
2023	208,000	3,502,245	147,094	2,372,070	3,649,339
2024	208,000	3,857,339	162,008	2,612,576	4,019,347
2025	208,000	4,227,347	177,549	2,863,182	4,404,896
2026	208,000	4,612,896	193,742	3,124,314	4,806,368
2027	208,000	5,014,638	210,615	3,396,414	5,225,252
2028	208,000	5,433,252	228,197	3,679,942	5,661,449
2029	208,000	5,869,449	246,517	3,975,378	6,115,966
2030	208,000	6,323,966	265,607	4,283,222	6,589,572
2031	208,000	6,797,572	285,498	4,603,996	7,083,070
2032	208,000	7,291,070	306,225	4,938,242	7,597,295
2033	208,000	7,805,295	327,822	5,286,527	8,133,118
2034	208,000	8,341,118	350,327	5,649,439	8,691,445
2035	208,000	8,899,445	373,777	6,027,594	9,273,221

INTERMEDIATE PLANNING

$5 Million Credit against Taxable Transfers: An Overview

The current federal transfer tax system allows an individual to make $5 million of taxable gifts (at death) without having to pay any estate tax. This credit is the reason that many estates—because they are worth less than $5 million—will have no tax liability in 2011 and 2012. Additionally, the credit is available to anyone, meaning that married couples may, in combination, transfer $10 million at death without having to pay any estate tax.

Because the Tax Relief Act of 2010 provided for reunification of gift and estate taxes, individuals may also take an advance on their credit for lifetime gifts of up to $5 million. Accordingly, anyone during his or her life has the one-time opportunity to gift up to $5 million without having to pay any gift tax. Note, however, that every dollar of lifetime credit used reduces the amount of the credit available at death. This $5 million/$10 million lifetime tax-free transfer is *in addition* to annual gift tax exclusion gifts of $13,000/$26,000 per donee.

The $5 million exemption ($10 million for a married couple) is not a family heirloom to die with. If you can afford to do so, you should consider transferring some or all of the credit during your lifetime. You pay a significant tax penalty by waiting until you die to use this credit because all of the appreciation in value is included in the taxable estate.

What if the estate tax exemption is decreased in the future after you have used your $5 million gift tax exemption? Will there be a "clawback"? The consensus is that Congress and/or the IRS will act to avoid any type of clawback or adverse consequences. Even if some type of clawback were to occur, it is still beneficial to make significant gifts because:

- The asset appreciation will be excluded from your estate

- Not having made the gift would have resulted in a larger tax

- Gift tax exclusivity—If you survive the date of the gift by three years, the gift tax is not in your estate

Let's assume that you can afford to use the credit now, instead of waiting until you die. If you transfer $5 million of assets out of your estate today, under the rule of 72 and an assumed 6% growth rate, the amount would double every 12 years. If you live 12 years after the transfer, the assets will have grown to $10 million; in 24 years, they will be worth $20 million; in 36 years, they will be worth $40 million; and so on. Therefore, as a result, the actual amount transferred tax free would be $40 million, not just $5 million. That is a potential tax savings of more $12,250,000 since the $40 million would have been included in your taxable estate.

The time is **NOW**. Most people are not aware of this opportunity to transfer and protect their wealth. This is also extremely timely, because, unfortunately, as a result of the recent economic downturn, many people are holding assets that are worth significantly less than they were just a few years ago. I don't recall a better time in recent history to engage in this type of proactive estate preservation. The combination of low valuations and historically low interest rates creates the perfect storm for the application of certain estate preservation strategies. These include advanced-level planning strategies, such as sales to intentionally defective grantor trusts (IDITs), GRATs, and intrafamily sales and loans, as well as sales and loans to grantor trusts.

We reiterate: the time to take advantage of these strategies is now. Once interest rates climb and stock prices, real estate values, and the values of certain closely held businesses return to previous levels and move beyond, these wealth transfer strategies will be much less effective. Furthermore, future legislation may reduce the amount of the lifetime gift tax exemption or may take away the availability of certain techniques or make them less effective.

> *The time to take advantage of these strategies is now.*

FAMILY INCOME TRUST (FIT)

Rather than making gifts outright to family members, you might consider a family income trust (FIT), also known as an irrevocable trust, as a receptacle of gifts. The terms and conditions of the trust, including income and principal distributions, can be flexible and may be tailored to your distribution goals. Additionally, the family income trust can ensure that assets left to your children will be protected and stay within your family bloodline.

This is often preferable over giving assets outright to family members. A family income trust can do the following:

- Provide liquidity to pay estate taxes by purchasing assets from the taxable estate

- Loan proceeds to estate to pay taxes

- Make bequests to heirs

- Equalize inheritances

- Protect assets from creditors, liability, divorce, and taxes

- Provide the trustee the use of gifted cash to acquire life insurance on the trust grantor(s) (this is a highly efficient method to provide for future payment of estate taxes)

Advantages

- Asset protection—protects gifted assets from creditors and predators of trust beneficiaries

- Receives assets transferred through the use of annual exclusion and lifetime gift tax exemptions

- Removes assets from estate taxation at the death of the grantor

- Removes growth of gifted assets from the estate

- Provides management assistance for beneficiaries

- Provides a fund of cash that can be used to loan money to or purchase assets from a decedent's estate, thereby creating estate tax liquidity

- Principal and income can be sprinkled to beneficiaries without the use of additional exclusion or credits through an independent trustee

- Avoids probate

Considerations

- The trust is irrevocable, and its provisions cannot be changed. However, the trust can be drafted to provide for flexibility in case of changing tax laws or personal circumstances through special "kick-out" distribution provisions for the beneficiaries and trust-to-trust merger provisions.

- Loss of control over assets once transferred into the trust—The chosen trustee directs the use of trust assets.

- Administration—To qualify for the annual gift tax exclusion, the trust should provide its beneficiaries with the right to withdraw gifts from the trust for a certain time (typically 30 days) after the gifts are made. These withdrawal powers are known as Crummey powers. By the way, if you already have an FIT, have you sent Crummey notices to all beneficiaries each year a gift was made?

ADVANCED PLANNING

Giving away the Best Parts of Assets

Basic and intermediate planning strategies essentially involve tax-free direct gifts of assets through annual and lifetime gifts. However, "pure" gifts alone cannot effectively manage most high-net-worth families' transfer-tax problems. John and Mary, for instance, can give away $10 million (through outright gifts) and supplement their lifetime credit gift with annual exclusion gifts of $26,000 × 8 beneficiaries = $208,000, as previously illustrated. But because of their success—and high net worth—John and Mary are just not able to give away enough assets to their children to eliminate their estate tax liability. Furthermore, to give away ownership and control of so much wealth could severely compromise their own financial independence.

So what are high-net-worth families such as the Prescotts to do? They can't give away enough assets to manage their estate tax problem. Let's look at giving away the best parts of an asset.

Simply stated, an asset can be divided into two parts: an income interest and a remainder interest. You can retain the income interest, that is, the right to receive income (such as rents, interest, and dividends) from an asset, but at the end of a certain number of years, the asset itself (reminder interest), plus growth, passes to a family member or trust for his or her benefit, free of any gift or estate taxes. On Wall Street, these kinds of exchanges are sometimes called arbitrage transactions. In estate preservation, these transactions are usually called GRATs, QPRTs, or IDIT sales. Each involves the same basic concept: exchanging an asset (hopefully for less than full price) for future payments at a given rate of interest. In practice, each of these transactions seeks to reduce estate taxes by transferring value and growth in exchange for something less.

GENERATION-SKIPPING TRANSFER (GST) TAX PLANNING

Under the Tax Relief Act of 2010, the GST tax has returned. It affects transfers to your grandchildren, future grandchildren, and beyond. The exemption is $5 million per donor ($10 million per couple), just like the gift and estate tax exemption. This creates extremely valuable planning opportunities for 2011 and 2012. In many instances, you can use your GST exemption to shelter $10 million (or more with advanced planning techniques) of your family wealth from estate, gift, and GST taxes—not just at your children's deaths but forever. Thus, proper planning of gifts and bequests to take advantage of this dramatic GST exemption increase will allow many families to achieve long-term tax savings of tens of millions of dollars while shifting great wealth to multigenerational and dynasty trusts with asset protection features.

Note that the Tax Relief Act's two-year life span creates continuing uncertainty as to the effect of the exemption after 2012, so generation-skipping transfers need to be carefully structured. Beware: the act preserves the "automatic allocation" rule, which means that many people are unknowingly wasting their GST exemptions by making gifts to nondynasty (GST) trusts. A thorough review of your gift-giving history and gift tax returns filed should be undertaken to properly plan for the use of your precious GST exemption.

GRANTOR RETAINED ANNUITY TRUST (GRAT)

A GRAT is an irrevocable trust into which you (the grantor) place assets and retain an annuity (income stream) for a fixed period of years. Principal, at the end of the specified period of years, will pass to your beneficiary, such as your child or another trust for his or her benefit. During this period, the trustee (which could be you) will pay the donor/grantor (you again) either a fixed amount with a GRAT or a fixed percentage of the value of the asset with a GRUT (grantor-retained unitrust) on an annual basis by using trust income and, if necessary, principal.

A gift is made to your beneficiaries upon creation of the trust. But since the trust principal will not be distributed to your beneficiaries (usually your children) immediately, the IRS permits a discount on the gift. GRATs work best in a low-interest-rate environment—like the one we are in right now! The measure of the gift is your beneficiaries' remainder interest, substantially less than the value of the asset today. At the end of the trust term, the trust may be terminated, with trust principal distributed to your beneficiaries, including all appreciation in value.

If you survive the trust term selected, significant tax and other transfer cost reductions may be realized. This technique works best on highly appreciating assets. Planning under the Tax Relief Act of 2010 is more favorable because of the higher gift tax exemption. You can choose to establish a lower annual payment or a shorter term to facilitate a successful outcome with greater ease.

GRAT EXAMPLE

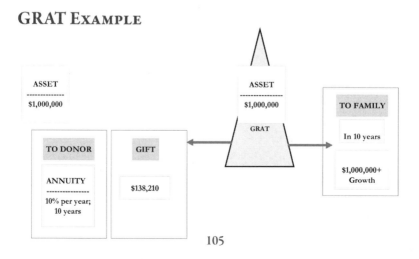

ASSET	ASSET	TO FAMILY
$1,000,000	$1,000,000	In 10 years
	GRAT	

TO DONOR	GIFT	$1,000,000+ Growth
ANNUITY	$138,210	
10% per year; 10 years		

Advantages

- No current gift tax due—Your $5 million lifetime gift tax exemption would be used to shelter the $138,210 gift, resulting in ZERO gift tax (of course, your $5 million would be reduced by $138,210 to $4,861,790).

- Leverage is provided by the time value of money with respect to the amount of the gift.

- Asset value and future appreciation are transferred outside of your taxable estate.

- Income from the trust is retained and payable to the grantor (you) during the trust term. The grantor chooses the term of years the GRAT will last. It can be as short as two or three years (Walton GRAT) or as long as 10, 15, or more years. Congress recently attempted to limit GRAT terms to 10 years, but final legislation did not address it.

Considerations

- Possible gift tax if you exceed the $5 million gift tax exemption— This risk heightens if any aggressively low valuation was placed on the asset transferred and/or valuation discounts are challenged upon audit.

- Loss of control of asset after GRAT term if left outright to beneficiaries—This can be mitigated if assets at the end of the GRAT term pour over into another trust. Note: Be wary of GRAT assets passing to grandchildren. This could inadvertently trigger a generation-skipping tax due to the so-called ETIP rule, which requires GST exemption to be allocated at the end of the GRAT term, not the beginning. As a result, the appreciation is potentially taxed for GST purposes.

- If the grantor (you) dies during the trust term, the asset's value and any appreciation are includable in your estate. (Recommendation: Don't die!)

- Your beneficiary receives your income tax basis, i.e., loss of step-up in basis upon your death.

- Annual asset value appraisal will be needed during the term of the GRAT (if there is not enough cash flow to make payments and, therefore, principal must be returned). This is simple if assets are easily valued, such as marketable securities. It gets a little more tricky and costly if hard-to-value assets are given away, such as closely held business interests. Competent third-party appraisals are necessary.

QUALIFIED PERSONAL RESIDENCE TRUST

A qualified personal residence trust (QPRT) is a method to transfer your personal residence or vacation home to a trust for a period of years and to your beneficiaries of choice with little or no gift or estate tax.

The trust would hold the real property for a term of years, during which you would live in the residence free of rent. This is similar to a GRAT in that you retain the use and enjoyment of the house rather than income since a personal residence does not produce income. At the end of the trust term, the residence would pass to your selected beneficiaries, typically your children. It may be passed outright or into another trust. At that point, you would pay fair-market rent to live there. (The rent would not be considered a gift and would further reduce your taxable estate.)

Advantages
- Now may be a good time to get an appraisal, with housing values being relatively low.

- Leverage is provided by the time value of money with respect to the amount of the gift.

- The residence and appreciation are out of your taxable estate.

- The property is available to use during the trust term without paying rent.

- To the extent that rent is paid after the trust term, it reduces the value of your estate.

Considerations

- Is a QPRT the best use of your lifetime gift tax exemption? Does your residence or vacation home have significant appreciation potential (or more rapid appreciation than other assets you could transfer)?

- If you die during the trust term, the value of your residence is includable in your estate, but offset gift tax credit is restored. With the larger gift tax exemption available under the Tax Relief Act of 2010, you may want to create a shorter-term QPRT, i.e., 10 years rather than 15 years. This uses up more of your exemption but reduces the risk of dying before the end of the trust term.

- Potential loss of control of asset after QPRT term if given outright to beneficiaries—To avoid this, QPRT can pour over into another trust after the term ends.

- Your beneficiary receives your income tax cost basis, i.e., loss of step-up in basis upon your death.

- Fair-market rent should be paid after the trust term, if you choose to continue to occupy the residence.

- Mortgages—Outstanding mortgages should not be transferred, so they should be paid off prior to transfer to QPRT, or you must become a personal guarantor and remain liable.

If the Prescotts transferred their beach house to a 15-year QPRT, here's what it would look like.

QPRT EXAMPLE

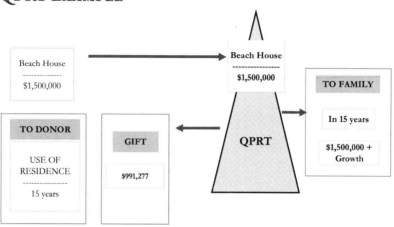

The $5 million lifetime gift tax exemption would be utilized, resulting in ZERO gift tax liability ($5,000,000 – $991,277 = $4,008,723 exemption remaining). Assuming that John (if he is the grantor; also Mary could be, or they can split the deed, with each spouse transferring a half interest) survives 15 years, the value of the beach house and any appreciation will pass outside of their taxable estates.

SALE TO AN INTENTIONALLY DEFECTIVE INCOME TRUST (IDIT)

What Is a Sale to an IDIT?

You (as grantor) can create a trust for the benefit of your family. The trust (IDIT) is designed so that assets owned by the trust will be out of your taxable estate but any taxable income retained by the trust would be taxed back to you as the grantor. The trust could then purchase income-producing, appreciating property from you in exchange for an interest-bearing installment note (or interest-only note with a balloon principal).

What Are the Benefits?

- No gain or loss is recognized on the sale to the trust.

- ◆ The grantor is taxed on trust income but not taxed separately on the interest received on the note.

- ◆ Appreciation of assets in the trust is not included in the grantor's taxable estate.

- ◆ Significant generation-skipping opportunities exist.

- ◆ Interest can be as low as the applicable federal rate (AFR).

An IDIT sale is the exchange of an asset for a promissory note. It is a sale, rather than a gift, to a trust. However, a separate gift is typically made to the trust equivalent to 10% of the value sold as seed money.

SALE TO IDIT EXAMPLE

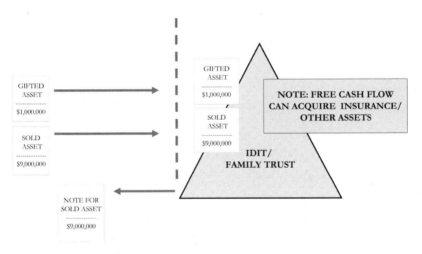

About now, the discerning reader might be thinking that there isn't much difference between a GRAT (an income-tax-free transfer of an asset to a trust outside the estate tax base in exchange for a determined series of payments) and an IDIT sale (an income-tax-free transfer of an asset to a trust outside the estate tax base in exchange for a flexible series of payments), and this would not be completely wrong. The primary difference between these two strategies is the interest/return rate required to sustain the transaction (often higher for GRATs) and the flexibility of payments

(IDIT sales can be amortized, interest only with a balloon, or something in between, but GRAT payments can only go up over time and are often level).

The benefit of lower interest rates for an IDIT sale is significant: if the asset grows at 8% and you have to take back only 5% interest, 3% necessarily is left behind (in estate preservation, a good result because the amount left behind is outside the seller's taxable estate, often in the hands of a trust for the benefit of your beneficiaries). So, if the required interest rate is 5% for a GRAT and 3% for an IDIT, an IDIT is 2% more efficient because more assets remain in trust.

The benefit of flexibility is less obvious. With an IDIT sale, the bare minimum requirement is to take back interest (and ultimately pay back principal, typically during the seller's lifetime).

Most IDIT transactions involve assets that will predictably generate enough cash flow to at least service interest during the worst of years. For a GRAT, the bare minimum is the stated annuity payment. If there's not enough cash, the seller has to take back equity (which may not sound so bad, but the idea in estate preservation is to leave the equity, or upside, behind, not take it back). Worse still, GRATs often require annual revaluations of equity *because* the seller is taking equity back. Bottom line: GRATs are often great tools, but their opportunity for success may not be the same as that of IDIT sales if the goal is to transfer more assets outside of your taxable estate.

Comparing IDIT and GRAT Results: Which is Better?

So, is an IDIT sale better than a GRAT? Maybe. But if an asset does not (and will not) provide enough cash flow to pay off the IDIT note, an IDIT can be disastrous, while a GRAT would be preferable. Conversely, for an asset or closely held business with good cash flow, a GRAT, with annual revaluation requirements (and a higher implied interest rate), would be a poor choice compared to an IDIT sale. Consider other pros and cons, such as generation-skipping planning opportunities (for which IDITs are superior) and audit risks. Bottom line: The increase in the gift tax exemption by the Tax Relief Act of 2010 has provided more flexibility than ever to design either a GRAT or an IDIT. You need to crunch the numbers, brainstorm, and determine which is best for you.

VALUATION DISCOUNTS

Many high-net-worth individuals understand that in business, the sum is greater than the parts—and the same holds true in estate preservation. For instance, voting stock is worth more than nonvoting stock (because control is better than no control). Additionally, half a beach house is worth less than 50% of the market value of the entire house (because sharing means losing complete control, and that sharing penalty should be reflected in how much is paid for the right to share).

In planning parlance, these attributes (partial ownership, unequal control, and lack of marketability) are called valuation discounts. Since the object of tax planning is often to decrease value for tax purposes, advanced estate preservation strategies often involve voluntarily breaking things apart (creating minority ownership), locking them down (removing marketability), or surrendering power (creating nonvoting interests) so that more value is preserved for your family.

STRUCTURING ASSETS FOR
ADVANCED PLANNING STRATEGIES

Family Limited Partnership (FLP) or Family Limited Liability Company (FLLC) with Minority Interest Discounts

Another area to explore would be the structuring of assets into an FLP or FLLC, in order to realize a substantial discount on current gift and future estate tax liability. Consolidating ownership and management of family assets and shifting future appreciation to other family members also help.

How to Implement

- Create an FLP or FLLC.

- Transfer assets to the FLP or FLLC (such as income-producing real estate or marketable securities).

- Gift limited partners' (LPs') interests to family members; retain general partner's (GP's) interests (with an LLC, similar terms are "managing" and "nonmanaging" members).

Advantages

- ◆ GP retains control.

- ◆ Gift taxes are reduced through discounting.

- ◆ Forming the FLP or FLLC is relatively simple.

- ◆ The partnership (or operating) agreement is flexible and amendable.

- ◆ Income shifting is possible.

- ◆ FLP or FLLC interests may have some protection from creditors under state law.

For example, if you isolate $15 million of assets in excess of exemption and assume that this $15 million doubles in value between now and the time of your death 12 years from now, you could have a tax liability of $10.5 million (on that $30 million at 35%). Conversely, if you transfer the $15 million of assets into an FLP today and claim a minority interest discount of approximately 35%, the gift is not $15 million but only $10 million, with no gift tax required. This discount technique includes further discounts for lack of voting control and illiquidity. If you again assume that this investment asset doubles in value to $30 million, then at your death, only $10 million is subject to tax (the discounted value when gifted), and $20 million escapes taxation. This results in a tax savings of $7 million ($20 million × 35%).

A proper appraisal or business valuation is necessary in order to substantiate the amount of discount claimed and to defend this position in the event of an IRS inquiry. This technique, coupled with the diminished values as a result of the economic downturn we have recently experienced, makes it a particularly timely and powerful planning technique.

FLPs and FLLCs could also be combined with other techniques, such as GRATs, sales to an IDIT, and other advanced strategies. A partnership's design may be enhanced with preferred partnership structures, where partnership interests are divided into preferred-income and common-growth portions. Preferred frozen interests have priority over fixed income and liquidation proceeds, with no appreciation potential. Common-growth interests are subordinate but capture all of the appreciation. There are many technical rules to be aware of in the design, but it is worthy of consideration when designing a partnership.

PRESCOTT FAMILY SALE TO IDIT EXAMPLE

John owns a real estate holding company (PresCo Realty), an LLC worth $5 million. It predictably provides John with a 7% annual cash flow return. Assume that John transfers 40% of PresCo Realty to a trust for his family's benefit. Because PresCo Realty is not publicly traded (and because 40% of PresCo Realty provides less than full control or even veto power), let's assume that 40% of PresCo Realty is subject to a 30% valuation discount. As a result, instead of having to sell or exchange 40% of PresCo Realty for $2 million, now John can sell 40% of PresCo Realty to an IDIT for $1.4 million without creating transfer tax liability (even though he exchanged $2 million for $1.4 million). Where did the other $600,000 go? To the trust, free of transfer taxes, for a $210,000 tax savings at 35%. Furthermore, if the $2 million PresCo Realty interest doubles to $4 million, all of the appreciation is outside of the Prescotts' estate. The result is another $700,000 (35% of $2 million) of savings in estate taxes. Alternatively, the Prescotts may choose to simply make a $1.4 million gift to a trust. This is well within their combined $10 million lifetime gift tax exemptions for 2011 and 2012. The IDIT allows for income retention through the note receivable. It also uses a minimal amount of their lifetime exemption, reserving their exemptions for other transfer strategies over time.

CHARITABLE PLANNING

If they find it consistent with their family values, high-net-worth individuals can transfer an unlimited amount of assets to qualifying charitable organizations during lifetime or at death without paying any gift or estate taxes. Income tax savings also apply for lifetime contributions. Let's explore five of the most effective charitable giving techniques.

1. **Outright gifts to charity** - Charitable gifts that you make directly to a charity during your lifetime will qualify for an income tax deduction. Note that this deduction may be limited in a single tax

year if it exceeds certain percentages of your adjusted gross income (AGI). For example, your deduction may be limited to 20%, 30%, or 50% of AGI, depending on whether you contribute cash or other property and the type of vehicle you make the contribution to. However, you may be able to use the excess deduction as a carry-forward for the following five tax years.

The Tax Relief Act of 2010 contains a special provision for IRA charitable rollovers. Taxpayers who are 70 1/2 or older can donate up to $100,000 directly from their IRAs to public charities without having to account for the distributions as taxable income and are not subject to AGI limitations. Therefore, it will be fully tax deductible.

2. **Charitable remainder trusts** - You can also establish a charitable remainder trust (CRT) during your lifetime or upon your death. You can transfer an asset to a CRT and retain the right to receive payments from the CRT for a certain period of time, either a specified number of years or, if you desire, for your lifetime and over your spouse's lifetime. Upon death, the assets remaining in the CRT will be transferred to one or more charities you designate. A CRT can be particularly attractive if you have assets, such as closely held business interests, publicly traded stocks, or real estate, that have appreciated significantly over your basis. The benefits of a CRT include:
   a. Avoidance (or deferral) of capital gains tax upon disposition of the contributed asset
   b. Charitable income tax deduction based on the actuarial fair-market value of assets contributed to the trust
   c. Reduced estate taxes
   d. Potentially increased income stream (100 cents of a dollar to invest, not reduced by income tax on sale of the asset)
   e. Substantial benefit to the charity/charities of your choosing

3. **Charitable lead trusts** - Another popular vehicle for those who wish to make current gifts to charity is a charitable lead trust (CLT). A CLT does the opposite of a CRT. It provides an income stream to a charity during your life or for a specified period of time.

After the trust term ends or upon death, the remaining trust assets pass to the donor or to family beneficiaries named in the trust.

4. **Private foundations** - You can also consider establishing a private foundation and funding it with appreciated assets, cash, or life insurance. Contributions to private foundations are eligible for an income tax deduction (subject to certain income limitations). Most foundations are required to pay out a percentage of their income each year to charity. Family members can be involved as trustees of the foundation and can earn reasonable fees for their time and efforts in the management of the foundation and selection of worthy charities.

5. **Wealth replacement trusts** - Even those with strong charitable inclinations can often feel that although the IRS is not receiving the assets directed to charity (which is a very good thing), their families are also not receiving the assets. To ameliorate this concern, families often establish a wealth replacement trust to replace the assets going to charity. Often, charitable techniques—CRTs, CLTs, private foundations—are coupled with an FIT, or irrevocable family income trust, sometimes referred to as a wealth replacement trust. In fact, the grantor can use a portion of the cash received from income tax savings, or the income stream retained in the case of a CRT, to make gifts to the wealth replacement trust. The trustee can then purchase life insurance on one or both donors to benefit the family and replace some or all of the assets passing to charity.

Charitable Remainder Trust (CRT)

If you have highly appreciated assets that inflate the size of your estate and are subject to capital gains taxes if sold, consider creating a lifetime charitable remainder trust (CRT) and making a gift of low-basis property to this newly created trust.

◆   A charitable remainder annuity trust/unitrust allows an individual to make a substantial deferred gift to a favored charity while retaining a right to payments from the trust for a period of time.

A unitrust would provide that the grantor receive annually a fixed percentage of the trust value. An annuity trust would provide a fixed dollar amount paid annually to the grantor.

♦ If you don't need income currently, you could create the type of CRT that allows you to defer the income to a future date. This is known as a charitable remainder unit trust with net income makeup provisions (i.e., NIMCRUT). Any income not taken (because not generated) currently can be taken at some time in the future.

   ♦ This feature may be more beneficial for the surviving spouse. For example, he or she could elect to begin taking distributions from the NIMCRUT to help replace a reduced pension benefit.

♦ You can replace assets vesting with charity that heirs fail to inherit through the use of a wealth replacement trust funded with life insurance.

CRT EXAMPLE

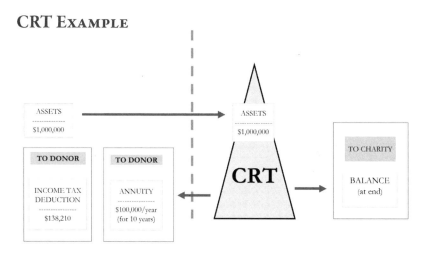

CRT Advantages

♦ You receive a lifetime stream of income that could increase or decrease, depending on your financial needs.

- You may control when to begin taking distributions (NIM-CRUT).

- You receive a significant income tax deduction that can be carried over five years, if needed.

- You avoid immediate capital gains taxes upon a sale of the appreciated property.

- You have the ability to reinvest the *full amount* of the proceeds from the sale of property into a diversified portfolio.

- Estate taxes are reduced because assets and the future growth of those assets are excluded from your taxable estate.

- You have the satisfaction of knowing that the trust assets will go to your favorite charities.

CRT Considerations

- You could possibly lose control of the asset.

- The trust must be valued annually (for unitrust).

Charitable Lead Trust (CLT)

A charitable lead trust (CLT) is a split-interest trust, with an income interest going to charity and the remainder interest going to a noncharitable beneficiary. It typically involves a lifetime transfer of cash and/or property in trust in exchange for an income interest payable over:

- A fixed term of years

- The lives of one or more noncharitable beneficiaries

- The shorter of either or the greater of either

The income interest is paid as either a fixed annuity amount (determined at the trust's inception) or a fixed percentage payout (determined at the trust's inception), recalculated annually.

Assets remaining in trust after the term of the trust pass to a noncharitable beneficiary (donor heirs).

CLT EXAMPLE

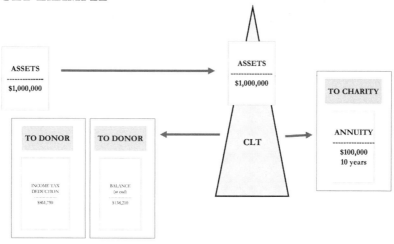

Advantages

- The combination of charitable intent and the wish to have the asset ultimately pass to heirs is met.

- The charity receives a benefit (via an income stream) without the asset being given away.

- Wealth transfer discount: gift and estate taxes can be diminished.

- An income tax deduction is available if the CLT is a grantor trust (the actuarial value of the present value of the income stream payable to the charity).

- CLTs can be created upon death (testamentary CLT).

- Flexibility in planning: the CLT term is not restricted like that of charitable remainder trusts. Furthermore, payout to the charity has no limitations. Also, the annual interest payment can be back-loaded.

- Valuation discounts can limit the value of the annuity to the charity and the associated gift or estate taxes.

Considerations

- CLTs are not tax-exempt trusts. Either the grantor pays the income tax generated in the trust or the trustee of the CLT pays the excess income generated in the trust above the amount paid to charity.

- An income tax deduction is received only if the trust is a grantor trust, meaning that the CLT's income is taxable to the grantor for amounts above the annual charity payout.

- CLTs must comply with many of the rules for private foundations.

- Debt-encumbered donated assets present a problem.

- Gifts maintain carryover cost basis (no stepped-up cost basis at grantor's death).

- The transfer to a CLT is irrevocable.

Grantor Trusts vs. Nongrantor Trusts
Grantor Trusts

- A charitable income tax deduction is equal to the present value of the charity's income interest at the time of funding.
  - An income tax deduction is limited to a percentage of adjusted gross income (30% for cash; 20% for appreciated property); excess can be carried forward for five years.
  - Death during a CLT term may result in a partial recapture of the income tax deduction.
- The gift or estate tax deduction is the present value of the lead trust.

Nongrantor Trusts

- The annual income tax deduction is the amount that is paid to the charity. Excess income is taxed at the trust income tax rates.

- The gift or estate tax deduction is the present value of the lead trust.

Private Family Foundation

A private foundation is any charitable organization that has not elected status under Internal Revenue Code §501(c)(3) as a public charity. Public charity status pertains to those organizations that qualify for the 50% income tax deduction (e.g., churches, schools, hospitals, medical research organizations, and, generally, other organizations that receive a substantial part of their support from the public or a governmental unit). Private foundations are subject to more restrictive rules than are public charities.

A typical example of a private foundation is a charitable organization funded by contributions from a small number of contributors (often family members) and income from investments and businesses unrelated to the foundation's charitable purpose. Such a foundation often makes grants to organizations that conduct charitable activities rather than conducting such activities itself.

Advantages

- A charitable deduction reduces income taxes.

- Family control is retained over assets dedicated for charitable purposes.

- Your family name is institutionalized as a legacy in the community.

- Assets and the future growth of those assets are excluded from your taxable estate.

- You have the satisfaction of knowing that assets placed in the foundation will eventually pass to your favorite charities.

Considerations

- An excise tax is imposed on a private foundation's net investment income, generally equal to 2% of the foundation's net investment income for the year. If certain requirements are met, the excise tax may be lowered to 1% of the foundation's net investment income.

- Tax may be due upon the termination of an organization's private foundation status.

SUMMARY OF THE PRESCOTT FAMILY PLAN

What were the outcomes for the Prescott family? As a result of experiencing the comprehensive wealth preservation planning process, the Prescotts accomplished the following:

- Creation of new A/B testamentary trust wills for both John and Mary. These updated documents provide:
  - Estate tax minimization
  - Generation-skipping provisions
  - Asset protection
  - Proper fiduciaries (and successors) in their proper places
  - Provisions to protect family wealth passing to children from divorce and creditors
  - Flexibility through powers of appointment
  - Trust protector

- $5 million of assets have been retitled from JTWROS to Mary's sole name to fully fund the trust created under her new will in the event she predeceases John.

- The $3 million of life insurance has been transferred to a newly created dynasty trust. In addition, the policy proceeds will escape taxation in their children's estates. Also, asset protection for the family has been achieved.

- A portion of PresCo Realty, LLC, has been sold to an IDIT. This strategy removes the real estate and future appreciation from the Prescott family taxable estate and protects it.

- The beach house has been gifted to a QPRT to preserve it for future generations to enjoy.

- The Prescotts have implemented an annual gift-giving strategy to transfer $208,000 (their maximum allowable annual exclusion gifts) to a dynasty trust. The trustees acquired a survivorship life policy in the face amount of $15,367,392 to help pay a significant portion of future estate settlement costs and preserve family wealth for future generations.

- To lock in the 15% capital gains tax rate, the Prescotts will sell some of their highly appreciated investments before 2012. They will also enjoy low tax rates on dividend income. It's anyone's guess where income tax rates will be two years from now.

- A charitable remainder trust will be established. When John sells his business in five years, a portion of the proceeds will be contributed to generate a sizable income tax deduction and also to remove those assets from the taxable estate. John's and Mary's alma maters and church, as well as cancer research, will benefit from their generosity.

- Current durable powers of attorney, living wills, and HIPAA release/authorizations are now in place.

Above all, John and Mary have tremendous peace of mind now that their affairs are in order. Their plan will be reviewed annually, or more frequently as circumstances change. They have retained control over their family wealth, have plenty of cash flow to meet their needs, and are proud of what they have accomplished. They have created a lasting legacy for their children, grandchildren, future generations, and charities.

Estate Tax Savings Summary

	Tax Savings
A/B will and retitling of assets	$1,750,000
Transfer of life insurance to trust	1,050,000
Sale of real estate to IDIT	210,000 (+ appreciation)
Annual gifts of $208,000/year	3,589,841
QPRT—beach house	180,000 (+ appreciation)
CRT ($3 million contribution)	1,050,000 (+ income taxes)
Total savings	$7,829,841

Nearly $8 million of tax savings was achieved plus additional tax savings on approximately 30 years of appreciation (John's and Mary's life expectancies) on PresCo Realty and the beach house. In addition, their family wealth objectives such as asset protection and proper distribution to children, grandchildren, and charities will be satisfied. They have successfully defended their wealth.

CHAPTER SUMMARY

The estate and GST taxes are back. They represent the largest threats to preserving and passing on your family wealth. The Tax Relief, Unemployment Insurance Reauthorization, and Job Creation Act of 2010 (Tax Relief Act of 2010) was signed by President Obama on December 17, 2010. It provides temporary relief by increasing and reunifying the gift, estate, and GST exemptions at $5 million ($10 million per couple) and establishing a 35% tax rate on the excess. This historic legislation answers a number of questions, eliminates some problems caused by the temporary repeal in 2010, and creates major planning opportunities for those who become informed and act decisively. The Tax Relief Act of 2010 creates a sense of urgency, as it is scheduled to expire on December 31, 2012. Thus, unless Congress acts again within the next two years, in the face of a presidential election, the provisions of 2001 estate, gift, and GST tax law may return. We may face another 55% tax rate on estates worth more than $1 million. The future is uncertain. The political tumult over taxation and concern over the $14 trillion federal deficit show no signs of abating.

Estate taxes threatened the Prescott family in ways they never imagined. All of their assets, especially their business, retirement plans, and even their life insurance, would be hit hard.

Outdated estate documents, asset titling problems, and lack of coordination contributed to their inability to defend their wealth properly. Their wealth was completely exposed to potential creditors and predators, and their children and grandchildren would be, too, if not properly addressed—and they initially thought they were OK. You should start by understanding the ingredients of your current wealth preservation plan: get a document audit of your wills, trusts, powers of attorney, health-care directives, etc.

Then create an inventory of your assets by ownership (yours, your spouse's, trusts, other entities you established) as part of your financial independence model. Determine who gets what after you're gone and after your spouse is gone. Calculate the estate tax. Create a flow diagram to track wealth distribution to your children and grandchildren. Do you like what you see? Will your family be able to pay estate taxes without liquidating valuable assets? Are assets exposed to forces outside of your family bloodline? What if it didn't have to be that way? What is your ideal family wealth plan?

Like the Prescotts, you have a choice. The estate tax is voluntary. Planning requires acceptance of the fact that we all die. However, you can control and protect your family wealth. Wealth preservation has three objectives:

1. Reduce the taxes and expenses associated with death

2. Distribute your wealth in accordance with your wishes

3. Ensure the existence of appropriate estate tax liquidity to avoid forced liquidation

There are many strategies and levels of planning, starting with:

1. Fundamental

2. Basic

3. Intermediate

4. Advanced

5. Charitable

You choose how high up the wealth preservation planning pyramid you want to go. We encourage you to be proactive and learn about the various techniques, their pros and cons, and how they may apply to your family's needs. Then, decide which to implement and DO IT! Getting lost in the technical jargon is easy, so find someone who can explain everything in terms you can relate to. It doesn't need to be complicated to be effective.

The difference between doing it or not doing it could be millions of dollars lost to taxes or exposed to other threats rather than passing to those you care about most: your family and possibly charitable causes.

Now is the optimal time to defend your family wealth by implementing a wealth preservation plan. We may never have another wealth transfer opportunity like this again. Ask yourself the following questions and get started today.

WEALTH PRESERVATION STRATEGIES

Questions—"Is Our Family OK?"

☐ Are your wills/trusts current? When were they last reviewed by someone other than the attorney who drafted them?

☐ Are powers of attorney, health-care directives, and HIPAA releases and authorizations up to date?

☐ Do you know EXACTLY how they work?

☐ Have you seen a flow diagram of how your assets will pass upon your death and your spouse's death, with actual dollar amounts to each family member and the IRS?

☐ Do you know how much the IRS will take if you and your spouse died today? In 10 years? At life expectancy?

☐ Are you concerned about paying estate taxes?

☐ Which assets do you want liquidated to pay for estate taxes?

☐ People are motivated to plan their estates for various reasons. What is your primary motivation? Rank in order of importance:

_____ To reduce estate taxes

_____ To increase inheritance for heirs

_____ To make charitable contributions

_____ To protect assets from creditors and predators

_____ Other_____

☐ If you could allocate your estate at death any way you wanted to among the following choices, what would be your ideal allocation?

_____ % your family _____ % IRS _____ % charity

☐ What are the most important financial values that you would like to pass on to your children?

☐ How should assets be managed at:
- Your death for your spouse?
- Your spouse's death for you?
- Both of your deaths for your children?

☐ Have you reviewed the ownership of assets (your name, your spouse's name, joint, trust)?

☐ Do you want to guarantee that your assets go to your children or allow your surviving spouse to decide?

☐ What are you doing today on a proactive basis to increase the likelihood that your children and grandchildren will be outstanding stewards of your wealth?

☐ How do you intend to equalize inheritances among children who are active or inactive in your family business, if applicable?

☐ When was the last time you received an objective second opinion of your overall wealth preservation plan?

☐ Have you calculated future required minimum distributions from your retirement plans and IRAs and what percentage will be lost to income and estate taxes after you and your spouse are gone?

☐ Have you calculated the long-term economics of gifting to your family?

☐ What steps have you taken to make sure that your family's knowledge, wisdom, and experiences, as well as your financial philosophy, will be transferred to your heirs?

☐ Are you concerned about leaving substantial wealth to your heirs and actually causing more harm than good (i.e., lottery winners)? What are your thoughts about this?

☐ What do you think about transferring assets to children and/or other heirs during your lifetime, when you may be able to share in the enjoyment of their use?

_____ I prefer to transfer assets to my heirs as soon as possible.
How much? _____
For any particular use? _____

_____ I prefer to transfer some assets today but will wait to transfer the largest portion of my estate at my death.

_____ I prefer to transfer all assets at my death or at the death of the survivor.

_____ I prefer to transfer assets at my spouse's death.

_____ Other (be specific) _____

☐ Which statement most clearly reflects your thoughts regarding your willingness to give up ownership or control of assets?

_____ I am uncomfortable with any strategy that interferes with my direct ownership or control of assets.

_____ I am comfortable relinquishing ownership as long as I maintain control

_____ and retain access to all income.

_____ and retain access to sufficient income to maintain my financial independence.

_____ regardless of access to income (i.e., I can continue to manage the assets).

_____ I am comfortable relinquishing ownership as long as I maintain control

_____ of investment policy.

_____ of distribution decisions.

_____ of future management decisions.

_____ I have no concern about relinquishing ownership.

☐ Your children's inheritance can be ,considered in terms of the amount of principal they receive or the capacity of the estate to deliver an amount of annual income that would be available to help maintain their standard of living. What amount of inflation-adjusted income would fulfill your definition of success for each child's inheritance?

☐ If you could leave any amount of wealth to your heirs, what is the total amount you would leave them?

$ _____ How did you determine this amount?

☐ In estate preservation, fair is not always equal, and equal is not always fair. Which statements most closely reflect your thoughts on the subject?

_____ Regardless of his or her individual circumstances or need, each child should receive an equal principal share of my estate at the time of my death.

_____ On the basis of the individual needs and circumstances of each child, an appropriate share should be distributed from the estate.

_____ Specific assets should go to certain children.

☐ You may be concerned that your heirs lack the necessary skills to manage inherited wealth. Which statement most closely reflects your view?

_____ I believe my children do not possess the necessary skills to manage wealth and

_____ I do not feel a responsibility to prepare them to do so.

_____ I do feel a responsibility to prepare them to do so.

_____ I prefer to pass assets in trust or by other means that assure professional management.

_____ I believe my children do possess the necessary skills to manage wealth

    _____ but I prefer to pass assets in trust or by other means that assure professional management.

    _____ and I feel comfortable that they will manage their inheritance effectively.

_____ I am unsure of the interest levels, skills, and abilities of my children to manage wealth.

☐ Your family wealth can be structured to protect inherited wealth from the claims of your children's creditors, divorce proceedings, and/or liability claims.

_____ This is an important goal in planning. What asset protection tools are you utilizing?

_____ I am not concerned about this aspect of my planning.

☐ If applicable, how do you feel about transferring assets to your grandchildren?

_____ I prefer to leave my estate to my children; they can determine whether passing a portion of the assets along to my grandchildren is appropriate.

_____ I am primarily concerned with providing for my children; however, if sufficient assets are available, I would consider leaving a portion of my estate directly to my grandchildren.

_____ I would like to make assets available for both my children and my grandchildren, with the flexibility to respond to their varying needs.

_____ I have already provided adequately for my children and would prefer to distribute the remainder of my estate to my grandchildren.

_____ I do not choose to transfer assets to my grandchildren.

Charitable Giving Questions - "Is Our Community OK?"

☐ As a family, you may have a history of charitable giving and volunteerism. Which statement most closely reflects your philanthropic history? Check all of the following statements with which you agree.

_____ I have a clear picture of why I made past gifts of money and time.

_____ I feel good about my philanthropic history.

_____ I believe that my efforts have made a difference.

_____ I have received little satisfaction from gifts I have made in the past.

_____ I have created a mission statement or charitable philosophy for me, my family, and my advisors relative to my giving.

_____ When I give to charity, I usually do so with a specific objective in mind.

_____ I usually prefer to make unrestricted gifts, as the organizations I support know best how to use those dollars for their greatest benefit.

_____ I hold charities accountable for gifts that I make.

_____ I prefer to have direct contact with the charities I support financially.

_____ I prefer to make anonymous contributions or those where no direct contact with the charity is required.

_____ I would like to be directly involved in the work of exploring and/or analyzing problems or shaping promising solutions with my philanthropy.

_____ I enjoy being recognized for my philanthropy.

_____ I prefer to make my charitable contributions during my lifetime, so that I can enjoy watching the impact of my philanthropy.

_____ I prefer to make my charitable contributions through my estate plan, so that I do not give up control of my assets during my lifetime.

_____ I think a private family foundation might be a good idea.

_____ I am interested in a private foundation but would prefer a less complicated alternative.

_____ Giving should be hands-on; I want my family to "walk the talk" of philanthropy.

_____ I have already established a family foundation and

_____ so far have been disappointed.

_____ have found the process compelling and rewarding.

☐ Which statement most closely reflects your thoughts regarding the transfer of charitable gifts through your estate plan?

_____ "Charity begins at home." I have no intention of providing for charitable organizations through my estate plan.

_____ I would rather direct money to charity than pay taxes.

_____ As long as my financial independence or intended family legacy is not compromised, I would consider charitable gifts as part of my estate plan.

_____ I would like to include charitable gifts in the distribution of my estate in some form; however, I am not interested in making those transfers today.

_____ To the extent possible, I plan to include charitable gifts in the distribution of my estate.

_____ Philanthropy is the focal point of my estate plan.

☐ What has been your level of personal involvement with charitable organizations, including volunteer time and/or money?

☐ Does your current wealth preservation plan accomplish your goals for charity?

CHAPTER FOUR

THE NEW ROLE OF LIFE INSURANCE

By Dan Prisciotta

WHY EVEN THE WEALTHY CONSIDER LIFE INSURANCE

"Why in the world would I need life insurance? If something were to happen to me, my spouse and children will inherit millions!"

We have heard this exclamation from many high-net-worth clients over the years. And do you know what? They're right! They absolutely do not **need** life insurance for the traditional purpose of putting food on the table in the event of a premature death. However, should you consider life insurance as part of your holistic wealth preservation plan on the basis of economics and tax advantages? The answer is a resounding YES! No other vehicle can achieve tax efficiency under U.S. tax law as well as an insurance product can. Structured properly, it is income, gift, estate, and generation transfer tax free. Even family offices, which typically represent families with at least $150 million in net worth (often most of it liquid), are huge buyers of life insurance. Why? High-net-worth families use life insurance for the following wealth transfer and preservation purposes:

- To fund the payment of estate taxes on a discounted basis

- To create additional liquidity so that valuable family assets do not have to be sold

- To create estate equalization among heirs, particularly when specific assets (such as business interests) are not going to be shared equally

- To develop business continuity/key person indemnification

- To enhance charitable gifts or wealth creation for family to replace assets left to charity; also to allow gifts to charity to continue after death

- To create specific bequests to heirs

- To address multiple marriages and provide for children from more than one spouse

- To leverage assets already in trusts, such as credit shelter trusts, GST trusts, and other living trusts previously funded with gifts or bequests

- To pay income taxes with respect to a decedent (IRD) and prevent erosion of income streams that continue after death, such as qualified retirement accounts, royalties, and stock options that trigger postmortem income tax liabilities

Today, protecting your family and your assets is getting more and more complicated. With all of the complex strategies available to solve your problems, sometimes we forget how useful a tool such as simple, plain, vanilla life insurance can be, especially when used in combination with and support of other sophisticated planning strategies. Do high-net-worth individuals want to acquire life insurance? Not really. But they do want what life insurance can accomplish in terms of defending their families, businesses, and wealth.

DISCOUNTED DOLLARS

Estate taxes represent a liability for individuals whose taxable estates exceed $5 million ($10 million for couples) in 2011 and 2012. Who knows for sure what the estate tax brackets or rates will be in the future? If judged on the basis of the current federal deficit, the U.S. Treasury is unlikely to ever want to give up the revenue that the estate, gift, and generation-skipping tax transfer system raises. So it is prudent to say that, at some point in the future, a significant estate tax will be levied on assets passing from one generation to the next.

What is unknown is the date on which the liability will come due. Prefunding a known liability certain to occur at some future date makes economic sense. Corporations set up reserves or sinking funds all the time. When the event that causes the liability is the death of the owner, life insurance is often the most viable funding vehicle because the liability could come due today, tomorrow, or 40 years from now. Only life insurance can instantly convert to cash and create a benefit to pay the liability no matter when the liability occurs.

Also, leverage exists in a life insurance policy as long as the death proceeds exceed the premiums paid plus opportunity costs. Maximum leverage occurs on the day a policy is issued and decreases slowly over the insured's lifetime. If death occurs prior to life expectancy, significant leverage still exists, so dollars to pay estate taxes are delivered at a substantial discount. With proper policy design and a reasonable rate for opportunity cost, discounted dollars can still be delivered even if death occurs well after life expectancy. Quite obviously, the earlier the death, the greater the discount—a great deal but nobody wants that to happen. Over time, a great deal slowly changes to a good deal but still offers considerable value even for deaths at advanced ages. Some clients plan ahead and acquire life insurance to help fund their estate tax liability while still in their 40s and 50s. Others will put off the acquisition until their 70s or 80s (believe it or not, several insurance companies will issue insurance policies on people up to age 90).

Why pay taxes with 100-cent dollars if the opportunity exists to use 20-, 30-, or even 80-cent dollars (representing an 80%, 70%,

> *Why pay taxes with 100-cent dollars?*

or 20% discount)? In fact, until premiums plus opportunity costs exceed 100% of the death proceeds, using discounted life insurance dollars to pay taxes would be preferable to liquidating estate assets. Furthermore, logical thinking would say that this concept is just as valuable for the liquid estate as it is for one that is illiquid. The IRS charges the same rate, currently up to 35%, whether your estate consists of cash, money markets, CDs, or closely held business interests and real estate.

INTERNAL RATE OF RETURN (IRR)

Insurance can be an attractive asset class when the internal rate of return (IRR) of premium dollars contributed to death benefit received is calculated. You give the insurance company pennies, and it pays in dollars, TAX FREE. While many factors affect the IRR of a life insurance policy (such as age, gender, health, etc.), it is reasonable to expect that many life insurance policies will provide returns between 6% and 8% at life expectancy. This IRR is both the gross rate and the net rate, as there would be no income taxes due. Depending on your tax bracket (probably the highest and getting even higher), the return on other assets would need to be between 11% and 15% to equal the IRR on life insurance. Compare this to the liquid, stable portion of your portfolio, as the insurance provides instant liquidity at maturity; comparing it to equities or hedge fund returns, which carry much higher risk, would be unfair. In fact, certain policies provide guarantees that take risk off the table entirely. Thus, life insurance provides an extremely attractive tax-free yield and a safe way to diversify and preserve your assets.

The following chart analyzes the tax-free IRR of a hypothetical life insurance policy on John and Mary Prescott:

Internal Rate of Return (IRR)

For John and Mary Prescott, both age 65

End of Year	Annual Premium	Insurance Death Benefit	Tax-Free IRR % on Death Benefit
1	$208,000	$15,367,392	7,288.17%
2	208,000	15,367,392	711.00%
3	208,000	15,367,392	281.48%
4	208,000	15,367,392	161.28%
5	208,000	15,367,392	108.56%
6	208,000	15,367,392	79.81%
7	208,000	15,367,392	61.99%
8	208,000	15,367,392	50.00%
9	208,000	15,367,392	41.43%
10	208,000	15,367,392	35.04%
11	208,000	15,367,392	30.12%
12	208,000	15,367,392	26.22%
13	208,000	15,367,392	23.06%
14	208,000	15,367,392	20.46%
15	208,000	15,367,392	18.29%
16	208,000	15,367,392	16.45%
17	208,000	15,367,392	14.88%
18	208,000	15,367,392	13.52%
19	208,000	15,367,392	12.33%
20	208,000	15,367,392	11.29%
21	208,000	15,367,392	10.37%
22	208,000	15,367,392	9.55%
23	208,000	15,367,392	8.82%
24	208,000	15,367,392	8.16%
25	208,000	15,367,392	7.57%

Note: *The* **guaranteed** *income-tax-free IRR on death benefit is 11.29% when John and Mary reach age 85, which is equivalent to 18.82% pretax in a 40% combined federal and state income tax bracket. By age 90, it is 7.57%, which is equivalent to almost 13% pretax.*

FOUR WAYS TO PAY ESTATE TAXES

As we briefly discussed in one of our examples in chapter 2, "The Value of a Planning Process," estate taxes can be paid in only one of four ways:

1. **Cash** - You can try to stockpile enough cash and cash equivalents (money market accounts, checking and savings accounts, short-term CDs, etc.) inside your estate to pay for the future estate tax bill. In addition to suffering a low yield on such accounts, you may find the main problem to be that the dollars set aside to pay estate taxes are themselves subject to estate taxes, i.e., tax *inclusive*. Therefore, to pay a $1 estate tax, you must keep more than $2 in cash, because that $2 is subject to estate taxes at 35%. If we assume that you devised and implemented a plan to transfer cash into a tax-exempt environment without the imposition of gift taxes, the cost would still be $1 per $1 of estate tax liability. Please see the chart on the following page.

2. **Sale of assets** - The estate tax is generally due and payable to the IRS within nine months of death. The U.S. Treasury accepts only cash, not bricks and mortar. Often, when cash is needed quickly, it forces assets to be sold for less than full market value. In addition, poor timing can result in a loss of value in a closely held business after the death of its founder, an overall market decline in real estate or stocks (as we have seen recently and throughout many market cycles), or opportunistic buyers (vultures). The objective here is to benefit your family, not someone who buys your most valuable assets at forced-sale prices because your family needs cash. If we assume a 20% reduction in value, i.e., 80% of market value realized, the cost per dollar of estate tax paid increases to $1.25 in this example. This is often the approach used when no planning has been done.

3. **Loans** - Let's assume that your family could find a lender willing to make a loan at such an unfortunate time. Lenders, of course, make a living by charging interest. If interest costs 6%, over a 10-year loan period, the cost per dollar of estate tax paid is $1.54.

4. **Life insurance** - Discounted dollars are provided through the use of life insurance as a means to pay estate taxes. Consider the total cash outlay (premiums paid since inception of the policy) compared to the death benefit check delivered by the insurance company and the cost per dollar of estate tax is discounted to 34 cents. Furthermore, life insurance provides certainty. Upon death, the policy automatically converts to cash.

Four Ways to Pay Estate Taxes

For John and Mary Prescott

Assumptions

Adjusted gross estate (in 2 years)	$35,000,000
Estate tax due	$15,367,392

Four Methods of Payment		**Cost per Dollar of Estate Tax Due**
1. Cash		
Assets needed	$15,367,392	
Total transfer cost	15,367,392	**$1.00**
2. Sale of assets at 80% of market value		
Assets needed—forced sale	19,209,240	
Total transfer cost	19,209,240	**$1.25**
3. Bank loans		
Interest rate	6.00%	
Total cash outlay (principal and interest)	23,734,037	**$1.54**
4. Life insurance		
Total cash outlay (premiums)	$ 5,200,000	
Initial death benefit	15,367,392	**$0.34**

We note that under Internal Revenue Code §6166, if the value of a closely held business exceeds 35% of the value of the entire estate, the estate tax may be deferred over 15 years if certain conditions are met. Principal payments may be deferred for five years and then are payable, plus interest, in installments for the next 10 years. IRC §6166 should not be relied upon; traps exist for the unwary.

THE ECONOMICS OF LIFE INSURANCE

High-net-worth individuals and their advisors are often pleasantly surprised by the positive economics of life insurance.

Consider additionally the tax advantages, predictability (especially in guaranteed no-lapse policies), and noncorrelation to investment alternatives and insurance begins to make a lot of sense as part of your overall wealth preservation plan.

As previously discussed in chapter 3, "Wealth Preservation Strategies," annual exclusion gifts are a simple way to reduce your taxable estate. The current annual exclusion amount is $13,000 per beneficiary in 2011 ($26,000 for a married couple). In addition to the annual exclusion, each person also has a $5 million lifetime gift tax exemption. This is not a family heirloom to be kept until death. Tremendous leverage and tax benefits can be gained through its use during your lifetime. Well-planned gift giving can dramatically reduce your estate tax liability. When gifts are used to purchase life insurance, lifetime giving truly increases the amount of money left for your heirs.

Recall the Prescott family plan. They have the desire, cash flow, and gift tax exclusions available to begin making maximum annual exclusion gifts of $208,000 per year ($26,000 × 8 beneficiaries).

The Economics of Life Insurance

For John and Mary Prescott, both age 65

Assumptions:

Annual outlay	$208,000
Pretax rate of return	7.00%
Income tax rate	40.00%
Estate tax rate	35.00%

The Economics of Life Insurance

Year	Annual Outlay (1)	Balance Forward (2)	After-Tax Earnings (3)	End-of-Year Investment Balance "Don't Do it" Leave in Taxable Estate (4)	Transfer out of Estate (5)	"Do It" Insurance out of Estate (6)
2011	$208,000	$208,000	$8,736	$140,878	$216,736	$15,367,392
2012	208,000	424,736	17,839	287,674	442,575	15,367,392
2013	208,000	650,575	27,324	440,634	677,899	15,367,392
2014	208,000	885,899	37,208	600,019	923,107	15,367,392
2015	208,000	1,131,107	47,506	766,099	1,178,613	15,367,392
2016	208,000	1,386,613	58,238	939,153	1,444,851	15,367,392
2017	208,000	1,652,851	69,420	1,119,476	1,722,271	15,367,392
2018	208,000	1,930,271	81,071	1,307,372	2,011,342	15,367,392
2019	208,000	2,219,342	93,212	1,503,160	2,312,555	15,367,392
2020	208,000	2,520,555	105,863	1,707,172	2,626,418	15,367,392
2021	208,000	2,834,418	119,046	1,919,751	2,953,463	15,367,392
2022	208,000	3,161,463	132,781	2,141,259	3,294,245	15,367,392
2023	208,000	3,502,245	147,094	2,372,070	3,649,339	15,367,392
2024	208,000	3,857,339	162,008	2,612,576	4,019,347	15,367,392
2025	208,000	4,227,347	177,549	2,863,182	4,404,896	15,367,392
2026	208,000	4,612,896	193,742	3,124,314	4,806,638	15,367,392
2027	208,000	5,014,638	210,615	3,396,414	5,225,252	15,367,392
2028	208,000	5,433,252	228,197	3,679,942	5,661,449	15,367,392
2029	208,000	5,869,449	246,517	3,975,378	6,115,966	15,367,392
2030	208,000	6,323,966	265,607	4,283,222	6,589,572	15,367,392
2031	208,000	6,797,572	285,498	4,603,996	7,083,070	15,367,392
2032	208,000	7,291,070	306,225	4,938,242	7,597,295	15,367,392
2033	208,000	7,805,295	327,822	5,286,527	8,133,118	15,367,392
2034	208,000	8,341,118	350,327	5,649,439	8,691,445	15,367,392
2035	208,000	8,899,445	373,777	6,027,594	9,273,221	15,367,392

Assume that John and Mary qualify for life insurance at standard rates. Their trustee may apply the gifts of $208,000 per year and acquire a guaranteed survivorship universal life policy with a death benefit (face amount) of $15,367,392.

The Prescotts have two decisions: do it or don't do it. In other words, if they acquire the insurance (and do so properly inside of an estate-tax-exempt trust, to be discussed later), their heirs will receive $15,367,392 completely income, gift, estate, and generation-skipping transfer tax free, **regardless** of the year of their passing (column 6 on the prior page), to help pay for estate taxes. If the Prescotts don't do it and leave the $208,000 inside of their taxable estate, it will accumulate, and its earnings will be subject to income taxes annually. In addition, whatever value it grows to inside of their taxable estate will be subject to estate taxes at 35% (column 4 when they die). If the Prescotts commit to making annual gifts to their trust, the investment balance will accumulate outside of their taxable estates. Their family will receive whatever the investment account balance grows to at the time of their passing. However, those accounts are subject to income taxes on interest/dividends earned each year. Any appreciation in value is taxed once realized upon sale because the trust does not receive a step-up in basis upon death of the grantor (gifts retain their original cost basis). The $15,367,392 of life insurance is received completely free of all taxes. **Bottom Line: Column 5 rarely, if ever, catches up to column 6.**

No other financial vehicle—no stock, bond, annuity, or hedge fund—can create and preserve wealth as well as life insurance can.

How Does the Insurance Company Do It?

Many high-net-worth individuals will look at the economics of life insurance and question how the insurance company affords to provide the benefits it does. Is it too good to be true? Many of us (myself included, when I was a practicing CPA) were raised to believe that life insurance was a lousy deal.

The first thing to realize is that a good deal for one party to the transaction (the insurance company) isn't necessarily a bad deal for the other party (the insured/family). The second thing to realize is that an individual is not capable of duplicating the financial results of the life insurance transaction on his or her own. For many reasons, the insurance company is capable of delivering financial results on a life insurance policy superior to what an individual can realize. How?

> *An individual is not capable of duplicating the financial results of the life insurance transaction on his or her own.*

1. **The law of large numbers** - An individual assuming the risk of insuring another is a gamble. This same transaction is of little to no risk to an insurance company because it insures so many people. There is no way an individual can duplicate the mortality component of the transaction. Actuarial tables are valid only for large groups; they have no relevance for an individual. You never know when your time is up (actually, with improvements in medical care and increased longevity, the cost of insurance has reduced significantly as life expectancy has increased).

2. **Economics of investing** - The insurance company approaches the investment marketplace with a significant amount of money—billions of premium dollars in its reserves. This enables the insurance company to participate in institutional investment transactions that we, as individuals, will likely never see. It also allows the company to realize pricing and transaction discounts.

3. **The insurance industry is tax favored** - Individuals do not quality for the tax breaks the insurance companies do. Congress considers insurance a socially desirable benefit because it delivers a respectable standard of living to widows and orphans. Historically, it has helped to preserve farms and small businesses, which are the financial backbone of this country and would otherwise be destroyed because of estate taxes. Also, insurance proceeds create capital that can be pumped back into the economy and used to create new jobs.

    The tax laws favor life insurance policies in three ways:
    - First, cash value increases credited to a policy holder are deductible to the insurance company but are not currently required to be reported as income by the policy holder.

In other words, the cash value grows tax free as long as the policy stays in force.

- Second, the death benefit proceeds can be structured so that they totally escape estate, gift, and generation-skipping transfer taxes.
- Third, death benefits paid out to policy beneficiaries (by reason of the insured's death) are income tax deductible to the insurance company but income tax free to the beneficiary.

4. **Not everyone qualifies for life insurance** - As anyone who has ever applied for a life insurance policy knows, the insurance companies will carefully weigh the health risks before they accept a new policy. The insurer is potentially on the hook for millions of dollars while the policy holder pays a relatively small premium over time. The insurance underwriting process has two phases.

- The first phase is medical underwriting. Depending on your age and the amount of insurance you applied for, the carrier will require various tests, ranging from a basic paramed exam to a more comprehensive medical exam, including x-rays and/or stress tests, etc. In addition, the insurance carrier will request and review your medical history obtained from your doctor(s). Over the years, underwriting requirements have become much more streamlined, simplified, and minimal. Still, the underwriters want to make sure that the insured is in reasonably good health. If not, a rating, or extra charge, may apply. Few people are declined outright. When considering survivorship/second-to-die insurance, a healthy spouse could make even an uninsurable risk attractive when joint life expectancies are considered.
- In the second phase, the insurance underwriters are very careful to review your financial qualifications. In other words, someone with a net worth of $10 million is not likely to be approved for $30 million of life insurance. The insurance company will consider your age at time of application, future income and growth of your estate, and, accordingly, your

future estate tax liability to determine how much insurance it will issue.

Bringing it all full circle, the combination of lifetime giving, discounted dollars, the economics of life insurance, and the use of various trusts form a powerful wealth transfer strategy. Below is our gift decision chart, which outlines the steps involved in evaluating your capacity to make gifts during your lifetime. We will also explore several highly effective types of tax-exempt asset protection trusts to receive those gifts.

Gift Decision Chart

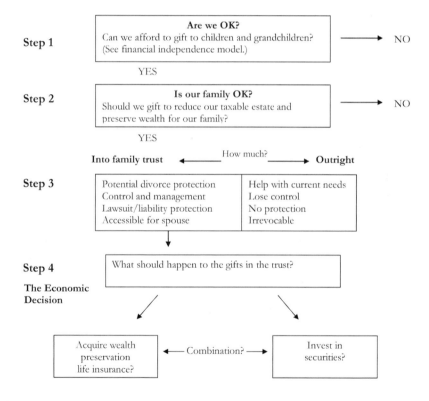

Tax-Exempt Trusts

Gifts can be made to any of the following tax-exempt trusts:

1. **FIT** - family income trust

2. **Dynasty trust** - designed to continue for several generations

3. **SLAT** - spousal lifetime access trust; have your cake and eat it, too

4. **IDIT** - intentionally defective income trust; gift and sell assets for potentially massive tax savings

These are excellent vehicles to defend your family wealth and will be explored in the following pages.

Family Income Trust (FIT)

As discussed in chapter 3, "Wealth Preservation Strategies," an irrevocable life insurance trust (ILIT), aka family income trust (FIT), can be the receptacle of gifts; your trustee can acquire insurance on your life as the grantor (and/or the grantor's spouse). Your FIT can accomplish the following:

- Receive assets (and all future growth) transferred through the use of your annual exclusion, lifetime gift tax exemption, and generation-skipping gifts

- Provide liquidity to pay estate taxes by using life insurance proceeds to:
  - Purchase assets from your taxable estate
  - Make loan proceeds available to your taxable estate

- Make bequests to your heirs

- Equalize inheritances among your heirs

- Protect assets from creditors, liability, divorce, and taxes during the trust term (for your children, grandchildren, and so on)

- Avoid the probate process and its inherent cost, delays, and publicity

Dynasty Trust

A powerful estate preservation tool to create a lasting legacy for your children, grandchildren, and future generations is a dynasty trust. It is basically an irrevocable life insurance trust (with all of the advantages described above) designed to benefit multiple generations and last a very long time. In certain states with no rules against perpetuity, these trusts can last forever. For example, a trust created in Florida can last up to 360 years. A trust established in Delaware can last indefinitely. It is no coincidence that many high-net-worth families have created trusts in states such as Alaska, Delaware, and Arizona.

How Is a Dynasty Trust Beneficial?

Assets transferred into your trust are kept outside of your taxable estate. You are allowed, in certain instances, to maintain control over the assets in the trust. In addition, the trust assets remain outside of your beneficiary's taxable estate for as long as state law allows. The best part is that even though these assets are out of your beneficiary's estate, each generation (your children, grandchildren, and so on) can have access to the dynasty trust's assets, subject to the terms of the trust. A dynasty trust can also provide protection from creditors of the trust's beneficiaries, such as a divorcing spouse or malpractice claim.

How Does a Dynasty Trust Work?

1. Establish a multigenerational, irrevocable life insurance trust (ILIT). As always, trusts should be drafted by an attorney experienced in this area.

2. Fund your trust by utilizing annual exclusion gifts and, perhaps, all or a portion of your lifetime gift exemption. Note that you should allocate your generation-skipping transfer tax (GST) exemption, up to $5 million per grantor, so that the assets in the trust can be passed to grandchildren, great-grandchildren, and others as they skip generations free of the GST.

3. The final step is for the trustee to acquire life insurance on your life, your spouse's life, or both. The use of life insurance significantly

leverages your gifts and thus creates more wealth for your heirs for generations to come. Of course, the proceeds from life insurance are not taxable for income, estate, or GST purposes.

What Is the GST Tax, and Why Is It important to Avoid?

Without the generation-skipping transfer (GST) tax, high-net-worth families could potentially circumvent the estate and gift tax system by making gifts directly to grandchildren or future generations, thereby avoiding the estate tax that would otherwise occur as each generation passes on. Obviously, the IRS would prefer a lineal transfer, with an opportunity to tax those dollars (and the growth) at the passing of each generation. In other words, a tax is due when you and your spouse pass on and leave assets to your children, a second tax is due when your children pass on and leave assets to your grandchildren, a third tax is due when your grandchildren pass on and leave assets to your great-grandchildren, and so on. The GST tax prevents families from doing an end run around multiple levels of taxation.

Fortunately, a $5 million GST tax exemption ($10 million for husband and wife) provides a significant planning opportunity to avoid the GST tax and accomplish an end run for $10 million of assets. With life insurance, the GST tax exemption of $10 million can be significantly magnified. The GST tax exemption is allocated against *annual gifts of premiums*, NOT the face amount of the insurance policy, creating tremendous GST tax leverage. For example, if you apply your $10 million GST tax exemption toward gifts of insurance premiums, the death benefits can be $100 or $150 million or more (depending on age, health, etc.), providing maximum wealth transfer.

Spousal Lifetime Access Trust (SLAT)

A spousal lifetime access trust (SLAT) is a variation on the traditional irrevocable life insurance trust (ILIT) and dynasty trust. If you are married and your spouse establishes a SLAT,

> *You can have your cake and eat it, too!*

you may have access to the trust income and principal during your lifetime. In other words, you can have your cake and eat it, too. The assets within the SLAT are completely outside of your and your spouse's taxable estates; however, you are still able to receive distributions to supplement retirement income or as an emergency cash reserve. Who knows what the future may bring? The SLAT provides maximum flexibility to potentially retrieve assets that were previously given away into the trust. This type of trust can be an excellent vehicle for those considering large lifetime gifts (approaching $5 million for each spouse) provided under the Tax Relief Act of 2010.

Advantages
- Future growth of the asset and asset income are removed from estate taxation.

- Access to funds can be retained for a lifetime through the noninsured spouse; the family has tax-favorable access to the cash value of the insurance policy or other trust assets.

- You have flexibility and access to principal if needed.
  - Ascertainable standards, i.e., for health, education, maintenance, and support, are available if spouse or spouse and children are trustees.
  - If an independent trustee is used, he or she may have absolute discretion to make distributions to any of the beneficiaries in any amount desired.
  - Probate is avoided.

- It provides a great way to hedge against possibility of future tax laws and economic changes.

- Both spouses can set up SLATs to retain access to trust income and principal.

Considerations
- For estate tax exclusion purposes, the grantor (you) should not be the trustee—but your spouse can be.

- It is irrevocable; trust provisions cannot be changed.

- If both spouses establish SLATs, beware of the reciprocal trust issue. Trusts may not have the exact provisions, so plan accordingly.

- If the grantor's spouse predeceases or divorce occurs, then access would no longer be available; however, trust assets can be distributed to trust beneficiaries.

Sale to Intentionally Defective Income Trust (IDIT)

One of the more popular techniques in recent years and one that provides tremendous leverage for wealth transfer is the sale of your assets to an intentionally defective income trust (IDIT). This strategy was covered in detail in chapter 3, "Wealth Preservation Strategies."

We will now look at ways to make a great strategy even better through the use of life insurance. As a quick review, an IDIT is a grantor trust for which trust income is attributed and taxed to the grantor (you) rather than the trust itself. For clients with income-producing assets, such as stock, real estate, or partnership interests, an IDIT can be an attractive planning tool because the trust is not depleted by having to pay income taxes. Therefore, the trust assets can grow unencumbered by income tax liability. By virtue of the grantor (you) paying the income taxes, this is another way to transfer wealth to the trust (and ultimately your beneficiaries) without the imposition of a gift tax. Furthermore, since the trust has the full amount of income generated on trust assets (after debt service) available, it can be used to acquire a life insurance policy on the grantor and/or the grantor's spouse. Selling or gifting income-producing assets to the IDIT, in addition to the life insurance policy, can be an excellent way to take advantage of the income tax benefits and provide additional financial leverage through the tax-free nature of life insurance.

How Does an IDIT/Life Insurance Combination Work?

The grantor can gift cash and income-producing assets such as stock or FLP interests to an IDIT. After gifting some assets, the grantor can also sell additional assets in exchange for an installment note. The trust can pay interest on the installment note based on the low government-prescribed applicable federal rate (AFR), properly structure the trust, and purchase assets at discounted values (anywhere from 20% up to 40%) from the grantor. The trust can then use the income earned on its assets, i.e., interest, dividends, rent, or other distributions generated by the underlying assets, to pay back the interest on the loan to the grantor, as well as the life insurance premiums on a policy to be owned and payable to the IDIT. Ultimately, the trust assets and all of their appreciation plus the life insurance can pass to the beneficiaries of the IDIT free of estate, gift, and generation-skipping transfer taxes. Unlike other techniques, such as the use of a GRAT, the IDIT can be structured as a dynasty trust to take advantage of multigeneration planning opportunities.

IDIT - LIFE INSURANCE EXAMPLE

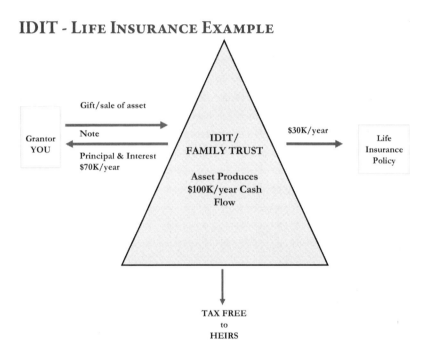

Life Insurance Funding Options

In the development of a comprehensive wealth preservation and transfer plan for the high-net-worth family, the use of life insurance in conjunction with other estate preservation strategies is often indicated. The challenge, sometimes, is how to structure and find the dollars to make the premium payments.

The challenge may come in two forms: (1) you may not have sufficient cash flow available or may have competing business opportunities for your available cash flow and therefore must become creative in finding the premium dollars and/or (2) cash flow is abundant, but gift tax exposure is a concern. The Tax Relief Act of 2010 provides a $5 million lifetime gift tax exemption ($10 million for couples), so gift taxes should not be too much of a concern. In fact, this is one of the tremendous planning opportunities available until December 31, 2012.

On the chart located on the following page, we will explore different financing options that can help the high-net-worth family acquire life insurance in the most cost-effective, tax-efficient manner. These options include (1) split-dollar arrangements, (2) private premium financing, and (3) commercial premium financing. See the chart for a quick comparison and explanation of each technique.

Note that these options will be discussed in an estate preservation context; however, they can also be used in conjunction with business planning techniques such as deferred compensation, buy/sell arrangements, and key person life insurance.

Life Insurance Funding Options

	Private Split Dollar	Private Premium Financing	Commercial Premium Financing
Lender	You	You	Bank
Description	You pay annual term costs or "economic benefit cost" and trust pays the difference, if any.	Intrafamily loan transaction	Approved third-party provides loan for purchasing life insurance
Loan Interest Rate or Annual Cost of Financing	Economic benefit cost	Applicable federal rate (AFR): short-term (0 - 3 years) mid-term (3 - 9 years) or long-term (9+ years)	LIBOR + spread (typically)
Gift Tax Impact	Minimizes gift taxes because loans are NOT gifts	Minimizes gift taxes because loans are NOT gifts	Minimize gift taxes because loans are NOT gifts
How It Works	You as a lender provide liquidity to pay large premiums	You as a lender provide liquidity to pay large premiums	Lender provide liquidity to pay large premiums
Benefits	Minimizes gift tax costs	Minimizes gift tax costs	No need to liquidate taxable assets to fund liquidity needed for premiums
Collateral	Policy	Not required	Policy and/or other assets
Potential Generation-Skipping Transfer (GST) Tax Impact	GST exemption should be allocated to gift of economic benefit amount	GST exemption should be allocated to gifts of interest	GST exemption should be allocated to gifts of interest

SPLIT-DOLLAR PLANNING STRATEGIES

A split-dollar arrangement, in its various designs, can be very useful in providing estate liquidity, as well as a strategy to minimize income, estate, and gift taxes.

Although life insurance can be owned by an ILIT so that the proceeds are not subject to estate taxes, the gifts of the premiums made to the trust may be subject to gift taxes if they exceed your allowable gift tax exclusion and exemptions. A private split-dollar arrangement can help to minimize or even eliminate the gift tax exposure. If you own a business, a similar arrangement may be entered into using business dollars.

What Is Private Split-Dollar?

A private split-dollar arrangement involves a split of the cost and benefits of a life insurance contract between you and an ILIT or dynasty trust. The trust owns a life insurance policy on your life (or joint life of you and your spouse). In these types of arrangements, you pay the annual premium. The plan operates much like a personal loan, except that the cost of the loan to the ILIT is based on an economic benefit as opposed to loan interest.

How Does It Work?

You and your spouse enter into a private split-dollar arrangement with your ILIT. The trustee of the ILIT will then acquire a life insurance policy. As security for the premium payments you make, you will be collaterally assigned the greater of the policy's cash value or cumulative premiums paid. Upon death, your estate will receive the repayment from the death proceeds. If possible, try to repay the loan during your lifetime. Numerous exit strategies can be developed using GRATs, IDITs, and other advanced planning techniques.

The value of the gift you make to the ILIT is based on the economic value of the death benefit, which initially represents only a fraction of the annual insurance premium. The economic benefit increases annually with your age and is derived from either a government rate table or an insurance company rate table. With a survivorship policy, the economic benefit can be extremely low since the value of the death benefit is based on two lives.

Finally, the gift of the economic benefit may be covered by your available annual gift tax exclusions, allowing you to avoid gift taxes entirely. Here's an example, based on $3 million of guaranteed survivorship universal life, of how much lower the economic benefit cost can be compared to the actual insurance premium.

Annual Gift Tax Cost with and without Private Survivorship Split-Dollar

Year	Annual Premium	Value of Gift with Split-Dollar (Economic Benefit)
1	$64,262	$186
5	$64,262	$395
10	$64,262	$1,279
15	$64,262	$3,147
20	$64,262	$7,496

Benefits of Split-Dollar Plans

- **Minimal gift taxes.** Gift taxes are minimized since the measure of your gift is based on the economic benefit or loan interest cost, not the full premium. These can be a fraction of the premium cost and can significantly leverage gift and GST exemptions.

- **Estate liquidity.** The insurance policy provides liquidity to pay future estate tax obligations.

- **Alternative to premium financing.** When a survivorship policy is used, the gift tax cost of the arrangement is even lower than a single-life economic benefit cost.

- **Planning flexibility.** You can lock in your insurability now, at a relatively young age, at a low gift tax cost.

Considerations

- **Cash flow required.** Cash flow is still required to pay the full life insurance premium. Therefore, depending on the arrangement, whether corporate or private split-dollar, the premium-paying party must have the cash available.

- **Increasing economic benefit cost.** The economic benefit cost increases with age, potentially increasing the tax cost of the arrangement. While the cost is low initially, it does increase as the insured(s) begins to approach and exceed life expectancy. You should develop a plan for a lifetime termination of the split-dollar arrangement; there are a number of ways to roll out or terminate split-dollar arrangements during the lifetime of the insured(s). The increased lifetime gift tax exemptions under the Tax Relief Act of 2010 provide an excellent opportunity to transfer assets to a trust to fund split-dollar terminations.

- **Estate inclusion of repayment.** When the collateral assignment amount is repaid, i.e., the premium-paying party is reimbursed for its outlays, that portion is includable in the insured's taxable estate.

Premium Financing

Private Financing

In certain cases, high-net-worth families have more than adequate cash flow available to pay for insurance premiums. However, they are concerned about avoiding gift taxes and finding a way to fund significant premiums without having to make large taxable gifts. In this instance, as an alternative to a split-dollar arrangement, private financing may be the answer.

What Is Private Premium Financing?

Private premium financing (also referred to as self-financing) is the funding of life insurance premiums through a personal loan between a family member and an ILIT or dynasty trust. Unlike commercial premium financing (to be discussed next), private premium financing does not have a third-party lender, such as a bank. Therefore, there is no need for collateral deposits, and the loan repayment itself ultimately remains within the insured's family.

How Does It Work?

The insured loans the premiums for a life insurance policy to an ILIT. The beneficiaries can be your children, grandchildren, and other family members. The ILIT pays loan interest based on the applicable federal rate (AFR) and principal in accordance with a repayment schedule. Upon the death of the insured, the loan is repaid using the death proceeds of the policies paid to the ILIT. As we do for a split-dollar arrangement, we recommend that a strategy be developed to pay the loan off sooner rather than later.

Premium financing may allow the funding of a large life insurance need at a low-interest cost without negatively affecting your current cash flow. It works very much like a personal loan; you become the bank.

Advantages

+ Gift tax cost may be avoided (or significantly lower) since the gift is only the loan interest and not the full premium.

+ The loan could be made by the insured to the trust in annual payments or in an upfront lump sum to create a sinking fund. The insured must have the cash flow to pay the full premium and/or must be able to make a lump-sum cash loan.

+ No loan approval process by a third party is necessary.

+ Regarding loan interest, consideration must be given to whether it should be paid annually or accrued and for how long.

+ No collateral is required to secure the loan.

+ The loan does not risk being called by a third-party lender.

Considerations

+ Regarding loan repayment, the loan principal is typically repaid at death, using the insurance death benefits. However, it may be advisable to repay the loan earlier to minimize the long-term costs of the arrangement.

+ The loan repayment portion may be subject to estate tax if the insured is the lender.

Commercial Premium Financing

How do you acquire life insurance to provide estate tax liquidity if you are tied up in assets that do not currently produce an adequate amount of cash flow? How can you secure the desired life insurance coverage without selling illiquid or high-performing assets? Commercial premium financing is a possible solution.

What Is Commercial Premium Financing?

Commercial premium financing is a way to borrow money from a third-party lender to pay the premiums on a life insurance policy owned by an ILIT. By doing so, you avoid selling your current investments and can then pay the loan off later, when investments have matured and your portfolio is more liquid.

How Does It Work?

You or your ILIT will pay loan interest each year on the amount borrowed at the interest rate set by the lender. Upon death, the life insurance proceeds are paid to your ILIT, net of the loan repayment to the lender. During the life of the loan, the life insurance policy cash value may be used as collateral for the loan. The lender may also require additional outside collateral and/or personal guarantees for the loan.

Advantages

Commercial premium financing may allow the funding of a large life insurance need at a low-interest cost without affecting your current cash flow.

- ♦ You may be able to borrow cash from a lender at a low interest rate (especially these days) without liquidating taxable investments that may be earning a higher rate of return than the loan interest cost. In other words, you can create arbitrage.

- ♦ It enables you to acquire life insurance without giving up the use of your assets. You can conserve your assets and use other people's money. Certainly, real estate investors understand this concept. Do they buy property with 100% cash? No! They pay the minimum down payment required and then mortgage the rest to enhance their rate of return.

Considerations

- The loan interest rate may fluctuate over the term of the loan (unless a fixed loan or a rate cap is negotiated).

- The loan interest is generally not tax deductible for income tax purposes.

- The lender may require additional collateral for a period of time until sufficient policy cash values accumulate.

PERMANENT COVERAGE VS. TERM INSURANCE

Permanent cash value life insurance is built to last a lifetime. A permanent policy can offer ongoing life insurance coverage for a lifetime to:

- Provide payment of estate taxes

- Plan for business succession

- Replace income for the family

- Cover the cost of care provided by a nonearning spouse

- Repay debt obligations

The Benefit of Cash Value Life Insurance

- Unlike term insurance, a permanent policy provides cash value accumulation that can be tapped to supplement income or to fund emergency needs.

- Term insurance provides only temporary protection, with limited opportunity for continuation of coverage at older ages.

- Unlike a term policy, a permanent policy does not terminate and can replace income from an earning spouse.

Features of Term and Permanent Insurance	Term	Permanent
Death Benefit Protection	Yes	Yes
Cash Value Accumulation	No	Yes
Acceleration of Death Benefit during Lifetime to Cover Long-Term Care Expenses	No	Yes
Death Benefit Protection for Life	No	Yes
Flexibility Based on Changing Needs	No	Yes

Here's when the use of term insurance is indicated:

♦   Younger ages, when cash flow is tight, i.e., newly married with children and a large mortgage

♦   Business loans, to cover the term of the loan

- Key person, when he or she is close to retirement

- Other temporary needs (1–20 years in duration)

SINGLE LIFE INSURANCE VS. SECOND-TO-DIE (SURVIVORSHIP) LIFE INSURANCE

Another major decision is the choice of insuring one or both lives for a married couple.

The advantages of single life insurance are

1. Creation of an additional security blanket for the surviving spouse and family in the event of a premature death. If, through present value analysis of objectives and resources, it is determined that a need exists for additional capital upon the death of a family member, then, clearly, the use of single life insurance is indicated.

2. Use of single life insurance provides flexibility to pay some estate taxes at first death. At first, this concept seems counterintuitive. Most plans defer the estate tax until the second death through the use of the unlimited marital deduction (if the surviving spouse is a U.S. citizen). However, deferral causes all of the assets to be added up when the second spouse dies, and thus, the estate will be pushed into the highest tax bracket. As an alternative, a surviving spouse could consider disclaiming certain assets and *creating* a tax on the first death to take advantage of the lower rates in the graduated tax brackets. The combined taxes through two deaths could be substantially less than deferring all of the tax until the death of the surviving spouse. The use of single life insurance could provide for payment of taxes due at first death if this disclaimer strategy is employed.

3. The presence of liquidity upon the first death could reduce the ultimate estate taxes due at second death through the purchase of hot assets, i.e., growth assets from the estate of the first spouse to die. Insurance available at first death can be used to acquire rapidly appreciating assets from the inheriting surviving spouse

or marital trust/QTIP. Those assets would then be placed into the ILIT and cash put in its place. Thus, the highly appreciating assets continue to compound and grow inside the estate-tax-exempt trust (ILIT) while the cash is conservatively invested to provide income for the surviving spouse and family inside the taxable marital trust/QTIP.

4. The proceeds of a single life policy inside an ILIT will be received when the insured dies. Those proceeds can be invested inside the ILIT for growth. Depending on when the surviving spouse passes away, the estate may have experienced substantial growth by the time estate taxes are due.

Advantages of Second-to-Die (Survivorship) Insurance

1. This form of insurance helps pay the ultimate estate taxes due on second death through maximum utilization of the unlimited marital deduction and tax deferral. The survivorship insurance premium is usually 40%–50% less than single life coverage.

2. It absorbs an uninsurable (or highly rated) spouse combined with a healthy spouse to acquire cost-effective insurance.

3. Survivorship insurance can be extremely efficient and provide greater bang for the buck from a cash flow and gift tax (and GST exemption allocation) standpoint; if a split-dollar arrangement is utilized, joint-life economic benefit costs are extremely low.

As part of a review of your wealth preservation plan, be sure to consider the use of both single life and survivorship. Existing policies should be reviewed carefully. In some instances, cash value in existing single life policies can be liberated and reallocated toward the acquisition of second-to-die policies.

IS MY EXISTING INSURANCE PERFORMING AS EXPECTED?

Regular Policy Reviews Are Necessary

Today's life insurance policies tend to be superior to earlier policies issued. Insurance companies have become leaner and meaner and more competitive; life expectancies have increased, resulting in lower mortality costs; and technology has driven down the cost of issuing and servicing policies, in addi-

> *The bottom line is that life insurance is no longer a buy-and-hold asset. It must be reviewed regularly, just like your investment portfolio.*

tion to many other improvements. The bottom line is that life insurance is no longer a buy-and-hold asset. It must be reviewed regularly, just like your investment portfolio.

For example, we recently completed a policy review for a client who had eight existing policies totaling $9.5 million in death benefits. He and his wife were paying more than $145,000 per year in premiums. By exchanging the cash value of the old policies to modern, more efficient policies, they found that the total death benefits increased to the needed $25 million while the annual premiums decreased to under $45,000. That's a savings of more than $100,000 per year for the next 30 to 40-plus years ($3–$4 million in savings) and a 250% increase in coverage.

Review your existing life insurance at least every three years for:

- Guaranteed and nonguaranteed elements of permanent policies
- Sufficient death benefit amounts and length of coverage
- Adequate funding/premium levels
- Appropriate type of policy (i.e., temporary or permanent)
- Cost and/or benefit analysis
- Appropriate ownership structure and beneficiary designations
- Policy loans that might affect premiums, cash values, and/or death benefits adversely

- Ensuring that the need still exists and the policy adequately meets those needs

- Coordination with business objectives

- Changes in circumstances or life events, such as:
  - Marriage, divorce, or birth of a child
  - Improving health and lifestyle changes, such as quitting smoking
  - Declining health; does your policy allow you to stop paying premiums sooner? Experienced advisors can help you manage your policy costs if you experience a significant change in health that impacts life expectancy.
  - Retirement or new job with changing fringe benefits
  - Buying a business or a change in business value

- Changes in the insurance industry can also affect your life insurance policy:
  - Reduction in the dividend scale or interest crediting rate
  - Reductions in policy expenses or charges (newer policies that are now available reflect reduced mortality rates, i.e., longer life expectancies or longer premium-paying periods)
  - Improvement in policy features availability, i.e., lifetime guaranteed death benefit and extended maturity options
  - Enhanced underwriting classifications (SUPER preferred available)
  - Changes in the tax and legislative environment; e.g., new regulations on split-dollar arrangements have affected all such policies and may need to be restructured or rescued
  - Consolidation of insurance companies

NOTE: You should not change or replace your existing insurance until a thorough analysis and review have been made and new insurance is underwritten and issued, if appropriate.

TRUST-OWNED LIFE INSURANCE (TOLI)

Policies placed inside trusts for the preservation of assets are at risk if not regularly monitored. As a result of changing regulations, many institutions, law firms, and other trustees increasingly find themselves with greater financial responsibilities and risk. Trust-owned policies may not meet their expectations. Policies purchased before 2001 were projected to perform based upon financial assumptions by both carriers and consumers that were made in a vastly different economic, regulatory, and industry climate than the one that exists today.

If a policy is owned by a trust, the trustee has fiduciary liability. They are fiduciaries for the trust beneficiaries, not the insured or the grantor of the trust.

Duties of the trustee:

+ Meeting trust objectives

+ Respecting the rights of all beneficiaries

+ Compliance with state and federal law

+ TOLI administration: gifts, notices, premium payments

Trustees may have issues if they fail or are perceived to fail to meet trust objectives.

Ultimately, the trust beneficiaries could hold them liable if problems arise with trust-owned life insurance.

Trustees usually fall into two categories:

1. Personal: family and friends

2. Professional: private banks, trust officers, attorneys, and accountants

It is startling to note that very few trustees, personal or professional, have a formal process in place to review policies. Trust-owned policies must be reviewed regularly.

Possible Reasons to Exchange or Replace a Policy

Below are common reasons to consider the exchange or replacement of an older policy. This list is not all inclusive.

1. **Lower-cost, more competitive plans are now available** - In any market, improvements are inevitable, and prices tend to decrease because of new innovations. Over time, insurers have cut expenses and distribution costs. When this is combined with other pricing improvements, it can lead to much more competitive policies, with lower costs and/or features and benefits not available on earlier plans.

2. **Excess cash value** - Some older policies have accumulated hundreds of thousands—sometimes millions—of dollars in cash value. Upon death of the insured(s), the cash value reverts to the insurance company; it is **not** paid to the policy beneficiary. The beneficiary receives the death benefit only. In certain cases, the cash value can be exchanged to a new, superior policy with significantly higher death benefits and perhaps lower premiums and stronger secondary guarantees.

3. **Secondary guarantees** - One of the newer policy design features for universal life includes the ability to guarantee the death benefit based on a fixed-premium structure. This guarantee applies even if interest rates experience a sustained drop or if the current cash value declines or disappears. The real benefit to this type of policy is that the insured can be assured that his or her death benefit will always be guaranteed, as long as the premium is paid according to schedule.

4. **Better mortality** - Along with dramatic improvements in medical science comes a corresponding increase in life expectancy. Because of this, many new policies have lower mortality expenses than existing policies do—sometimes significantly lower.

5. **Special underwriting programs** - If you are currently rated and the existing company won't remove the rating, you could possibly qualify under a special underwriting concession program. This is

a program where rated cases (through a certain table rating, often table 3 or 4 to standard) will automatically be issued a standard rating. If your health has improved from a previous rating, you might benefit from a program like this.

6. **Company strength** - One of the most important factors an insured should consider is the strength and stability of the issuing life insurance company. The higher the ratings of a company are, the better able the company is to keep its promises to its policy owners.

7. **Preferred and preferred-plus underwriting** - When universal life was introduced 25 years ago, only two classes of standard underwriting were available: smoker and nonsmoker. Since that time, these classes have been subdivided into preferred, preferred plus, and, in some instances, even preferred select plus. This occurred first for the nonsmoker class and later for the smoker class. If you fall into one of the preferred classes, you might benefit from the lower mortality charges in an exchange.

8. **Loan treatment** - Having a significant loan on a policy may seem insurmountable, but this doesn't have to be the case. Under the 1035 exchange rules, the IRS allows for the transfer of a loan along with the cash value from an existing life insurance policy to another life insurance policy, so long as the insured and the owner are the same. Some insurance policies offer attractive loan interest rates that might not be available on the existing policy. A wash loan may even be an option, meaning that interest credited on the loan amount is the same as that charged for the loan. This could be important if you do not plan to pay back the loan. Another potential benefit is the ability to use cash withdrawal to completely or partially pay back the loan.

9. **Extended maturity** - Many existing policies have an age 85, 90, or 95 maturity date. When a policy matures, the policy cash values will become payable to the owner of the policy, and taxes will be due on any gain. The insurance contract will be completed, so the face amount will not be paid.

THE LIFE INSURANCE DISCOVERY PROCESS

The life insurance discovery process provides a framework to understand how life insurance works and why it works the way it does. It is considered an excellent primer on the fundamentals of life insurance and is a decision-making tool to be used as you consider the acquisition of new insurance and also as you review your existing policies.

First Discovery: Understand What You are Buying (or Have Bought)

To understand what you are buying, first you should understand the three components and the three variables of every permanent insurance contract.

Components

1. **Premium:** the amount of money paid for a policy

2. **Cash value:** the balance that may accumulate, tax deferred, in the policy; the performance of the policy is largely determined by the amount of cash value

    ◆ Cash value can give the policy owner flexibility to skip premiums or create a tax-advantaged withdrawal stream. Greater cash value creates greater flexibility in these areas.

3. **Death benefit:** the cash paid to the beneficiary, usually income tax free, at the death of the insured(s)

Variables

1. **Investment performance** - Investment results of the insurance company impact the performance of dividends and interest crediting. The better the company's investment results are, the better able the company is to provide higher-credited interest rates to its policy holders.

2. **Mortality** - The more diligent an insurance company's underwriting practices are, the better its mortality experience and the resulting performance of its insurance policies are. This creates better long-term value for its policy holders.

3. **Expenses** - Expenses consist of the overhead expenses of the insurance company associated with creating and administering the policy.

The amount of cash value and death benefit delivered, per premium dollar expended, is a function of the actual long-term outcome of these three variables. Who do you think bears the risk of adverse (less favorable than originally assumed) results: you or the insurance company? It depends on the second discovery, policy universe, discussed below.

The degree of interest, mortality, and expense risk that you assume will impact policy performance. If you bear no risk, the contract you acquire will have a lower but more predictable cash value and death benefit per premium dollar expended. As you bear more risk, the contract you acquire will deliver potentially greater increases in cash value and death benefit, depending on the performance of the three components. The risks and guarantees depend on the type of product you choose and the level of funding in the policy. It's like comparing Treasury bills to small-cap stocks; T-bills are guaranteed, pay a comparatively low interest rate, and give a lower return than do small caps, which have the potential for higher return but with higher risk.

Second Discovery: Policy Universe

The type of policy and how it's funded determine the risk and performance of your insurance. There are four main policy universes to choose from.

1. **Whole life** (current interest credited/participating whole life)
   - Premiums are generally guaranteed not to change from the illustrated rate. The face amount of the contract is generally guaranteed not to go below a specific amount if the guaranteed premium is paid every year.
   - Cash value and death benefit have substantial floor guarantees; the rate of dividend interest credited to cash value is generally guaranteed at 4%–6%. If the contract experiences favorable dividend/interest rates and lower mortality, the favorable experience is credited directly to the policy. Favorable dividend/interest and mortality rates significantly increase cash

value and death benefit per dollar of premium. In addition, while premiums are due and payable each year, whole life can provide flexibility if premiums need to be reduced or skipped once sufficient cash value can be applied to pay premiums.

♦ Premiums must be paid every year to maintain guarantees, however.

2. **Universal life**

♦ Premiums, cash value, and death benefit are not always guaranteed at the illustrated rate in traditional universal-life products. In some cases, the face amount of the contract can be guaranteed not to go below a specific amount if a specified premium is paid.

♦ No-lapse protection riders in certain universal-life contracts protect policies against declining dividend/interest rates. This feature protects the death benefit from declining or lapsing, as long as the policy owner pays a specific premium. The life insurance carrier guarantees the contract to maturity with this no-lapse feature.

♦ Premiums may be skipped, depending upon the structure of the policy. This is very flexible for the policy holder.

3. **Variable life**

♦ Premiums, cash value, and death benefit are not guaranteed at the illustrated rate. Generally, this type of contract has the potential to accumulate the highest cash value per premium dollar. The owner of a variable-life policy is responsible for choosing and allocating cash values among various subaccounts (usually 30–40 to choose from), which are mutual fund–like investments. These contracts have the fewest guarantees and the greatest volatility because the policy owner, rather than the insurance company, bears the investment risk.

♦ Variable policies have the opportunity to enjoy upside potential if their subaccounts perform well and increase the cash in value and/or death benefit.

- Certain variable policies provide guarantees to protect the policy death benefit in a declining-rate-of-return environment through the addition of a no-lapse protection feature noted previously.

So, with variable life, the policy holder chooses how to invest premium dollars. With traditional universal life, premiums are conservatively invested in the insurance company's general reserve account (mostly bonds).

4. **Temporary coverage** (term)
   - This type of contract provides the highest death benefit per premium dollar. Premiums generally increase dramatically over time, with no cash value. This type of coverage may quickly become more expensive than a permanent contract. Coverage is not available at life expectancy. Therefore, it is appropriate for short-term needs, such as loan repayment, income for minor children, etc.
   - Our experience has been that no matter how much risk high-net-worth individuals take to create their estate, they generally gravitate toward more conservative ways to protect it when it comes to life insurance and estate preservation.

Now that you understand the policy universes, which one do you feel most comfortable with? Note: You may use different policy types for different purposes.

Third Discovery: Length of Guaranteed Death Benefit

Once you decide on the policy universe, you have to decide how long you want the death benefit to be guaranteed. It can be guaranteed until age 90, 95, 100, 105—even up to 126 with some carriers. Is this necessary? Some people have significant health issues that should be considered. Others are in outstanding health, with an excellent family history of longevity. Keep in mind that most universal-life and variable-life policies do not guarantee the death benefit unless the no-lapse protection feature is added. Guaranteed policies generally accumulate relatively low cash values.

For how long should your death benefit be guaranteed? Age 100? Beyond?

Fourth Discovery: Premium Duration

Next, you have a choice as to the number of years of out-of-pocket payments to pay. Every policy requires an annual premium to cover the cost of insurance to life expectancy. The question is whether the premium comes from your pocket or from the policy's existing cash values. The number and size of the out-of-pocket premiums determine the magnitude of the long-term benefit. For example, premiums can be paid one time (single premium), 10 times, 20 times, or every year for the duration of the policy (often referred to as a full-pay design). A full-pay design amortizes premiums over the entire life of the policy, thus resulting in the lowest-possible annual premium. It usually creates the highest IRR, as you have the least out-of-pocket amount to support the policy.

Do you have a preference as to the number of years that you would like to pay premiums?

Note: These premium durations are different from the old whole-life concept of vanishing premiums. The problem with vanishing premiums is that they didn't vanish! That design was entirely dependent on policy dividend rates. When the dividend rates declined from the 11.5% levels of 1989 to the 6% levels of today, the policies required out-of-pocket payments. This left many policy holders dismayed because the policy may not have been explained properly. The premium durations I refer to above in our example are *guaranteed*, not predicated on dividend performance.

Fifth Discovery: Focus on Death Benefit or Cash Value?

Is the primary focus of the coverage to maximize death benefit or cash value? Each policy will stress one or the other. Which one to focus on depends on the primary purpose of the coverage. In general, greater emphasis should be placed on the death benefit for estate tax purposes. If access to cash value is important, say, for deferred compensation or in a SLAT design, then a policy that accumulates maximum cash value would be preferable.

What is the main purpose of the policy: cash value accumulation or death benefit?

Sixth Discovery: Policies in a Similar Universe will Tend to Illustrate Similarly

Review illustrations (aka projections or quotes) from multiple carriers. When you review different policy illustrations, focusing on cost differences is easy. In other words, if policy A is cheaper than policy B, policy A must be better. This is not necessarily the case. In most instances, if policies look radically different, they may not be in the same universe or might be illustrated using different assumptions.

The important decision is not to focus on cost alone but to determine the correct policy universe and how that policy should be designed within that universe. Let's face it: insurance companies compete for business, just like any other industry. They will price their policies to attract new buyers. Some carriers are well priced at certain ages and designs and accept ratings well, etc. The key is to compare apples to apples.

If you approach your insurance decision-making process in this manner, your conclusion will be sound and will help you accomplish your planning goals with acceptable risk (or no risk in the case of no-lapse protection).

Seventh Discovery: Quality of the Insurance Company Issuing the Coverage

Make sure that you are placing your coverage with a reputable company with high-quality ratings. Be sure to check the independent rating companies that have ranked the company/companies you own or are considering as among the highest caliber, such as:

- AM Best

- Moodys

- Standard & Poors

These ratings can be boiled down and evaluated together in a 0–100 measurement known as a COMDEX. Consider companies with a COMDEX of 80 or higher.

Other measures can also help to determine how sound a life insurance company is and to gauge their ability to meet future claims such as size and solvency. An experienced insurance advisor will understand the ratings, reputation, and capabilities of numerous insurance companies. The advisor will also manage the overall underwriting process, reinsurance, applications, and other necessary forms. Also consider diversifying among multiple insurance companies when acquiring significant amounts of coverage.

Are you aware of the quality and strength of the insurance company you own or are considering?

Eight Discovery: Talent, Integrity, and Professionalism of the Advisor Representing you to the Insurance Marketplace and Servicing the Policy

You will want to make certain that the insurance advisor helping you acquire the proper insurance for your needs takes you through a process as outlined here, as opposed to being transaction oriented and selling you a policy that you may not fully understand or that may not address your true long-term needs. A qualified professional will be objective and act as your advocate to represent you to the insurance marketplace to secure the right policy for your needs at the most competitive cost. A good advisor will truly understand the underwriting process and competitive advantages among multiple carriers and policies. Most importantly, he or she will make certain that you actively participate in the decision-making process as you are educated about the alternatives and the effects these discoveries have on policy selection and ultimate performance.

Finally, an advisor will coordinate your life insurance with the balance of your estate documents, tax planning, premium financing strategies, and overall wealth preservation plan.

CHAPTER SUMMARY

For the affluent, life insurance is no longer a necessary evil acquired to replace income for your family in the event of a premature death. Today, it has become a highly efficient wealth preservation tool to transfer wealth completely free of income, gift, estate, and generation-skipping transfer taxes (if properly structured). No other financial vehicle—no stock, bond, annuity, or hedge fund—can create and preserve wealth as well as life insurance can.

Tax laws favor life insurance, and therefore, the economics are attractive. Certain policies provide guaranteed returns. They can be used to pay remaining unavoidable taxes after all of your other wealth preservation planning is done to reduce the ultimate tax liability. Life insurance represents discounted dollars. Of the four possible ways to pay estate taxes, life insurance is the clear winner, if you qualify.

You can structure the ownership and payment of the life insurance premiums in many ways. By using the gift tax laws to your advantage, you can transfer dollars to various estate (and GST) *tax-exempt* trusts. These trusts protect the insurance proceeds not only from taxation but also from creditors and predators you or your family members may be threatened by. Which type of trust you choose depends on your family's needs.

Life insurance premiums can be paid by you, your company, your trust, or a third-party lender such as a bank. Financial leverage, as well as tax leverage, can make the life insurance transaction even more financially appealing.

Choosing the right type of policy among all of the varieties available today can be confusing: single life or second to die? Term or permanent? Which type of permanent to choose? How long should you pay premiums? How long should your policy last?

What about the insurance you acquired in the past? Life insurance is no longer a buy-and-hold proposition. It must be reviewed regularly, just like your investment portfolio. Modern policies are often more cost effective and offer better guarantees than previous generations of policies. Review older policies and consider exchanges to more competitive plans if warranted.

The Tax Relief Act of 2010 will cause many who acquired life insurance for estate tax liquidity purposes to review their policies. When the annual premium notice arrives, questions will arise: should this premium be paid? Do I have the right amount of insurance? Is it structured properly to avoid estate and GST taxes?

Whether acquiring or reviewing your existing coverage, you should follow a well-defined discovery process. This will allow you to:

1. Fully understand what you are buying (or have bought)

2. Learn about the four policy universes

3. Determine the appropriate length of guaranteed death benefit period

4. Choose a premium payment duration

5. Focus on death benefit or cash value performance (or both)

6. Make proper comparisons among policies in the same universe

7. Evaluate the financial strength of the insurance carrier (more important than ever!)

8. Choose the right insurance advisor to help you implement your plan

Properly structured life insurance can help you address the single largest threat to your family wealth and preserve your assets for future generations.

THE NEW ROLE OF LIFE INSURANCE

Questions

☐ Do you have life insurance? ☐ No ☐ Yes—For each policy, please answer the following questions:

☐ The primary reason(s) you purchased insurance coverage is to address the following: (check all that apply)
   ☐ Estate tax payment (Have you analyzed the four ways to pay estate taxes?)
   ☐ Survivor/family income
   ☐ Debt repayment
   ☐ Children's/grandchildren's education
   ☐ Pension replacement
   ☐ Business succession (buy/sell)
   ☐ Estate equalization to heirs
   ☐ Key executive/employee
   ☐ Collateral for loans or bonding

- ☐ Charitable gift
- ☐ Supplemental income at retirement
- ☐ Tax-favored accumulation of cash value

☐ What types of policies are they?
  - ☐ Term
  - ☐ Whole life
  - ☐ Universal life (guaranteed or nonguaranteed?)
  - ☐ Variable universal life
  - ☐ Single life or second to die

☐ How much is your death benefit? $_____

☐ How much is your premium? $ _____

☐ Do you intend to pay the next premium?
  - ☐ Out of your pocket (gifts)
  - ☐ With trust-owned assets
  - ☐ Through a split-dollar arrangement

☐ How much cash value is currently in the policy? $_____

☐ Who is the owner of the policy?
  - ☐ You
  - ☐ Your spouse
  - ☐ Business
  - ☐ Trust
    - ☐ Family income trust
    - ☐ Dynasty trust
    - ☐ SLAT
    - ☐ IDIT
    - ☐ Other or unsure

☐ The last time you had a formal life insurance review of all your existing policies was:
  - ☐ Within the past year
  - ☐ Within the past three years
  - ☐ Within the past five years

    ☐ Longer than five years ago
    ☐ Never

☐ Have you had a recent ledger or point-in-time illustration run to identify how your policy will perform? How many additional premiums are required to be paid up? What are the policy guarantees?

☐ The following statement best describes your feelings regarding the amount of life insurance you have on your life:
    ☐ You have more than you need to cover estate taxes.
    ☐ You are inadequately insured for your current estate preservation needs.
    ☐ You have the correct amount of life insurance to meet today's estate tax liability.
    ☐ You are not sure whether you have too much or too little.

☐ The last time you had an analysis to determine the appropriate amount of coverage needed was:
    ☐ Within the past year
    ☐ Within the past three years
    ☐ Within the past five years
    ☐ Longer than five years ago
    ☐ Never

☐ The death benefit of your life insurance must be guaranteed.
    ☐ Yes ☐ No
    ☐ If yes, the duration of the guaranteed death benefit needs to be:
        ☐ Lifetime (no end to guaranteed duration)
        ☐ Age 105
        ☐ Age 100
        ☐ Age 95
        ☐ Age 90
        ☐ Other age _____

☐ You agree/disagree with the following statements:

A life insurance policy requires that premiums be paid every year. The premium can be paid out of pocket by you or by the policy's values (cash value and/or dividends).
☐ Agree ☐ Disagree ☐ Not sure

Lower premiums may increase the risk you have with an insurance policy.
☐ Agree ☐ Disagree ☐ Not sure

The financial strength of an insurance company is an important consideration when buying a policy.
☐ Agree ☐ Disagree ☐ Depends on cost factors

The talent, integrity, professionalism, and commitment of the person representing you and servicing your life insurance are important to you.
☐ Agree ☐ Disagree ☐ Not sure

☐ You would prefer that the cash value growth in your policy be based on:
  ☐ A guaranteed rate, i.e., with no risk
  ☐ A bond-based portfolio based on the insurance company's investment results, i.e., low to medium risk, with potential of average return
  ☐ An equity-based portfolio based on a portfolio of stock funds, i.e., medium to higher risk, with potential of highest return

☐ The focus of your life insurance should be on:
  ☐ Death benefit
  ☐ Cash value
  ☐ Both
  ☐ Not sure

☐ You understand how your life insurance will be taxed at your death.

☐ Agree   ☐ Disagree   ☐ Depends on cost factors

☐ What questions or concerns do you have regarding your life insurance coverage?

CHECKLIST OF POTENTIAL PROBLEMS WITH YOUR EXISTING INSURANCE

Do any of these situations exist for your policy/policies?

☐ Excess rating/risk class based on your health

☐ Improper policy universe for your risk tolerance

☐ Level vs. increasing death benefit

☐ Outstanding policy loans (interest expense is not tax deductible)

☐ Deteriorated DB due to policy loans or split-dollar obligation

☐ Incorrect primary beneficiary

☐ Incorrect contingent beneficiary or lack thereof

☐ Incorrect beneficiary wording (per capita vs. per stirpes)

☐ Incorrect policy owner

☐ Policy subject to estate tax

☐ Current premiums do not support policy for desired duration

☐ Policy doesn't have a no-lapse provision

☐ No waiver of premium provision if insured becomes disabled

☐ No automatic premium loan provision

☐ Dividends being used incorrectly

☐ Convertibility window closing (term to permanent)

- ☐ Not reporting economic benefit under split-dollar arrangement, for income and gift taxes

- ☐ Not reporting table I costs (group term)

- ☐ Three-party interest (if owner, insured, and beneficiary are separate parties)

- ☐ Transfer for value (causes death benefit to become income taxable)

- ☐ No Crummey notices sent

- ☐ Policy subject to GST tax

- ☐ Timing of distribution of death benefit incorrect to beneficiaries

- ☐ Proceeds subject to claims of creditors/predators

- ☐ Non-top-tier insurance carrier(s)

- ☐ Lack of annual review/service

- ☐ Incorrect policy *design* based on objectives

- ☐ Incorrect policy *type* based on objectives

- ☐ Incorrect policy *amount* based on objectives

- ☐ Incorrect issue age

DEFEND YOUR BUSINESS WEALTH

CHAPTER FIVE

BUILDING, PROTECTING, AND TRANSFERRING YOUR BUSINESS

By Dan Prisciotta

CASE STUDY

Planning for the Closely Held/Family Business

Company History

The company started in 1945 in Brooklyn, New York. The Dodgers were still at Ebbetts Field. Like most New Yorkers, the family who started this small business worshiped their beloved "Brooklyn Bums." It helped cheer up a woman, Blanche, who became a widow at an unfair young age with two children to feed. She and her two boys, Robert and Gene, hatched an idea to find used equipment, recondition it, and sell it. Over the years, the company grew exponentially and moved during 1964, in need of more space. They bought several acres of land and built a 160,000-square-foot manufacturing plant somewhere in the swamps of Jersey, years before the region became heavily industrialized. In 1975, the matriarch passed away and left the company to her two sons. At that time, gross sales had just topped $1 million. They hired aggressively and grew from three employees to, ultimately, 350. Since 1979, they have run three shifts per day. Gross sales today are in excess of $75 million per year.

Family History

Robert has three sons, Herb, Lenny, and Ken. The first son, Herb, came into the business for a brief period of time and realized it was not for him. He ultimately left the business and the country. The second son, Lenny, graduated from college under a work/study program and worked for several years for a large public company to get his feet wet and learn the business world. The understanding was that he would come into the family business, which he did in his early 20s. He is excelling and is the driving force behind the business today. The youngest son, Ken, also came into the business after college and is doing quite well. Gene also had a son, Louis, who was active in the business.

Family Tree
> **Blanche**
> > *Children*
> > > **Robert**
> > > **Gene**
> > *Grandchildren*
> > > **Robert: Herb, Lenny, Ken**
> > > **Gene: Louis**

Business Valuation

When I met the owners in 1990, the company never had a formal business valuation. At the time, annual gross sales were in excess of $22 million. The net profits were several million dollars per year, including owners' compensations. Furthermore, the company had a very strong balance sheet; little bank debt; and a growing, diverse customer base. Conservatively, the business may have been worth $20 million.

Succession Planning

Robert and Gene had a stock redemption buy-sell agreement with a ridiculously low and outdated value of $500,000 each. A major concern was that if one of them died, the corporation (to the benefit of the surviving brother) could buy the business for a dramatic bargain price. Furthermore, neither family was prepared to pay the enormous estate tax that would result. As the brothers were now well into their 70s, this was becoming eminent. Also, becoming apparent was the fact that the next generation of children could not work well together. All three sons were paid equally, even though Robert's sons, Lenny and Ken, were working much harder and more effectively than Louis. The bothers disagreed vehemently on compensation issues. Gene thought that all pay should be equal. Finally, this disagreement boiled over, and Gene said, "Buy me out!"

Family Buyout

The objective was to buy out Gene and, at the same time, not increase Robert's already sizeable taxable estate. The solution was to design a buyout during Gene's lifetime. Rather than having his 72-year-old brother buy him out and inflate his taxable estate, the recommendation was to have the two sons, Lenny and Ken (who were in their mid-30s), buy out their uncle. A reasonable value was placed on Gene's 50% interest, and he was bought out through a promissory note over 10 years at a fixed imputed interest rate. Lenny and Ken used cash flow from the business, as S corporation dividend distributions, to buy out their uncle (and rid themselves of their cousin) while increasing their ownership percentages and tax bases. Robert still owns 33%, while his two sons now own 33% each.

New Buy-Sell Agreement

Creating a buy-sell agreement between Lenny and Ken was now imperative. A cross-purchase agreement was created and funded appropriately with life and disability insurance to protect the corporation, the shareholders, and their families.

Key Employees

Lenny and Ken's future success became focused on retaining and rewarding the key people who helped with the continuity of the business. The top eight employees were identified by the sons as key to the future success and growth of the business. While the company paid a fair wage, we needed to design a benefits program to "handcuff" and reward these eight key employees for staying with the company until retirement age and to provide incentive to reach specified profitability and performance milestones. We designed a two-step program as follows:

1. A nonqualified deferred compensation plan to selectively benefit the key employees only. The plan provided supplemental retirement income, disability income, and death benefits to their families if they should become disabled or die while employed by the company. The plan has proven to be highly effective; they have not lost a single employee since adopting it 15 years ago. Sales, profitability, and business value have increased dramatically, as well.

2. A 401(k)/profit-sharing plan for all full-time employees. During enrollment, employees were educated to fully appreciate the income tax benefits and retirement resources being provided by their employer.

The Future Is Bright

The industry is changing rapidly. As competitors continue to go out of business and/or consolidate, this company is thriving and expanding. It has made several acquisitions of synergistic businesses and now operates four facilities, in addition to the company headquarters and primary manufacturing plant. It has a fleet of more than 100 trailers that deliver product all across North America, although the New York/New Jersey metropolitan area still represents the majority of the market served. In 2010, the company achieved $76 million in gross sales.

The biggest challenge today is that the company is outgrowing its current facilities and has reached capacity.

Raising Capital

The company is on a major growth path and is in the process of acquiring a new plant. This will stimulate the local economy and create new jobs. The company qualifies for various tax credits from which tax benefits will be realized over the next 10 years. It has partnered with a strategic investor to help finance its expansion plans. A portion of the stock was recently sold to the strategic investor at seven times the adjusted EBITDA multiple. The owners received cash, retained control, and still own all of the business real estate (which is in a separate legal entity). They have also received additional working capital and salary continuation and have maintained all perks.

The new expansion plans include construction of a 500,000-square-foot facility on 95 acres, with enough space to park 450 trailers and access to eight rail cars. They have created over 200 new jobs in 2011. Sales are projected to soar past $100 million.

Conclusion

Let's review some of the major problems and threats encountered in this case study:

1. Lack of proper business valuation to ensure that the first shareholder to die did not lose tremendous value for his family

2. Need to buy out the uncle and, ideally, avoid inflation of Robert's taxable estate

3. Establishment of a proper buy-sell agreement between grandchildren at a reasonable value and funding it to carry out the terms of the agreement in the event of death or disability

4. Reduction of estate taxes and settlement costs to avoid involuntary liquidation of business and real estate to pay the IRS

5. Retention of key employees to provide second-line management strength for continued business success and achievement of future expansion plans

6. Search for growth capital and a strategic partner (this resulted in a partial sale, i.e., an equity recapitalization)

Results

- A formal business valuation was completed to establish fair-market value for transfer tax purposes and buyouts.

- A nonqualified deferred compensation plan was implemented, including retirement benefits, key person life insurance, and disability insurance for the top eight employees.

- New wills, durable powers of attorney, and living wills were executed for all shareholders.

- Business real estate was sold to an intentionally defective income trust to reduce estate tax liability on assets passing from Robert to his sons (this technique was covered in chapter 3, "Wealth Preservation Strategies").

- FLP/GRATs were implemented to further reduce estate tax exposure (and transfer 16% of Robert's stock to his sons).

- A 401(k) plan was created to provide for retirement savings of owners and all eligible employees.

- Personal life insurance was purchased for family members.

- Investment planning began for future financial independence.

- Equity recapitalization raised much-needed capital for expansion.

- The Tax Relief Act of 2010 provides tax incentives to purchase business equipment. A 100% write-off is available for eligible property purchased after September 10, 2010, and before January 1, 2012. This is very timely, as the business is planning to purchase equipment for its new plant.

- These themes and many others will be more fully developed throughout this part of the book, as well as in the section on wealth preservation.

WHAT IS BUSINESS SUCCESSION PLANNING?

Did you know that as the baby boomer generation approaches retirement age, more than 7.7 million business owners will exit from their businesses during the next 10–15 years? Some estimate that these businesses represent more than $10 trillion in wealth. Unfortunately, studies conducted by MassMutual, PriceWaterhouseCoopers, Marquette University, and others show that 75% of these business owners do not have a formal plan to deal with the single most important financial decision of their lives: their business succession.

> *75% of these business owners do not have a formal plan to deal with the single most important financial decision of their lives: their business succession.*

Business succession planning encompasses all of the areas of wealth preservation planning described earlier, with emphasis on:

- Family business planning, if the desire is to keep the business in the family

- Exit planning, which includes investment banking or M&A (mergers and acquisitions), if the objective is to sell the business

- Personal financial planning

- Risk management

- Advanced estate preservation

- Comprehensive tax planning (including reduction/avoidance of capital gains, gift, estate, and possibly generation-skipping transfer taxes)

Business succession planning may be further defined as the orderly and economical transfer of business ownership, under both *voluntary* and *involuntary* circumstances. Voluntary circumstances include the lifetime sale of the business, retirement, or the creation of an ESOP. Involuntary circumstances may occur as a result of death or long-term disability.

Planning in this area must address each major contingency. Resolution of the contingencies is accomplished through the adoption of a formal plan. Like family and personal wealth planning, business succession planning requires frank and collaborate discovery conversations about the attitudes, goals, and preferences of all stockholders. It represents the intersection of all areas of personal financial planning, business planning, risk management, M&A, and wealth preservation.

What a Business Succession Plan Accomplishes
A proper business succession plan addresses and satisfies the following objectives:

- Establishment of an acceptable business value for sale or federal gift and estate tax, buy-sell, and succession planning purposes

- Development of a plan to transfer the business to family members, if that is the owner's objective

- Shift of business growth out of the owner's taxable estate, while effectively retaining control

- Prevention of forced liquidation of the business to pay estate taxes and settlement costs

- Development or updating of a buy-sell agreement with any partners or coshareholders to ensure the orderly transfer of the business in the event of death, disability, or other trigger events, to guarantee that surviving family members receive cash for business interests

- Development of a plan to maximize use of the business for attainment of personal objectives and also to:
  - Improve fringe benefits for ownership and employees
  - Provide a qualified retirement plan for ownership and employees that is also cost effective for the business
  - Attract and retain key executives and employees
  - Build successor managers/owners

- Development of a plan to compensate owners and senior management personnel, with a package of fringe benefits that are affordable, easy to implement, and easy to manage

- Ability and preparedness to sell the business for maximum value in a desired number of years

THE VALUE PATH

The value path summarizes the life cycle of a business and highlights its various needs at each stage. Entrepreneurs often spend the better part of their adult lives nurturing and growing a business. They take on significant risk because they are passionate about their ability to compete in the marketplace and win on the basis of their ideas, products, and services. Their companies survive, thrive, and ideally pass through the early stage, to the growth stage, to the late stage, and then to the point of exit.

Early Stage

The early stage is typically characterized by 24/7 workweeks and a high degree of owner control and autonomy. The owner is often overextended and undercapitalized, while trying to keep creditors at bay, minimize taxes, and reinvest profits to finance future growth, often at personal sacrifice. Unfortunately, the majority of businesses do not survive the early stage.

Growth Stage

The growth stage is characterized by a new feeling of success. The business has made it. Survival is reasonably secure. However, the owner cannot afford to rest on his or her laurels. The challenges of running a growth-stage business include:

- Attracting, training, and retaining employees

- Obtaining additional capital, as needed

- Building more infrastructure, inventory, equipment, and real estate

- Staying one step ahead of competitors

Late Stage

During the late stage, the business owner has become a respected and influential member of the community. He or she now enjoys success and begins to think about how to convert the equity built up inside the business into resources for new opportunities, retirement, transfers to family, or the ability to satisfy charitable intentions.

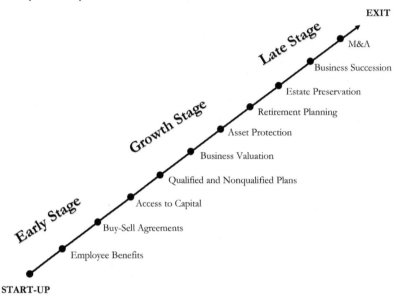

EXIT

Late Stage

M&A

Business Succession

Estate Preservation

Growth Stage

Retirement Planning

Asset Protection

Business Valuation

Qualified and Nonqualified Plans

Access to Capital

Early Stage

Buy-Sell Agreements

Employee Benefits

START-UP

© 2011 Equity Strategies Group

Value Path Process

As a business owner, your single largest asset is most likely your business. The value path process is focused on maximizing the value of your business and helping you transfer that value ultimately to

> *The value path process is focused on maximizing the value of your business and helping you transfer that value.*

your personal balance sheet, to your family, or to whomever you want to transfer it. Various concerns confront you from start-up (or whatever stage you are currently in) to growth stage, late stage, and, ultimately, your exit plan. Along the way, you build maximum value by:

+ Saving income taxes

+ Increasing operating efficiency

+ Attracting, retaining, and rewarding key employees

+ Taking advantage of all applicable company fringe benefits

+ Having ready access to capital

+ Protecting your business and other assets from creditors and predators

+ Preserving your wealth, allowing you to pass it on to your family (or charity)

+ Finally, developing an exit strategy so that when you are ready, you can exit your business and obtain maximum dollar value to enjoy your vision of the lifestyle you expect

Determine Your Stage

+ When did you start your business?

+ Why did you go into business for yourself?

+ How did you capitalize it initially and subsequently?

+ What is your 5/10/20-year plan?

Address Your Concerns/Issues

+ What would you like to develop further in your business?

+ What challenges do you face in taking your business to the next level?

+ If you could change one aspect of your business, what would it be?

+ Do you need access to additional capital to grow and expand?

+ What is your exit strategy?

Follow the value path diagram and consider your answers to the questions under each bullet point.

1. **Employee Benefits**
   - What fringe benefits does your business provide to you and your employees?
   - When were the programs last reviewed?

2. **Buy-Sell Agreement**
   - Do you have one?
   - What type?
   - When was it last reviewed?
   - Is it properly funded with life and disability insurance?

3. **Qualified Plan**
   - What type does your business have in place?
   - Are you happy with the investment performance and administration?
   - It is in compliance with ERISA and DOL rules?

3b. **Nonqualified Plan**
   - Do you have one?
   - Which employees are key to the survival and success of your business? What have you done to attract/retain/reward them?

4. **Access to Capital**
   - Who is your current bank or other lender?
   - What loans/lines of credit are outstanding?
   - Are the terms competitive today?
   - Do you need more capital?
   - How do you plan to take your company to the next level?

5. **Business Valuation**
   - What's it worth?
   - How did you arrive at that number? Have you ever had a formal valuation?

6. **Retirement Planning**

- What is your vision of retirement and the quality of life you expect to have?
- What cash flow/asset modeling have you done? Are you on track?

7. **Estate Preservation**
   - How do you intend to pass on your business at your death?
   - How will estate taxes be paid?
   - What steps have you taken to reduce taxes? Have you done all you can?

8. **Business Succession Planning**
   - Do you have a formal (written) succession plan? With whom? Is it funded?
   - When was the last review?

9. **Mergers and Acquisitions**
   - Do you plan to grow organically or possibly accelerate your business growth through mergers and acquisitions of other businesses?
   - How do you locate acquisition opportunities?
   - How do you know whether they are a good strategic fit and valued properly?

10. **Exit Strategy/Sale of Business**
    - When you started your business, did you have an exit strategy in mind?
    - What is your current thinking relative to exit?
    - What is the time frame?
    - Will you sell? To whom? Will it be 100% or just taking some chips off the table?
    - Which of the items along the value path interest or concern you most at this time?

The Needs of Business Owners

Business owners face a multitude of issues that require them to work *on* their businesses and not just *in* them, including:

- Competing in an increasingly challenging marketplace

- Planning for business succession

- Raising capital to support the growth of their businesses

- Developing an acquisition strategy for accelerated growth

- Deriving liquidity from the significant amount of their wealth locked up inside their business equity

- Reinventing when necessary

These challenges suggest the need for sophisticated strategies and experienced advisors to help design and execute exit strategies, estate/wealth preservation plans, and strategic plans for the sale of your business and to coordinate financial independence and investment advice. Oftentimes, today's pressing concerns about business growth and the capital needed to promote such growth dominate the minds of business owners. Business owners are focused on surviving under the intense pressures of today's economy. Owners are also concerned about maximizing their value as shareholders and, ultimately, keeping their businesses in their families or converting business equity into cash when they exit from their businesses, depending on their specific goals.

Much emotion is tied into this process. It's not all dollars and cents, which is what the transactional community often reduces it to. Your business may be an essential part of your identity, or it may be your "baby"—

> *Much emotion is tied into this process. It's not all dollars and cents.*

oftentimes it is part of your worth as a person. Solutions consistent with your *visions, values, and goals* are a critical element to successful implementation of financial strategies. Your advisors need to know what makes you run; what keeps you awake at night; what brings you joy; and how you define happiness, success, and fulfillment. With this vital data and intimate knowledge, along with keeping your best interests at heart, financial advisors can help you bridge the gap from traditional advisory roles to establishment of working relationships with investment bankers, mergers and acquisitions advisors, and other specialists who can help you examine all facets of a proper business growth and exit plan.

Raising Capital

One of the greatest challenges business owners face is financing their businesses. In today's economic environment, credit is tighter than ever. Whether financing is used to fund a start-up, provide necessary working capital for current operations, or fund growth or an exit strategy, the appetite for capital is omnipresent. It is important to understand how to raise capital beyond the founder's own money, family, and friends. The likely first source, of course, is banks. Banks have a process to approve loans on the basis of their established loan policies, credit scoring, approval systems, and loan committees, and business owners need to know how banks approve loans before submitting applications. Various loan durations are available, matching the need with the useful life of the underlying collateral. Other popular loans include lines of credit that establish a maximum amount that can be borrowed, real estate loans, equipment loans, constructions loans, and inventory loans.

Almost without exception, banks will require personal guarantees from the business owners or the largest stockholders. If traditional banks decline to lend, additional sources of borrowed capital include (1) local, state, or federal governments (numerous programs exist, including the Small Business Administration [SBA]) and (2) asset-based lenders who provide equipment loans, leases, and accounts receivable factoring. These lenders take much greater risks than traditional banks, and lending rates are commensurately higher.

Finding someone who can help raise capital is a great boon to entrepreneurs, and some financial advisors now include capital raising as a nontraditional but necessary service. A professional with intimate knowledge of your business, all of its owners, and the transaction has a real advantage in helping your business attract money. However, the quest for financing is but one piece of your puzzle; the qualified advisor who considers the entire puzzle and helps determine what would best fit into the open space is a truly valued resource for you.

Other Sources of Early-Stage Capital

While raising capital will often be a primary issue for a business throughout the value path, early-stage capital is often the most difficult to raise. When lending sources are unavailable or insufficient, equity partners could be the solution.

1. **Angel investors** are high-net-worth individuals seeking high returns who typically invest $100,000–$350,000 or more in early-stage businesses. An angel usually has in-depth knowledge of a business or industry he or she is investing in through prior experience in management of a similar type of business. Angels often want to mentor or participate in management or serve as board members.

2. **Venture capital** (VC) firms are typically the largest cash investors in early-stage entities when banks and other lenders are unwilling to make sufficient capital available. VCs raise the capital they invest from institutions such as pension funds and insurance companies, which earmark dollars for such high-risk/high-return investments. VCs generally have specific industries they favor, such as technology, health care, or consumer goods. VC minimum investments are usually $100,000 to $4 million, and maximum investments are $250,000 to $50 million. Most investment activity is in the range of $1 to $20 million. Their annual return targets range from 30% to 40% or more, and time horizons to liquidity are generally five to seven years. VCs often have certain demands of the business, such as substantial equity positions and board of directors seats.

3. **Private equity groups** (PEGs) are another source of capital for businesses. They are pools of capital usually funded by money management firms, pensions, other institutions, and select high-net-worth investors. PEGs sometimes fund early-stage investments. Most often, they will fund growth-stage and late-stage businesses in need of mezzanine financing (subordinated debt layered between senior bank debt and equity) or buyouts in management-led transactions and leveraged recapitalization

(the reverse of management buyouts, where management ownership is reduced). PEGs also, of course, acquire companies outright.

Private Placements: Debt and Equity

A private placement of debt or equity can be done for private or public companies. In a debt-financed private placement, the company must have predictable cash flow to service the borrowings. In an equity private placement, the company must have a thorough business plan and a strong, experienced team of managers.

Considerations

- Is the company enjoying strong growth?

- Does the company wish to raise capital to support such growth?

- Does the company need to finance an acquisition?

- Recapitalization: Owner seeks liquidity but not a total sale of the business.

- The public markets may not be suitable as a result of offering size or other constraints.

Furthermore, if a business owner has had difficulty raising capital through traditional banking channels, alternative financing methods such as private placements should be considered.

WHAT COULD GO WRONG FOR THE FAMILY BUSINESS?

Death of a Shareholder

The day you walk out, the government walks in. Your family is locked into a business that is not readily salable but immediately taxable.

> *The day you walk out, the government walks in.*

Estate taxes are probably the largest impediment to keeping the business in the family.

If your business transfers to a surviving spouse, estate taxes may be deferred until the surviving spouse dies, assuming that the owner is married and his or her business interest passes to the surviving spouse, utilizing the unlimited marital deduction.

The objective of retaining a business interest in the family gives rise to several planning considerations that need to be addressed.

If the stock is to be retained by the surviving spouse, the following considerations arise:

- What will the source of income be for the surviving spouse? If the spouse does not carry out duties commensurate with the salary, upon audit, salary payments likely will be recharacterized as a non-deductible dividend. Further, sales and profitability could decline as a result of the absence of the deceased owner, increasing the risk to the survivors.

- If children are active in the business, conflicts could arise. The surviving spouse will generally prefer security and dividend distributions, while the children may wish to pursue an active growth strategy, often requiring cash and entailing more risk.

- All of the business growth, presumably attributable to the children's efforts, will be included in the survivor's estate. The children will be burdened with unnecessary estate tax on wealth they created.

If your will transfers your business interest to all of your children:

- Inactive family members may own a portion of the business, which could lead to conflict.

- You lose the benefit of a trustee to help manage the business.

- If you've appointed a corporate trustee who will have no interest in or ability to maintain your business, this may force a sale.

If the stock is to be bequeathed to the active children at the first death, the following considerations arise:

- What will the source of income be for the surviving spouse?

- Estate taxes may be due upon the stock passing to the children. To the extent that this exceeds the available unified credit, cash will be required within nine months of death to pay estate taxes.

- You can transfer only your portion of the business. Any ownership interest your spouse has must also be addressed.

- The greater the portion of the estate represented by the business, the greater the likelihood of unequal estate distribution, including possible disinheritance of the inactive children, after estate taxes are paid from liquid assets.

If the stock is to be sold to the active children at the first death, the following considerations arise:

- Any ownership interest your spouse has should also be considered in the sale agreement.

- Will the children or business have the cash necessary? If an installment note is required, will the business be able to support the payments, especially after the death of the principal spouse/owner?

- Relying on installment payments places the surviving spouse in a vulnerable position.

- The sale must be at arm's length; otherwise, a taxable gift may arise.

Careful consideration must be paid to where the stock will go upon your death. Does this flow match up with your objectives? If your spouse and your children get along well now, is it important that they continue to get along after you're gone? Will key employees want control of the business and threaten to quit if they don't get it? How will your customers deal with someone else? How will relationships with bankers and suppliers change?

Lack of a Business Succession Agreement
All too often, owners with partners or coshareholders (co-owner members in an LLC) do not have a written plan in place to deal with the continuity of their businesses. A business has far greater value as a going concern sold

to your surviving partner(s) than could be realized upon its liquidation. Without a plan, you may not have the time or the bargaining power to receive maximum value for the business.

Nothing assures that a purchaser can be found who will buy at a price and on terms satisfactory to owners and their families. A buy-sell agreement creates a market for closely held business stock that otherwise would be difficult for owners or their families to sell. Families' financial security will otherwise be threatened, with business owners' salaries cut off and the uncertainties of a sale negotiation. In addition, provisions are often not made for the payment of taxes that may be due upon transfer. Survivors may be forced to liquidate the business at a price substantially below fair-market value.

In summary, the lack of a business agreement may bring the following consequences:

- It may fail to set a fair price for the business or may encourage disagreement and delays at the worst possible time. Cash is not guaranteed in order to buy the interest of a deceased, disabled, or retired partner.

- It allows the IRS to contest the value and thereby potentially increases the estate for estate tax purposes.

- In the event of the death of one of your co-owners, you must do business with one of your former co-owner's relatives, who has little or no knowledge of your business. Alternatively, if you want or need to buy out the deceased co-owner's survivor, the value and terms are uncertain.

- In the event of the death of one of your co-owners, you must accept your co-owner's relative's sale to an outsider to recoup the share. You could be in for the challenge of your life.

- In the event of the death of one of your co-owners, important management decisions could be delayed. Heirs of owners have very different concerns but still retain their voting rights.

- In the event of the death of one of your co-owners, you may wind up doing all of the work while sharing the profits equally.

- In the event of the death of one of your co-owners, you may seek capital to meet additional expenses but with a substantially weakened credit rating.

- In the event of the death of one of your co-owners, you could be forced to operate with credit temporarily cut off because the bank wants to wait and see or because outstanding loans and/or lines of credit may be called.

- The business may suffer irreparable loss in the period between the termination of your service and the completion of a sale.

- Additional tax and administrative costs may severely limit the net dollars received from your business interest.

The Importance of Valuing Your Business

In cases where no binding agreement was in place and where the estate was left to contend with the valuation issue after the death of the shareholder, the risk is that the IRS will challenge the taxpayers' valuation and force their own valuation.

Tax court history shows a risk that costs will increase greatly and that the time delays of settlement will be substantial. If you do not peg the value of your business for estate tax purposes, the government will.

| | Share Value | | | |
Title of Class	According to Tax Payer	According to IRS	According to Court	Elapsed Time in Years
Buchanan, Estate of Reba S.	160	478	478	4
Edwards, Caroline W.	200	310	310	5
Ewing, Estate of Anna C.	2,400	6,530	4,750	7
Helmers, Estate of George J.	500	1,000	900	5
Huntington, Estate of Henry E.	10,638	16,650	16,110	10
Tebb, Estate of Thomas W.	100	146	146	6
Levinson, Estate of David	253	1,033	900	6
Springer, Estate of Henry	200	290	250	4

This kind of exposure is an estate litigator's dream! A properly drafted buy-sell agreement can help to establish, or peg, a value for estate and gift tax purposes. It may not be binding on the IRS under certain circumstances, but it certainly helps the estate's argument.

Lack of a Disability Buyout Provision
With or without a business agreement, the threat of an owner's disability is often ignored. The likelihood of a business owner becoming disabled is significantly higher than death before age 65. If we assume multiple business owners, all will be adversely impacted.

Active Owner Considerations
- The disabled owner's interest is not guaranteed to be purchased.

- The disabled owner's family may want to come into the business and take an active role. (Are they qualified?)

- The disabled partner may want back in once recovered after several years of business changes.

- Outsiders may want to purchase the disabled owner's interest. (Is the sale restricted? Are the value and terms spelled out?)

Disabled Owner Considerations

- ❖ The disabled owner needs current income rather than business growth.

- ❖ The sale of ownership interest has no definite market; the disabled owner has no one, other than healthy owners, to sell interests to.

- ❖ Value is not guaranteed; without a carefully drafted disability buy-out provision that determines business value and payment terms, nothing is binding.

- ❖ How is disability determined? A definition of disability needs to be drafted in the agreement to avoid disputes.

THE VALUE OF KEY EMPLOYEES

The death of a key employee can cause serious problems for your business. Small and medium-sized businesses consider finding qualified employees one of their biggest problems. To protect against this loss, at least from a financial perspective, the business can acquire a life insurance policy on the life of the key employee(s).

The business entity owns the policy and pays the premiums. The company has all rights to the policy's living benefits, such as access to the cash values if a permanent policy is used. Death proceeds are received income tax free. The life insurance proceeds received by the company can be used for a variety of purposes, including attracting and compensating replacement talent.

Many guidelines can be used to determine the dollar value of a key employee. These include a multiple of the person's compensation, estimating profits lost, or the replacement methods as examples. Sound planning should examine all of the methods to determine the appropriate amount of insurance coverage needed to insure the key employee.

- ❖ **Contribution method.** How much is the key employee contributing to the profits of the company?

- ❖ **Replacement method.** What will replacing the key employee cost?

- **"Five years of salary" method.** Calculating five years of salary provides a rule-of-thumb formula to value a key employee.

Competing for Talent in the Private Sector
Nonqualified Deferred Compensation

Retention of key employees is critical to the future success of your closely held businesses.

Business succession planning at private employers poses unique challenges in contrast with public companies. In a highly competitive environment for talent, the ability of private owners to attract, retain, and motivate senior executives is critical in defining the success of an organization. Supplemental executive retirement plans (SERPs), which fall in the arena of *nonqualified* executive benefits, are instrumental in leveling the playing field for private companies when competing with public companies for senior executives to manage their companies. Public companies rely on equity-based benefits extensively, which is a handicap at private companies. In this regard, SERPs serve an increasingly important role in enhancing executive benefits packages at private companies that cannot be provided with *qualified* plans.

The many benefits of implementing an SERP to the private employer include:

- Attracting, retaining, and motivating senior executives

- Avoiding distribution of stock as compensation

- Controlling cash compensation costs

- Competing with public companies offering alternate forms of benefits

- Aligning the interests of the executives with those of the employer

- Having full discretion to determine eligibility for participation

- Offering complete flexibility in deciding how to informally fund the plan's obligations

- Maximizing the sale price of the company by locking in senior management with SERPs

- Rewarding long-tenured senior executives with SERPs at the time of sale of the business

From an executive's perspective, the benefits of an SERP offered by a private employer include:

- A financially secure retirement delivered via a customized SERP program

- A supplemental benefit in addition to taxable cash compensation

- A form of benefit in lieu of equity-based benefits

- The ability to participate in the financial success of a company as a nonowner

Why SERPs?

Government limits on tax-qualified retirement programs severely restrict the ability of employers to offer comprehensive retirement benefits from qualified plans. Some of these restrictions include the limits on the maximum compensation that can be taken into account in qualified plans and limits on employer contributions to defined-contribution plans. As a result of government limitations, highly compensated executives face a form of reverse discrimination, whereby their retirement income from qualified plans is proportionately much less than that for lower-compensated employees. In addition, a greater percentage of final compensation is required in order to retire comfortably. For private employers, the deficiencies of qualified plans can thus be addressed only by implementing SERPs to supplement executive retirement income and for retention purposes.

SERP Designs

SERP designs are highly customizable, allowing private employers to deliver benefits commensurate with their needs. In general, SERPs are designed in either of the following two key configurations:

1. **Nonqualified defined-benefit (DB) SERP.** A DB SERP provides the participant a specified percentage of final average compensation, similar to a pension plan. The employer has considerable flexibility in specifying what benefit amount is to be provided, whether by a formula or as a specific dollar amount. The employer also has the option to fund the future liability informally by utilizing mutual funds, institutionally priced life insurance, etc. A key characteristic of a DB SERP is that the employer is subject to the investment risk since the benefit to the participant is specified.

2. **Nonqualified defined-contribution (DC) SERP.** Under a DC SERP, the employer makes specified annual contributions into a participant's account on the basis of a formula or metrics designed by the employer. In this case, the employer may also informally fund the obligation by utilizing a funding vehicle. On the basis of the initial annual rate of return assumptions, the contribution amounts are predetermined, but the final benefit amount to a participant may vary. The participant is usually given some control over the investment choices for the account. Under this type of DC SERP, the participant is subject to the investment risk since the benefit received at retirement is dependent upon the performance of the selected investment options.

SERPs allow private employers to compete with public employers by implementing a valuable succession planning vehicle. Given the many advantages of SERPs, they are widely utilized by private employers to attract, retain, and motivate senior executives.

> *SERPs allow private employers to compete with public employers.*

Introduction to Exit Planning

Exit planning is a process resulting in an owner's transition out of a business. At that time, every owner wants to receive the maximum amount of value in order to accomplish personal, financial, and estate preservation goals.

Five Business Exit Paths

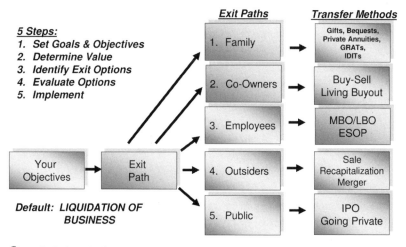

© 2011 Equity Strategies Group

Exit Planning

At some point in the life of the business, typically during the late stage, the owner must consider his or her exit path. Everyone exits—either voluntarily or involuntarily (vertically or horizontally). Thus, understanding the key principals of exit planning as a process, not a one-time event, is helpful.

> *Everyone exits— either voluntarily or involuntarily (vertically or horizontally).*

1. **Set your goals and priorities.** A few of the questions to be asked are: What do you want to do next with your business? To whom do you want to transfer your current business?

- **Family**: Are children ready, willing, and able to take the reins?
- **Employees**: Does sale to management or an ESOP make sense?
- **Co-Owners**: Do they want to and are they financially able to buy you out?
- **Outsiders**: Do you want to sell for maximum value to a strategic or financial buyer? Do you want to sell a portion or all of your business?
- **Do you want to go public?**

Are you emotionally and financially ready to exit? When? For how much?

What are your plans for life after you exit your business? Some owners find this to be a difficult question to address. It often creates an emotional response that touches on outside interests and relationships. Perhaps another business or investment is on the next horizon. What is your definition of "retirement"?

2. **Conduct an analysis of your current condition and determine the value of your business.** Is the business ready to be transferred or sold, or are interim steps necessary to cure weaknesses and enhance value? The creation of a **marketability assessment** prepared by advisors experienced in exit planning and investment banking provides an excellent view of this. It can give you a realistic estimate of a range of values your business may be sold or transferred for and can provide a study of sales of comparable businesses and prevailing multiples to analyze valuation methods.

3. **Identify exit options, choose the right one, and execute.** Education is important in order to become aware of available strategies and their advantages and disadvantages. The diagram of exit-planning scenarios summarizes your exit options, along with possible transfer channels and methods. Once a course of action is chosen, an advisory team must be assembled to carry out that strategy properly.

Step Two: Determining Business Value

In the course of running a company, business owners are accustomed to understanding profit margins, operating expenses, gross revenue, and the other expense categories on their financial statements. At the end of the reporting period, these categories all point to the bottom line or net earnings.

A common management tool used by savvy business owners involves using one or two simplified indicators that let them know at a glance whether the month or year is going to be profitable. It might be the cost of a particular commodity or wages as a percent of cost of goods sold. They may likely have a "spot indicator" tool as well. Whatever it is, many times it works like clockwork and the owner begins to rely and depend on it. However, when looking to understand the price or value of a business, owners naturally expect an accountant or other advisors to provide them with the same type of spot indicator or a formula that is as simple to understand.

Many times, forecasting a company's valuation in real time, as well as the unforeseeable future, is like trying to predict the weather. Because of the fact that many business owners are control oriented, their take-charge position may become larger than business marketability logic. This coupled with unrealistic valuation expectations and poor planning could cause them to overlook and miss opportunities to realize goals and objectives when they present themselves.

Determining business value is part science, part art, and part emotion, but some realistic techniques can be used to predict what the value range might be, giving consideration to all the tangible and intangible assets, current industry indicators, and current economic conditions.

What's My Business Worth?

Many different approaches exist to approaching valuation, depending on the owner's objectives for the future of the business and, therefore, the purpose of performing a valuation. Since closely held businesses are not traded on a public stock market, the perspectives of the players matter.

Fair-Market Value

The IRS determines fair-market value under Rev. Ruling 59-60 as "the price at which the property [your business] would change hands between a willing buyer and a willing seller when the former is not under any compulsion to buy and the latter is not under any compulsion to sell, both parties having reasonable knowledge of relevant facts."

Most people believe the axiom that fair is fair, so the statement by the IRS is a reasonable summation of the principles of exchange as they relate to the nagging questions, "Did I get a fair price?" and/or "Did I settle for less than I should have?"

Value depends largely on the purpose of the valuation, using different value worlds.

Where do we start? When a business owner receives an offer for his or her company, how do we know that the indicated value offered is fair, high, or not worth the paper it is written on?

- **Owner's value:** what you think it's worth

- **Collateral value:** what the bank says it's worth when you apply for a loan or business line of credit

- **Investment value:** what your employees think it's worth if you were to sell it to them

How Do You Get the "Right" Value?

The value of your business can be determined in a number of ways. Each method, in its own perspective, proves reliable, depending on the type of business, value of assets, technology considerations, and other factors specific to the value model.

In order to establish a baseline for value, a few methods are most commonly accepted in the business valuation process, lender calculations, and financial arena in general. This section looks at a few formulas, methods, and typical approaches, but the bottom line for the transaction will likely be value as referenced by the value world you are operating in.

Earnings-Based Formulas (EBITDAs)

One of the most common calculations involves the adjustment of the earnings of the company, based on the concept that all businesses are created equal and the owner's decisions are what make them more or less profitable.

The acronym **EBITDA** stands for **E**arnings **B**efore **I**nterest, **T**axes, **D**epreciation, and **A**mortization and is one of the most frequently used formulas because it can be applied to almost any business. Many times, a capitalization rate, or a multiplier, is applied to the EBITDA to determine the price that you would receive. For example, if EBITDA was $1 million and the multiplier was 5, the value would be $5 million. For the sake of this discussion, assume that we are talking about a lower middle-market business ($10–$100 million). This means that unless otherwise agreed to, all operating assets will be transferred and accounted for in the calculation.

The formula is

- **EBITDA** = gross revenue – business expenses (excluding interest, tax, depreciation, and amortization).

Typically, in this calculation, there may also be add-backs for items such as excess earnings of the owners, one-time capital expenditures, excess rent, and any other expenses that are nonrecurring or not necessary for the operations of the business—essentially hidden profit that would be available to the business (and a purchaser) otherwise.

The idea behind adjusted EBITDA is to provide a true picture of the future potential profitability of a company before expenses from creditors are taken into account, since every owner has his or her own level of risk and quantity of resources. Bear in mind that any number of options you choose will change the profitability of your company and thus change the EBITDA.

Which EBITDA Do You Use?

- **Reported EBITDA:** reflects your historical results

- **Recast EBITDA:** includes the aforementioned add-backs

- **Synergized recast EBITDA:** captures the synergies a potential buyer would realize as a result of purchasing your company. The additional profitability is extracted through cost savings as a result of economies of scale, increased market share, pricing, etc.

Example: A business sold for six times

			Transaction Value
Reported EBITDA of $2 million	× 6	=	$12 million
Recast EBITDA of $3.5 million	× 6	=	21 million
Synergized recast EBITDA of $5 million	× 6	=	30 million

An experienced M&A advisor or investment banker will represent your company to the marketplace, negotiate on the basis of the highest EBITDA, and fight for the best price and terms.

Other methods used to determine value are:

- **Discounted cash flow (DCF)**—In a DCF valuation, the value of your company is measured by estimating the expected future cash flows and then discounting those future flows by the desired rate of return in order to determine the present value of the future cash stream.

- **Capitalized earnings approach**—This approach measures the expected return on the buyer's investment.

- **Tangible assets approach (balance sheet items)**—This approach determines the business value on the basis of total assets, or adjusted book value, which may be adjusted to the estimated fair-market value for the replacement cost of equipment or other assets.

- **Value of specific intangible assets**—This approach is generally used when the buyer sees value in a customer list, reputation, etc., and the company has just a few tangible assets. This could also be called the goodwill of the business. You may have also heard the term "blue sky" used for these intangible assets. The difference between the two is that the value of the goodwill can be calculated by a rate of return from the excess profitability of the business over the actual return on the tangible assets. Blue sky, however, cannot be calculated, as it is the value beyond the return.

EXIT PATH 1: FAMILY TRANSFERS

Many people find no greater satisfaction than passing a family business along to the next generation. If children are interested, motivated, and capable of running the business, this is often the objective.

If your decision is to transfer your business to family members, it will take years of careful planning to accomplish.

Keeping the Business in the Family

The decision to keep the business in the family creates a number of issues, such as:

1. How you will derive an income at retirement?

2. How you will provide income for your spouse if you should happen to die prematurely?

3. How you will equalize the distribution among children involved, and those not involved, in the active management of your business?

4. Ultimately, where the dollars will come from to pay the estate taxes so that the business does not need to be sold in a forced liquidation to pay the estate taxes due?

Planning Priorities

The primary concern is usually to provide for your own financial security and your spouse's. When considering your objective to keep your business in the family, the main questions are:

Can you afford to? Are you and your spouse OK? Therefore, some personal financial planning is necessary.

Step 1: Identify your cash flow needs - create a personalized financial independence model to track your income and expenses. Before you make any decisions, you must run the numbers to see whether the proposed action is feasible.

Step 2: Inventory of your financial resources - Review your assets and liabilities.

Step 3: Evaluate your long-term situation - Run multiple "what-if" scenarios. If you can achieve financial independence without counting on the proceeds from the sale of your business, then you may be in a position to give it to your children during your lifetime or after you are gone. If, on the other hand, a shortfall exists for you and your spouse without the proceeds, family gifting is not an option. You need to consider an intrafamily sale or other exit options involving a sale to outsiders.

Fact: Many business owners can't afford to give away their businesses during their lifetimes.

Should I Give Company Stock to My Children?
Advantages
- Children may be more motivated to make the company succeed with vested equity interest.

- Business growth is removed from your taxable estate, and exposure to future estate taxes is reduced.

- Valuation discounts (potentially 20%–50% for minority-interest transfers, lack of marketability, lack of voting control) are allowed to be used.

Disadvantages
- Control/privacy is potentially lost.

- Income from business distributions is reduced.

- Proceeds are reduced if a parent later decides to sell.

- Children assume parents' income tax basis (carryover).

- There are costs of valuation, tax reporting, administration of additional entities created, e.g., family limited partnership, LLCs, etc.

- This choice is irrevocable; you can't take it back once given away.

How to Give Away Company Stock

You can transfer stock during your lifetime, via gifts to family members (or preferably trusts for their benefit) through the use of the annual $13,000 gift tax exclusion ($26,000 if made jointly) and, possibly, your lifetime $5 million gift tax exemption ($10 million if made jointly). Transfers during lifetime, via intrafamily sales, can be structured using installment sales, private annuities, and SCINs (self-canceling installment notes).

Transferring a business to family members can take many forms, including the acronym soup of estate preservation: GRATs, GRUTs, FLPs, IDITs, etc. These were covered more fully in the estate preservation section of this book.

Gift (Bequest) at Death

Another option is to hold on to the business stock until you (and your spouse) die. As previously discussed, this option raises a number of planning issues that need to be addressed:

- Grooming your successor
  - Is someone else capable of running the business?
    - What are your distribution objectives?
    - What are your projected estate tax costs? Do you have sufficient assets to pay the estate tax, equalize the estate, and keep the business? If not, what are your options?
    - Do you have the appropriate legal documents to achieve this? A will or trust with specific language dealing with the business is needed. All too often, the business is lumped in with other assets.
    - Have you taken full advantage of all tax relief and incentive provisions?
    - Do you have an adequate amount of properly structured life insurance to deal with payment of estate taxes and

equalization of inheritance among children? Without life insurance, all other assets may need to be liquidated, leaving some children with little to no inheritance.

Equalization

The problem of equalization arises when you have more than one child and some are actively involved in the family business while others are not.

Example: Business owner is a widow who dies in 2011 with three children; one is active in the business. If the business is left only to the child who is active in the business, the estate may be unequally distributed between that child and the others who are not active in the business.

Taxable estate	$30,000,000
Three children, one active in business	
Estimated estate tax	$ 9,000,000
Business value	$21,000,000
IRS receives	$ 9,000,000*
Active child receives (business)	$21,000,000
Child 2 receives	$ -0-
Child 3 receives	$ -0-

*assuming 2011 $5 million estate tax exemption and 35% tax rate

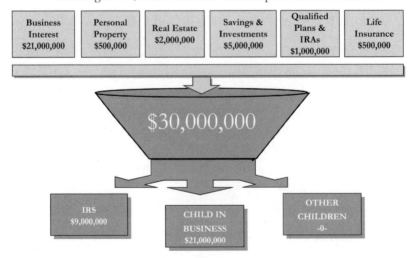

218

Ways to Equalize Your Estate between Active and Inactive Children
Consider a number of techniques, such as:

- Gift company stock to all children, with an agreement for the stock to be purchased later by your active children.

- Gift other estate assets, if enough exist, to equalize.

- Gift nonvoting preferred stock to inactive children.

- Gift nonvoting S corporation stock to inactive children.

- Create an estate equalization clause in your will/trust.

- Transfer business real estate to inactive children, subject to a long-term lease with the business.

- Use life insurance to create liquidity to pay estate taxes and equalize.

Lifetime Sale to Children
If you plan to sell your business to your children during your lifetime, the source of payments and taxation present challenges.

Installment payments may impose a substantial burden on your business, especially when expressed in terms of the sales required to generate the after-tax profits necessary for the principal payments. The portion representing principal is nondeductible for income tax purposes; only interest is deductible.

Example:

Company earns $1 net after-business expenses and pays it to son/ daughter.

Son/daughter pays total income and payroll taxes of 35%, which leaves 55 cents.

Son/daughter pays 55 cents to you.

You pay capital gains tax at 20% (federal and state), which leaves 44 cents of the original $1.

This method of transfer costs the family 56 cents in taxes on each dollar of value sold.

If payments continue after the principal's death, the surviving spouse's financial security will be held hostage to the children's ability to continue making the payments.

If an installment obligation remains upon the death of the survivor, it will be includable in the survivor's estate for estate tax purposes, and up to 35% will be lost to the U.S. Treasury.

Timing: Sale of Stock at First Death (before Your Spouse Dies)

+ Any ownership interest your spouse has should also be considered in the sale agreement.

+ Will the children or business have the cash necessary? If an installment note is required, will the business be able to support the payments, especially after the death of the principal spouse?

+ Relying on installment payments places the surviving spouse in a vulnerable position.

+ The sale must be at arm's length; otherwise, a taxable gift may arise.

Sale to Family with a Private Annuity
What Is It?

A private annuity involves the sale of the business interest, an interest in real estate, or other asset to a family member in exchange for an unsecured income stream for the life of the seller. The annuity is private, meaning that it is between buyer and seller, and does not involve an annuity company.

Private Annuity
How It Works

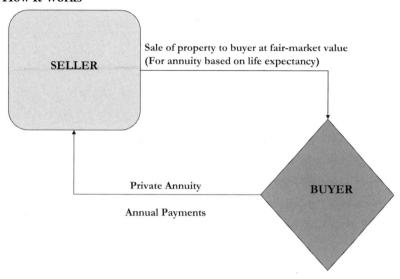

Advantages

- Since payments terminate at the death of the seller, it generally has no value and can escape estate taxation at the seller's death.

- The seller is assured that payments would be made even if the seller outlives his or her life expectancy.

- It freezes the value of an asset if growth subsequent to the sale appreciates in excess of the annuity payments.

- An early death reduces the transferor's estate.

- A high estate tax rate can potentially be converted to the lower capital gains tax rate.

Considerations

- The time of the seller's death gives a wide variation in results (i.e., likelihood of under- or overpaying).

- The purchaser's basis is equal to the total annuity payments made.

- The interest paid is not deductible to the purchaser.

- Interim-basis calculations are needed for asset sales and depreciation during the annuitant's life.

- The promise to pay must be unsecured, although it is a legally enforceable contractual obligation.

- The seller loses the right to report gain on an installment basis if payments are in any way secured (taxes will be due on the entire gain in the year of the sale).

In 2006, the IRS issued proposed regulations that would essentially eliminate the *income tax* advantages of selling appreciated property in exchange for a private annuity by causing the property seller's gain to be recognized *in the year the transaction is effected* rather than as payments are received. These rules generally apply for transactions entered into after October 18, 2006. For this reason, we have seen very few private annuity transactions in the past several years. However, if stock market assets and real estate values have declined, would the recognition of a lower amount of gain, or no gain, justify the transaction?

A private annuity may be a good strategy for an individual with a short life expectancy. However, the mortality component of the valuation tables cannot be used to determine the present value of an annuity if the person with the measuring life is terminally ill when the gift is completed. An individual who is known to have an incurable illness or other deteriorating physical condition is considered terminally ill if there is at least a 50% probability that he or she will die within one year.

Sale at Death to Children

You may want to plan to sell your business to your children upon your death. This is typically done through a buy-sell agreement under which stock in your company is sold to a child or children who desire to buy it in exchange for cash or an installment note to your estate. Life insurance is often used to fund the arrangement. It provides:

- Immediate cash to buy stock

- Cash to the surviving spouse

- Liquidity to pay estate taxes

- Cash for equalization or buyout of other children

Considerations
- Will you need to keep and control the business until you die?

- If so, do you have a buy-sell agreement?

- Is the funding sufficient?

- If unfunded, will the business be forced to sell to a third party to pay estate taxes?

Business Acquisition Trust (BAT)

If you are the sole owner of a business, you can consider creating a business acquisition trust (BAT) to purchase business interests from your estate. This trust may act to relieve many common concerns, such as flexibility, gifting of value with retained control, prearranged distribution (control even after transfer), generation-skipping tax savings, creditor protection, liability protection, and divorce proofing. You can transfer stock into the trust during your lifetime (utilizing your unified credit and annual gift tax exclusions) or wait until death to sell to your BAT.

Here's an example using lifetime gifts to a BAT followed by a sale of the remaining business interests at death:

- Immediately gift 2% of the corporate stock to the BAT, utilizing minority discounts.

- The remaining 98% could be equally distributed between you and your spouse. Each year, you could gift stock equal to your current annual exclusion and/or unified credit amounts to the trust, utilizing minority and lack of marketability discounts (30%–40% discount).

  - In order to maintain management control, the remaining 98% of the stock can be divided into voting stock and nonvoting stock. The portion owned by your spouse, equal to half the value, would be the nonvoting stock, while you retain the voting stock.

♦ Since you are each gifting a small portion at a time, you may take a marketability/minority discount each time you gift stock to the trust. Therefore, if we assume a 40% discount, a gift of $100,000 per year could actually be valued at $60,000 for gift tax purposes. Compare this amount to the current annual exclusion amount.

♦ In addition, you could consider gifting all or a portion of each of your unified credit exemptions (along with the future increases in value) to the trust. In this manner, you could freeze a substantial portion of your business from growing in value inside your taxable estate.

Upon your death, this trust can purchase the remaining shares from your estate. This will:

♦ Provide cash to pay estate taxes

♦ Provide cash to your spouse so that he or she is not dependent on the business for future income

♦ Provide trust protection for voting stock

♦ Provide management structure to assure continued profitability and fair-market value of the business (trustees and board appointees make business decisions and vote the stock)

♦ Business operations remain in the hands of trustees and the board until business interests are distributed or the business is sold. The valuation purchase price can be based upon adjusted book value, capitalization of earnings, or another method to pay your family a fair price. The purchase can be funded, in part or in full, through life insurance on you, owned by the BAT.

Exit Path 2: Co-Owners

Buy-Sell Agreements—Generally

If you have partners or coshareholders, creation of a buy-sell agreement is critical to defending your business wealth.

Before turning to a discussion of a specific type of buy-sell agreement, an understanding of the general utilization of shareholder agreements in closely held entities is appropriate. A well-written buy-sell agreement will accomplish two basic objectives:

1. It will provide a basis, or a peg, for the value of a share of stock for both a lifetime sale and a transfer at the death of a stockholder.

2. It provides certainty of action by stipulating in exact terms the obligations of all parties to the agreement. It creates a guaranteed market for the sale of a business, in the event of one of the triggering events (death, disability, retirement, divorce, bankruptcy of a shareholder). It prevents company stock from falling into the hands of people who are not desirable as owners, including a deceased shareholder's widow and/or children who are not active or knowledgeable about the business operations.

For the purpose of having the agreement qualify as acceptable in the eyes of the IRS with respect to the value of a share of stock, the agreement must:

- **Be for a business purpose.** It should provide for effective continuation of the business, create a market for the stock, etc.

- **Be an arm's-length transaction.** This refers to the situation at the time the agreement is signed and basically states that the agreement must be between a willing buyer and a willing seller for a price mutually agreeable to both, where neither party is under a prior obligation to buy or sell.

- Provide a **definite commitment** on the part of each stockholder not to sell or otherwise dispose of his or her stock during his or her lifetime without first offering it to the corporation or other shareholders at the stipulated price.

- Provide a **definite commitment** on the part of all the stockholders, in which they agree, binding their estates, that they or the corporation **will buy** and the deceased stockholder's estate **will sell** and transfer the shares of stock owned by the deceased stockholder prior to his or her death.

- Provide a **definite commitment** as to the purchase price to be paid for the shares that is **reasonable** and is either
  - a fixed and agreed-upon price per share or
  - a formula for valuation of the price per share

Buy-Sell Agreement Objectives

- Provide for your family's financial security

- Establish a predetermined sales price (value)

- Allow your business to continue with minimal interruption to your customers in the event of your death or disability

- Provide for orderly transfer of your business to your successors

- Allow for long-term retention of your key employees

- Eliminate a nonparticipating spouse or family members from the business

Buy-Sell Alternatives

1. Do nothing
   - Often the plan, never the solution

2. Liquidate the business
   - Forced sales generally yield only 30%–50% of inherent value

3. Gift/bequest business
   - To whom?
   - Transfer tax considerations

4. Set up a buy-sell agreement
   - Creates predictability and removes uncertainty
   - Guarantees market for closely held stock
   - Guarantees liquidity when needed

Stock Redemption Agreements

This type of agreement requires the entity to buy back the stock in the event of a triggering event. For example, Howard and Stan are 50/50 stockholders in a business worth $50 million. At Howard's death, his stock passes to his estate. **The business is obligated to purchase his interest from his estate.** Let's assume that the corporation planned ahead and acquired a $25 million policy on Howard's life, which is owned by and payable to the corporation as beneficiary. Upon Howard's death, $25 million of cash is paid, tax free, to the corporation. Under the terms of the stock redemption agreement, the corporation tenders $25 million to Howard's estate in exchange for $25 million of stock (Howard's entire interest in the business). This stock is surrendered to the treasury, and Stan becomes 100% owner of the business.

STOCK REDEMPTION AGREEMENT AT DEATH

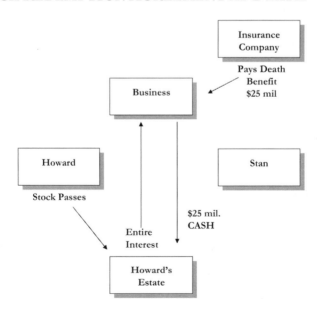

Advantage: Stan now has 100% ownership and control of the business.

Disadvantage: There is no step-up in basis for the survivor. If Stan were to sell the business in the future to outsiders, his basis is still the original basis from when he and Howard started the business many years ago. This exposes him to a potentially enormous capital gains tax. Much of this tax could be avoided through another form of buy-sell agreement.

Cross-Purchase Agreement

Assume again that Howard and Stan are 50/50 owners in a business worth $50 million and growing. Under a cross-purchase agreement, in the event of a triggering event, such as death, **the surviving shareholder is personally obligated** to purchase the interest from the decedent's estate. With proper planning, Howard is the owner and beneficiary of a policy on Stan, in the amount of $25 million, and vice versa. In the event of Howard's death, the stock passes to his estate. The insurance proceeds on his life are paid directly to Stan. Stan then pays cash to Howard's estate, pursuant to the cross-purchase agreement. In return for the cash, Howard's executor transfers the stock to Stan. The result is the same as the stock redemption agreement; i.e., Stan is the 100% owner. However, the big difference from an income tax perspective is that Stan receives a stepped-up basis of $25 million for the interest he acquired from Howard's estate. It does not matter that the cash came from the proceeds of an insurance policy on Howard's life; what matters is that Stan, in fact, paid $25 million, and this establishes his new cost basis for purposes of calculating any future capital gains taxes when Stan sells the business to outsiders.

CROSS-PURCHASE AGREEMENT AT DEATH

```
                                    ┌──────────────┐
                                    │  Insurance   │
                                    │   Company    │
                                    └──────────────┘
                                    Pays Death
          ┌──────────────┐         Benefit
          │   Business   │         $25 mil.
          └──────────────┘              │
                                        ▼
  ┌──────────────┐              ┌──────────────┐
  │    Howard    │              │     Stan     │
  └──────────────┘              └──────────────┘
                                       ↗
    Stock Passes      Entire              $25 mil. Cash
                      Interest   ↗
          ┌──────────────┐
          │   Howard's   │
          │    Estate    │
          └──────────────┘
```

Advantage: Stan has 100% ownership and control of the business. In addition, he has a full step-up in basis for the $25 million interest he purchased from Howard's family. If he decides to sell the business later, his capital gains tax exposure on the $25 million is zero.

Wait-and-See Buy-Sell Agreement

Since none of us has a crystal ball and we do not know what the future holds, consider a buy-sell agreement today that addresses all of the possible contingencies while providing maximum flexibility for shareholders. With a wait-and-see buy-sell agreement, only one thing is left for future determination: identification of the purchaser. Everything else is put in place, drafted, executed, and defined. However, the identification of the

> *Since none of us has a crystal ball and we do not know what the future holds, consider a buy-sell agreement today that addresses all of the possible contingencies while providing maximum flexibility for shareholders.*

purchaser, whether the entity or the surviving stockholder(s), is left open, usually through a series of rights of refusal. At the time of death of a stockholder, the survivors and their advisors can determine who the optimal purchaser should be.

If the tax laws favor a cross-purchase, then that is what will be chosen. If the tax laws at the time of the triggering event favor a stock redemption, then that approach may be taken. This is typically done through a series of rights of first refusal that expire after, say, 30 days and then move to the next option:

1. Option to purchase given **to business**

2. Option to purchase given **to other shareholders**

3. *Obligation* to business **to purchase**

"WAIT-AND SEE" BUY-SELL AGREEMENT AT DEATH

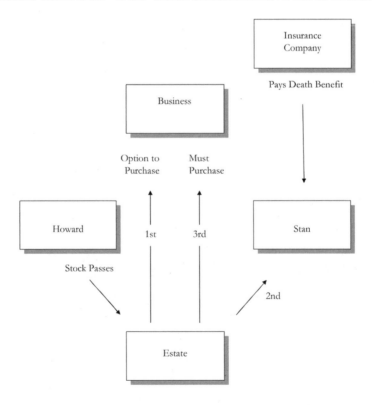

Trusteed Agreements

You could also consider the use of a trustee in a buy-sell agreement. This could avoid potential problems in carrying out the terms of the agreement. While all shareholders are alive, the trustee can be given the responsibility of obtaining the premiums to pay insurance when they come due and can also serve as the custodian of the insurance policy, subject to the agreement. After the death of a shareholder, the trustee will be the beneficiary of the insurance proceeds and can then act as an independent party to pay over the purchase price for the decedent's interest to the executor of the estate and then transfer the business interest to the purchaser. Note: Be careful to avoid the transfer-for-value problem regarding life insurance acquired by the trustee; a number of safe harbors exist.

Buy-Sell Agreement Funding Alternatives

In all buy-sell agreements, certainty of result is important. A properly drafted and executed agreement is the starting point. The final, critical step is to fund the agreement with the proper amount and type of life and disability insurance. Insurance provides cash when it is needed most—at the death (or disability) of a shareholder. Life insurance is typically the least expensive method of funding a buy-sell agreement, assuming shareholders are in reasonably good health.

Let's look at the alternatives:

1. **Cash or Surplus**
   - Will it be available at an undetermined time?
   - The government taxes the accumulation of excess cash held in certain corporate entities.
   - An active partner may need cash for working capital or loan repayment, and therefore, it will not be available to purchase stock.
   - The corporation must recognize gain on any assets liquidated.

2. **Future Corporate Earnings**
   - The corporation has an after-tax obligation.
   - The corporation's borrowing capacity is decreased.

- The corporation is obligated for principal payment plus interest on buyout.
- The assets of the business become collateral for installment obligations.
- The family of the deceased shares the business risk.

3. **Borrow from the Bank**
   - This has many of the same problems from above but an even higher cost (interest rates) and collateral. Fewer banks will make these loans today. Rather, they will likely look to call in outstanding loans when a shareholder dies.

4. **Insurance Funded**
   - The cost is pennies on the dollar.
   - It provides the cash while the partners are working.
   - It creates a surplus account via the cash value buildup.
   - It eliminates the need for the deceased stockholder's family to assume business risk.

Example of Buy-Sell Funding Alternatives for 50/50 Partners

Assumptions

Current business value	$15,000,000
Original business price (basis)	1,000,000
Percent of business to buy	50.00%
Inflation rate	2.00%
Current gross sales	$75,000,000
Profit as a percent of sales	1.00%
Loan interest rate	8.00%
Loan period (years)	20
Annual insurance premium	104,000
Years premium paid	25

Funding Comparison

Cash Flow (from business working capital)		Borrow (installment note)		Insurance	
Business Cost	$7,500,000	Business Cost	$7,500,000	Business Cost	$7,500,000
Current Sales	$75,000,000	Loan Duration	20 years	Premium	$104,000
Net Profit on Sales	$750,000	Loan Interest Rate	8%		
Net Profit as a Percentage of Sales	1.00%				
Total Payments	$7,500,000	Total Payments	$15,277,832	Total Premiums	$2,600,000
New Sales Required to Fund Corporate Redemption Buy-Sell	$750,000,000				

Existing Insurance Funding

In many cases, an analysis of existing life and/or disability insurance previously acquired for business purposes reveals these shortcomings:

- The coverage is not cost-effective. The insurance industry has repriced, and newer policies, with stronger guarantees, are available today.

- It has incorrect ownership and beneficiary designation. The owner and beneficiary of the policy should correspond to the buy-sell arrangement.

- It is the wrong type of policy for this agreement.

- The agreement is funded by an inadequate amount.

- The death benefit is potentially subject to the alternative minimum tax (AMT; in the case of a C corp).

- The insurance is an asset of the corporation and is subject to claims of business creditors (in the case of a stock redemption agreement).

- A potentially large number of policies is needed to accomplish goals (in the case of a cross-purchase).

- It is free from claims of the corporation's creditors but subject to claims of the individual shareholder's creditors (if cross-purchase).

- Transfer-for-value considerations may exist upon the death of the first shareholder. This can cause insurance proceeds to become income taxable.

A thorough policy audit or review should be conducted at least every three years to determine whether insurance funding is optimized.

Exit Path 3: Sale to Employees

Management Buyout (MBO)

A business owner may express a desire to sell his or her business to existing management and key employees. This can often allow the culture of the business to continue and strengthen as employees acquire an equity interest.

Management buyouts are acquisitions of an operating company or corporate unit in which the senior management of the business participates as a significant equity partner in the acquisition.

Considerations

- Does an internal or external management team want to buy a company or a division of a company?

- Does an internal management team want to acquire or substantially increase an equity position?

- Does a minority shareholder(s) desire to buy out a majority (older, retiring) shareholder(s)?

The downside is that management typically does not have the capital or access to credit to make the transaction happen. The selling owner is at risk and may not receive full price for the business. Furthermore, good employees don't necessarily become good owners. They may not have the tolerance for risk or the entrepreneurial spirit necessary to be successful.

Finally, the U.S. Treasury often takes 69 cents in income taxes in an internal buyout of $1 of business value. The employees must pay taxes on income earned and then buy out the seller, who also must pay taxes.

For example:

	Taxes Paid
Buyer: To net $1, business must gross $1.54 @ 35% tax bracket	$.54
Seller: For each $1.00 received from sale, pays 15¢ and nets 85¢	.15
Total taxes paid	$.69

69¢ in taxes paid for $1 of business value

Employee Stock Ownership Plan (ESOP). An ESOP is a qualified retirement plan with vesting schedules, contribution limits, and other ERISA requirements. What makes it unique is that the purpose of an ESOP is to buy company stock, is authorized to borrow money to do so, and is not concerned about investment diversification. ESOPs can borrow money to buy stock of a private company. Since owners can sell stock to an ESOP on a tax-favored basis and avoid capital gains, an ESOP offers many creative uses to explore. If you sell 30% or more of your company to an ESOP, you get to defer the capital gains taxes if you roll over the proceeds to qualifying securities. If you hold on to these securities until death, your heirs will receive a step-up in tax basis and never pay capital gains taxes.

- An ESOP creates a tax-sheltered private market for partial shares in a company when entrepreneurs and family business owners want to reduce the risk of having "all their eggs in one basket."

- The selling shareholder can usually retain substantial control over the company and maintain his or her business and personal philosophy even after a company is partially or wholly owned by an ESOP.

- An ESOP can protect valued employees from potential layoffs that usually result when third parties purchase closely held companies.

- Repayment of the principal of loans taken out by ESOP companies may be made wholly or in part with pretax dollars, which reduces the cost of borrowing for both the ESOP purchase of the shareholder's interest and general borrowing.

- Employees of the ESOP-owned company will have a substantial tax-sheltered retirement benefit that will grow with the company.

Considerations

- The owner desires to create a market for his or her stock without losing control.

- The owner is seeking a method to compensate and reward long-term employees with equity.

- A fairly large and sophisticated pool of employees is necessary.

- There is a desire to defer capital gains taxes, indefinitely under certain circumstances.

- Often, additional leverage (borrowing) is undertaken.

- Annual valuations and disclosure to employees must be made.

Exit Path 4: Sale to Outsiders

A sale to outsiders allows an owner the best opportunity to cash out at the highest price and sever risk of ownership.

The reasons most owners decide to sell include:

- A desire to cash out and remove chips from the table. Most owners have 80%–90% of their net worth locked up in a closely held illiquid business. The prospect of becoming liquid and building a diversified portfolio becomes alluring.

- Fatigue, burn out, or an eagerness to start a new chapter in their lives

- Decreased tolerance for risk—especially today as the credit markets tighten and banks put pressure on business owners. Personal guarantees become more stressful and put personal assets at risk.

- Spousal pressure or divorce. These have caused more than one owner to sell.

- Unwillingness (or inability) to take the business to the next level. The old saying goes, "If the business is not growing, it's dying." What does it take to grow? Often more capital, risk, and hard work.

- Lack of a successor. If the owner does not have children or the children have other business or career objectives, then a sale is inevitable.

- Health issues. A change in health could force a sale.

Why would owners consider their exit *now*? Today's tax and economic factors are quite attractive:

- The Tax Relief Act of 2010 extends the favorable long-term capital gains tax rate of 15% for 2011 and 2012.

- Interest rates are still at the lowest levels in more than 30 years; therefore, the cost of capital for purchasers is low.

- Foreign buyers are keenly interested in entry to U.S. markets.

- Private equity groups are holding billions of dollars that need to be invested. If not invested, monies must be returned to investors.

- Larger corporations are hoarding cash. In certain instances, they are using that cash to make strategic acquisitions for growth.

Growing by acquiring established businesses is often faster and easier than growing organically.

Presale Planning

Before you embark on the selling process, you should engage in presale planning. This allows you to clearly define your options and implement strategies that will enable you to exit your business on your own terms and at the most appropriate time. Minimizing income taxes upon sale is the number 1 issue for most owners. Strategic presale planning can reduce the IRS's cut. The second major goal in each transaction is to maximize the value of the business and create liquidity for the owner, whether a stock or asset sale, a merger, a partial sale, or recapitalization. Ideally, a plan to reinvest those proceeds should be developed prior to the transaction. Steps in presale planning include:

1. Conducting a legal and accounting review to make sure that everything is in proper order—this will avoid problems arising during buyer due diligence

2. Updating and revising, as necessary, your overall tax and estate preservation plan

Business owners should *not* try to sell their businesses on their own. A team, led by a client's exit planning advisor, can retain the services of a competent investment banker who will identify and qualify potential buyers; create and defend a higher valuation; and create a controlled, confidential auction of the business.

Services also include negotiation and structuring of the transaction and facilitation of due diligence and the closing process with your transaction attorney and accountant. The investment banker will add value to the transaction in ways too numerous to list. (See chapter 6, "Exit Planning: Maximize the Sale of Your Business.") If liquidity is paramount, then a sale of the business for cash is superior to all other alternatives.

Far too many owners fail to plan for their eventual exit from their businesses in a timely manner. They buy into the myth that a knight in shining armor will come along and make them an all-cash offer for some outrageously high multiple of earnings (EBITDA) at the precise time they are ready to exit. Others simply get so wrapped up in the day-to-day operations that they never take time to plan for the future. An owner should be prepared to sell at any time and shouldn't wait too long to sell, if that is the ultimate exit objective. Too many owners missed out on the opportunity to sell during 2005–2007 only to see the value of their businesses plummet during 2008 and 2009. The environment for selling businesses today has improved considerably. There is lots of cash available and too few viable sellers.

Now is the time to review your business with an exit-planning advisor to make sure it is marketable and ready to sell for an acceptable price. Any deficiencies should be addressed and corrected well in advance of a sale (refer to the "Company Assessment V-Number" at the end of the next chapter).

Considerations

- Do you desire liquidity?

- Are you considering retirement in the near horizon?

- Is family/management succession questionable?

- Are you concerned about the need to obtain or reinvest capital to stay competitive?

- Has your company been approached by a potential buyer?

- Are you concerned about the concentration of your personal wealth tied up in your business? Do you desire diversification of your assets?

Multiple affirmative answers, or the presence of these situations, are indicators that you are a candidate for a sale or equity recapitalization of your business.

EXIT PATH 5: GOING PUBLIC

Initial Public Offering (IPO)
Only the strongest middle-market or larger companies may even consider this. An IPO is really a financing tool to grow a business rather than a direct

exit plan. In the short term, the owner may be able to take some chips off the table, but the real payoff may not occur until several years later because of selling restrictions on publicly traded stock. IPOs require a tremendous amount of effort, commitment, and compliance, both before and after going public. However, IPOs have many advantages, including:

- Increased valuation

- Public stock giving the business acquisition currency

- Public stock options used to attract and reward top talent

- Infusion of capital deployed to grow the business further

Considerations

- The company is enjoying rapid growth and anticipates strong, continued growth.

- Capital is necessary to maintain momentum.

- The owners do not require immediate liquidity.

- The company has compelling products or services with proven markets.

- The company has a strong management team that recognizes responsibility to stockholders.

- The company has recognized backers (e.g., well-known venture capital investors).

- Being public could enhance the company's position with customers and employees.

There are numerous transactions that go beyond the scope of this book, including joint ventures, strategic alliances, restructuring activities (i.e., divestitures, carve-outs, spin-offs, etc.). Changes in ownership may also take place through leveraged recapitalization, dual-class recapitalization, and share repurchasing.

Sorting all this out to help achieve maximum value from your desired exit transaction requires the engagement of an experienced investment banker or M&A advisory firm.

Once an exit strategy is chosen, well-defined procedures need to be followed in order for the process to be efficient and orderly. Some of the obvious steps that need to be taken by the exit-planning team are:

- Identifying your goals

- Valuation of the business

- Recasting of financials

- Preparation of pro forma financials

- Development of a professional narrative description and overview of the business and the market (offering memorandum or book)

- Identification of potential buyers (could be hundreds)

- Discussions with prospective buyers

- Negotiation with qualified buyer(s)

- Obtaining a letter of intent

- Conducting due diligence

- Execution of purchase agreement

- Closing the transaction and follow up

Understanding the taxation of a particular exit strategy is also crucial. Some considerations are:

- Asset sale vs. stock sale

- Avoiding double taxation

- Tax-free reorganizations

- Reverse mergers

- Spin-offs

- Preserving net operating losses

- Personal goodwill vs. corporate goodwill

- Consulting and noncompete agreements

- Use of charitable planning tools, such as remainder and lead trusts and foundations

The next chapter, "Exit Planning: Maximize the Sale of Your Business," will explore this topic in greater detail and provide a real-life case study.

CHAPTER SUMMARY

As an owner, your business ownership can represent up to 70%–80% of your personal net worth. As a highly precious asset, it has been your main source of wealth generation, income, perks, passion, and future legacy. Defending your business wealth and transferring it represent major life events. You don't get a "do over"; you get one chance to do it right.

> *You don't get a "do over"; you get one chance to do it right.*

It all begins with a proper business succession plan. This plan changes throughout the life cycle of a business. Initially, the business is in survival mode. As it grows, new challenges emerge that require attention to raising additional capital, attracting and compensating employees, and providing selective benefits and addressing contingencies. These contingencies include the disability, death, or retirement of the owner(s) and the creation and funding of buy-sell agreements, nonqualified deferred compensation plans, qualified retirement plans, and asset protection strategies.

As the business (and its owner) matures further, thoughts go to business valuation, exit strategies, retirement, and estate planning. Owners ultimately choose an exit path and pursue the corresponding transfer methods to facilitate transfer to the chosen party:

1. **Family members** - Family succession requires years of careful planning to transition successfully. Decisions such as giving stock to children, selling to them during life, or bequeathing at death

need to be addressed. Equalization among inactive children, timing, and tax planning are crucial.

2. **Co-owners** - Buy-sell agreements are needed to protect you, your family, and your coshareholders and ensure continuity of the business. Proper design and insurance funding are necessary.

3. **Employees** - Identification of a strong management team with the financial wherewithal is the first step. Structuring of the sale to minimize taxes and provide you with security of receiving payments comes next.

4. **Outside buyers** - A sale to outsiders yields the highest price. Our next chapter will address the key steps in this process.

5. **Public offering** - The IPO is losing popularity today. Only the largest companies can consider doing so.

Understand your options and work with your advisors to implement strategies that enable you to exit your business on your own terms, at the most appropriate time, with minimal tax consequences, and at the right value. Be proactive in developing your business succession plan.

1. Identify and communicate your objectives.

2. Obtain a professional valuation of your company for internal transfers or a marketability assessment to understand its value if considering a sale to outsiders, an equity recapitalization, or an IPO.

3. Create a comprehensive financial independence plan to help meet your long-term goals of financial security and preservation of wealth for your family. Your plan should include a financial independence model before you commit to an exit path, in order to help:
    *   Provide a long-term perspective
    *   Demonstrate various what-if scenarios at different values and evaluate your net cash flows after you transfer or sell your business
    *   Help prepare you for your future after the business transition is complete

- • Consider presale planning strategies to reduce income and estate taxes

Don't put off succession planning. Implement today to build, protect, and transfer this precious asset.

BUILDING, PROTECTING, AND TRANSFERRING YOUR BUSINESS

Questions

- ☐ Do you know what your business is truly worth in today's market environment?

- ☐ Are you the sole owner, or do you have partners?

- ☐ Do you have a buy-sell agreement?
  - ☐ What type? ☐ Stock redemption ☐ Cross-purchase ☐ Wait-and-see
  - ☐ When was it last reviewed?
  - ☐ Does it adequately address all contingencies (retirement, disability, death, divorce, termination of employment, bankruptcy of a shareholder, disputes, etc.)?
  - ☐ Is it properly funded with insurance (life and disability buyout)?

- ☐ What would happen to your business if you were unable to show up to work tomorrow? Would it be able to go on? How would your family and your employees be impacted?

- ☐ Do you have any formal documentation or a written strategic plan as to what you would like to happen to your company in the future? When was it last reviewed?

- ☐ Is your business properly capitalized?

- ☐ Have your existing advisors discussed exit planning and your preferred timing, valuation, and strategies to enable this to happen successfully? Or have they been silent?

Succession Planning Questions

☐ Do you plan to *keep* the business for your family or *sell* it at some point?

If keep:

☐ Do you have a family member to whom you would like to pass your business?

☐ How will you derive income after retirement?

☐ How will you provide for your spouse if you die?

☐ Have you provided for payment of estate taxes due so that the business will not be forced into liquidation?

☐ How do you intend to equalize your estate distribution with children not involved in the business?

☐ Are you prepared to give up control of your business to your child?

☐ What documents do you have in place to make sure that this strategy is executed under all circumstances?

☐ What steps have you taken to prepare your heirs to succeed you successfully?

If sell:

☐ To whom would you sell your business? Who will help you identify potential buyers, qualify them, negotiate, and close the sale?

☐ Have you ever received an offer to sell your business? What happened? Was it firm and in writing? Why didn't you accept the offer? Was confidentiality maintained?

☐ Do you know how to realize maximum value? Are you familiar with the competitive auction process of selling a business?

☐ Are you represented by an investment banker or M&A advisor who is experienced in your industry, has a track record of success, and can help you sell for maximum value?

☐ What is your time frame? Are you doing all you possibly can to position your business for sale at maximum value when you are ready?

☐ What terms do you prefer: lump-sum cash or installments?

☐ What is your plan to manage the tax liabilities arising from a sale?

☐ How long do you plan to work for the business after the sale?

Employee Incentive Plans

☐ What have you done to attract, retain, and reward employees?

☐ Do you have a qualified retirement plan?
    ☐ What type?
        ☐ SEP-IRA
        ☐ SIMPLE-IRA
        ☐ Profit-sharing/money purchase
        ☐ 401(k)
        ☐ Defined-benefit (DB) plan
        ☐ Cash balance plan
        ☐ §419 plan
        ☐ Other _____

☐ Do you have a nonqualified deferred compensation plan for yourself or key employees?
    ☐ Who is covered?
    ☐ Is your plan funded or unfunded?
    ☐ How does the vesting schedule work?
    ☐ How are plan assets invested?
    ☐ Do you have a plan document?
    ☐ Do you have a plan administrator?
    ☐ What benefits does it provide?

☐ Have you given equity to employees (stock, options, warrants)?

☐ Are your existing employee incentive plans working?

CHAPTER SIX

EXIT PLANNING: MAXIMIZE THE SALE OF YOUR BUSINESS

By Mark Gould and Mark Jordan, VERCOR Advisors
and Dan Prisciotta

CASE STUDY

"Fortunately, I am not one of those business owners who made a multimillion-dollar mistake by thinking I could sell my company without the assistance of an M&A advisor. My M&A advisor helped me realize the true value of my company and designed a process to result in the best outcome for me. I am extremely thankful for the professional advice and guidance I received throughout the sale process, which in the end yielded a transaction value well beyond what I had initially imagined possible."

The quote above is from a client whose service business was recently sold. It is with good reason that he professes his thankfulness to his M&A advisor: **We sold his business for 82.3 times the company's past 12 months EBITDA and 13 times the following year's projected EBITDA—an unheard-of multiple in any industry.** Several factors were leveraged in the transaction to result in such an unbelievable value for the client's company. What follows is a case study of the sale path and process for this client.

The client's company was about five years old and growing rapidly in the medical services field. It was competing with a handful of much larger publicly owned companies. The client realized that in order to continue on its growth trajectory, the company would need the infusion of some substantial and much-needed working capital in the range of $4–$6 million. The client had planned from the beginning to build the business to be sold, but he felt that it was still too early in the building process to undertake selling the company because the revenues and profits had not yet reached the levels that traditional valuation models suggested could result in a transaction sizable enough to satisfy the client's objectives and help him achieve financial independence.

At this point, the client's financial advisors at Sagemark Private Wealth Services suggested that an M&A advisor be brought in through Equity Strategies Group (ESG) to evaluate the business and help the company satisfy its working-capital needs.

ESG began the process of capital raising and presale planning by initially conducting a series of interviews with the business owner to clearly establish objectives, gain a deeper understanding of the business and industry, and create a marketability assessment. You would be amazed by what can be accomplished through teleconferences and videoconferences! Technology enabled ESG to ask the owner questions about the major factors that would affect the sale of the business (explained further in this chapter), assess the business, establish capital needs, and develop a range of market values for the business (which greatly exceeded the owner's estimate of the value of his business). Ultimately, ESG introduced the owner to several highly qualified M&A advisory firms in its national network. The choice of firms was made on the basis of several important criteria:

- Industry expertise (medical devices, in this case)

- Type of transaction desired (capital raising, leading to a sale of the business, either 100% or partial sale through an equity recapitalization)

- Size of the transactions proposed (you don't want an M&A advisor that is either too big or too small to meet your needs; you want a fit that is "just right," a firm that will provide senior-level attention to your business)

- Personality and chemistry of parties involved

- Finally, geography (because the firms chosen had multiple offices near the client's location, working together was convenient and cost-effective)

After interviewing several of ESG's possible candidates face-to-face, the owner chose the regional office of an internationally respected and seasoned M&A advisory firm to represent his company. After reviewing the company at length, the M&A advisor agreed that the company might be worth much more than the client had anticipated. This was due in part to the company's high growth rate, knowledge capital, systems and processes in place, and geographic competitive advantage. A two-pronged plan was implemented: working capital would be sought while at the same time feelers would be put out to a handful of private equity groups (PEGs) and synergistic companies to get an idea of market interest in an outright acquisition.

Initially, the outreach was to traditional funding sources, consisting primarily of companies that specialized in higher-risk capital such as mezzanine and PEGs. The client was thrilled by the strong response level that was received. However, upon carefully reviewing the proposals that came in from this initial outreach, the client realized that he would have to give up more equity than desired in order to obtain the amount of working capital preferred. This is where things started to become very exciting.

After consulting with the client, the team decided to focus more intently on the possibility of an outright sale of the company. Some of the PEGs initially contacted as funding sources had expressed an interest in an outright or majority purchase. They were to be recontacted for further dialogue about that possibility. Additionally, the client was aware of at least one other large synergistic company that had an interest in entering the space. That company was contacted to open a dialogue about the possibilities of utilizing the client's company as its platform for entrance into the market space. Both of these avenues could be explored without tipping off the industry competitors as to the client's intentions, and this is exactly how the process unfolded.

Similar to the intense interest received while seeking proposals to satisfy the company's working capital needs, the opportunity for an outright acquisition of the client's company resulted in equally heated competition. Proposals were submitted by quite a few PEGs, as well as the synergistic company looking to enter the space. These opening proposals, although varying to great degrees in their value propositions, all fell inside the range of what would be considered the market value of the company, based on generally accepted valuation metrics. It was now time for the M&A firm to earn its fee.

At this point, the M&A advisor put together a valuation package to share with the PEGs and the synergistic company that were vying to purchase the business. The results were magnificent. The analysis estimated the value of the company to a PEG industry competitor and on a discounted future-earnings basis. All methodologies employed in the analysis were based on solid assumptions but pushed the envelope a bit on traditional thinking. As a result, the company's range of values derived in the analysis was far in excess of the offers previously submitted by the PEGs and the large synergistic company. Clearly, the contenders knew that their current proposals would need to be significantly enhanced if they wanted to stay in the running to purchase the company.

The M&A advisor's analysis proved to be very persuasive. Shortly after the analysis was distributed and a few questions were answered, new offers started coming in from the PEGs and the synergistic company. The new offers represented improvements on the original offers by 25%—to as much as 100%. Yes, that's right! One of the contenders actually doubled its initial offer, which was to the tune of an increase of $25 million. The excitement was palpable.

But did the M&A firm stop there? No. Fast-forward a bit and the client accepted an offer for an additional increase of $5 million ($55 million total) from the large synergistic company, representing a value more than four times the client's initial value estimate for the company. Now this is where things really got interesting. During the period after the initial proposals to purchase the company were received but before the client was locked into a no-shop period, an outreach was made to one of the company's primary competitors to determine whether it might have an interest in acquiring the company. This particular competitor was targeted because it was owned by a large multibillion-dollar revenue company, the competitor was known to be suffering from some operational difficulties, and its parent company was on a mission to acquire competitors, evidenced by the fact that the parent company had already completed numerous acquisitions in other industries throughout the current year and in the past few years. Some limited financial information was shared with the competitor, and a few cursory discussions occurred, but before any meaningful dialogue could be established, the client had to act on the synergistic company's current offer, which included a no-shop period. The synergistic company's offer was too good not to sign acceptance; thus, dialogue with the competitor was ceased in compliance with the no-shop provision of the accepted offer. Would the client and his advisors be left wondering forever what might have been with the competitor if only the process could have evolved further down the path? Well, the simple answer is no.

The competitor refused to be deterred by the fact that neither the seller nor anyone on his team could talk about a transaction. Apparently, the competitor was very enthused about a potential transaction to acquire the client's company, and the lack of a dialogue or information exchange was not going to stand in its way. This became evident when a purchase proposal showed up from the competitor, even though no one was in contact with the company at that time because of the no-shop provision in the accepted offer. The competitor's initial purchase proposal represented a $5 million increase over the synergistic company's offer, which had already been accepted. Fortunately, the no-shop provision in the accepted offer was based only on elapsed time on the calendar. As such, the ability to open a new dialogue with the industry competitor was only a few weeks away, and everyone determined that this was the right course of action, once the legal commitment to the synergistic company was satisfied.

After anxiously sitting out the waiting period for the no-shop provision to expire, the client and competitor promptly worked through a new letter of intent. From there, things progressed quite quickly to a completed transaction. The client, together with his advisors, was confident that the competitor was the best fit to purchase the company and lead it into the future. As it turned out, the client stayed on board with the competitor to lead not only his own company that had been acquired by the competitor but also the competitor's competing business in the same space. This is a transaction where both sides were happy with the outcome. The client got what he wanted, a transaction at top value and much-needed working capital for organic growth, and the purchaser got what it wanted, elimination of a competitor, market share, and knowledge capital to lead it into the future.

The seller (client) has said: "Thank you for all your hard work and good counsel this past year. This deal could not have happened without your keen ability to detect and project the hidden value in our business."

His attorney added: "I have been impressed by your energy and creativity and by your attention to the details great and small that can make or break a deal."

Lessons Learned

Several lessons can be learned from this case study, including:

- **Don't go it alone.** As identified in this case study, the final purchase price ended up close to $70 million, whereas the highest financial buyer's offer was around $40 million. The seller would have initially been satisfied with $20 million, so you can imagine his appreciation. The cost of an experienced and capable M&A advisor will generally be more than offset by better deal terms and a price that will be obtained on the basis of only the M&A advisor's experience, efforts, and contribution.

- **It is important to define and control the sale process.** In the above example, potential buyers and offers were already in hand when the competitor was contacted. This created a competitive landscape and may have helped in obtaining a better offer than would have been made in the absence of such competition.

- **Keep an open mind about potential transaction types that might meet your goals and objectives.** In this example, the client initially was most interested in obtaining working capital. The M&A advisor was able to demonstrate that an outright sale might also meet the client's goals and objectives, so both avenues were pursued.

* **Don't underestimate the importance of timing.** The client was trying to fulfill his own need for working capital but was also counseled by the M&A advisor to consider what was happening in the market space, as well as with some competitors. By considering a broader spectrum of items and issues beyond his own immediate need, the client realized that the timing was great for an outright sale.

THE M&A PROCESS

Anyone who has ever owned a business knows that it demands a tremendous amount of time and energy. Needless to say, many people contribute to the growth of a business. Many sacrifices are made along the way. But from the day the business owner sets out a shingle to the moment the doors are closed forever, that business itself takes on a life of its own. It's a round-the-clock job that demands the business owner's constant attention and focus. Regardless of the level of success achieved, every business owner ultimately reaches the point at which he or she asks, "What's next?"

The answer is a function of perspective. Some owners are simply tired of pushing the ball up the hill, while others are looking for a new challenge. Still others feel that they lack the skill set to develop the company beyond its current state. When a business owner contemplates selling a company, many factors, such as retirement, lack of capital, gaps in management, changing industry factors, or desire for greater liquidity, eventually lead him or her to consider several questions. "Should I sell my company now?" "Would I get more money if I waited until the next quarter?" "Who is the right buyer?" These questions can continue ad infinitum.

A business owner is faced with an abundance of decisions when considering selling his or her company. These decisions can be overwhelming. The focus of this section is to provide insight on the mergers and acquisitions process *after* making the decision to sell your business.

Once you have decided to sell your business, your journey could take as little as a few months or up to several years. As with any journey, the more realistic your expectations are, the more likely you are to be pleased with the outcome. In light of that, make your first course of action one of gaining clarity with regard to the life cycle of the entire business sale process.

After gaining clarity, create a sense of structure and order out of what may seem like a disjointed collection of steps that need to be taken. Following a proven five-step process will ensure that you retain a clear vision during what could easily become an extremely frustrating endeavor.

The first step is selecting an investment banker with whom to work through this process. Second, you and your investment banker will compile a plan for the actual sale of the business, including such items as defining your business's value and determining how to handle offers. Third, you will release information on a confidential basis about your company to generate buyers' interests. Fourth, once you have decided on a buyer, you will negotiate the terms and conditions of the sale. Finally, you will work with your investment banker, attorney, and other individuals to complete due diligence and close the deal.

As you gain greater clarity as to what to expect during the process of selling a company, our desire is that you will be more prepared to make the myriad decisions you will face throughout the journey. Deciding who will handle the process is your first major decision. You can either manage the process yourself or delegate it to an intermediary, typically referred to as an investment banker or a mergers and acquisitions (M&A) advisor. We will use the terms "intermediary," "investment banker," and "mergers and acquisitions advisor" synonymously.

M&A Success
The key advantages to utilizing an intermediary are best expressed with the acronym SUCCESS:

1. Strategic fit

2. Understanding the process

3. Creating multiple options

4. Communication and negotiation

5. Expectations are realistic

6. Stay focused on the business

7. Sustain momentum

Let's consider each of these benefits in more detail.

Strategic Fit

A strategic fit means that a synergy exists between the buyer and the seller. Synergy could take many forms, but examples include product, distribution, geographic, and management synergies. Product synergy occurs when the purchaser and seller have complementary products that, when combined, create greater value. Additionally, distribution synergy occurs when the purchaser's products can be distributed through the seller's customer base.

Another type of strategic fit is geographic synergy. This is when a purchaser needs a new geographic presence—where the seller is currently located. Finally, management synergy occurs when management gaps close upon the purchase of a new company. By striving toward a good strategic fit, the business sale yields greater value.

A skilled, experienced intermediary is adept at discovering synergy between buyers and sellers. He or she accomplishes this through a clear vision and definition of strategic marketability.

Understanding the Process

Understanding the process of selling a company is, in many respects, the most vital component to a successful divestiture. Since most business owners have experienced building a company, they naturally assume that they fully comprehend all of the aspects of selling the company. The reality is that they do not. An investment banker, who handles deals constantly, naturally understands the process to a far greater degree.

Let's examine the process in more detail. The following steps illustrate the typical flow of a deal from beginning to end:

Step 1: Initial meeting with investment banker

Step 2: Financial review of the company to determine viability

Step 3: Finalization of engagement agreement with investment banker

Step 4: Presale planning

Step 5: Deal marketing

Step 6: Negotiation and execution of letter of intent

Step 7: Due diligence

Step 8: Closing

Steps 1 and 2, the initial meeting and financial review, are conducted to determine the probability of success and potential fit between the mergers and acquisitions firm and the seller before an agreement to work together is established. ***Step 3 is the finalization of the engagement agreement*** between the intermediary and the seller. The core process of selling a company begins with ***step 4***, otherwise known as ***presale planning***, and concludes with ***step 8, closing***.

Presale planning is a vital part of establishing direction. It involves extensive company fact finding and industry research. The objective of this step is to complete a deal book that outlines key information regarding the company.

Selling a business requires a tremendous amount of *deal marketing* while utilizing many different avenues, including industry contacts, deal databases, and private equity.

Negotiating requires management of all relationships in a transaction with a keen understanding of each party's goals and objectives. There is no magic formula to succeed in this area, but just as in every other area of selling a business, good negotiation involves a specific process that will steer even the most knowledgeable individuals away from potential pitfalls.

The final step is ***closing the deal***. Frequently and somewhat ironically, the most difficult step in the entire process is moving all of the interested parties to a successful closing. Even in the best of circumstances, this is a complicated process.

Creating Multiple Options

Creating multiple options relates to the ability to gather and manage several buyers at the same time. The most common mistake a business owner makes when selling a business is dealing with only one interested party at a time. This limits not only an owner's likelihood of landing a successful deal but also the number of potential offers.

If the marketing outreach process is managed effectively, it leads to a greater probability of securing several interested parties on each deal. Garnering multiple interested parties provides much greater clarity in evaluating the merits of each offer, and it increases the likelihood that a strong, reasonable value will be received.

Communication and Negotiation

Communication and negotiation are the foundation of every deal. Since many business owners see themselves as first-class negotiators, this is by far the most common stumbling block to the process. Much more goes into getting a good deal than one's ability to communicate.

Consider, for example, the owner who focuses exclusively on price in his or her negotiations. He or she may very well get the asking price, not realizing that the purchaser gladly agreed to it because the structure of the deal heavily favored the buyer. Another common development is "sowing the seeds of discord." In this instance, in an attempt to negotiate the best position, the purchaser or seller unintentionally insults the other, thereby creating an antagonistic relationship that impedes the ability to resolve future disagreements.

Another serious pitfall is disclosing an asking price too soon. Business owners often disclose their asking price too early in the process, thereby eliminating the possibility of securing a value beyond their desire.

Expectations Are Realistic

Few sellers have realistic expectations about the process in general. The questions abound: "Is it reasonable to ask for a confidentiality agreement before releasing any information?" "How much information should I release initially?" "When should I meet with the buyer?" "When should I expect a letter of intent, and what, exactly, should that contain?"

"What about earnest money—how much should I ask for and when?" "Who drafts the purchase agreement?" "When do I tell my employees I'm going to sell?" "How long should I allow for due diligence?" "Who pays for due diligence?"

These are just a few of the questions that come up during the process. Knowing what is reasonable dictates how you will respond to the buyer and demonstrates your skill level. Your response also dictates who controls the process, who bargains from a position of strength, and whether you generate an acceptable outcome.

Stay Focused on the Business

The biggest risk a business owner faces when attempting to manage the process himself or herself is the inability to stay focused on the business during the sale process. The owner typically becomes distracted in two ways: time and mental energy. Given the time-consuming nature of the process, an owner might wake up one day to find that he or she is spending a majority of time on the transaction. In addition, when managing the process, the owner frequently becomes mentally drained. Both of these situations create a scenario in which the business suffers during a highly critical time.

Sustaining Momentum

Selling a business is like any other process in which sustaining momentum is critical. When you have positive momentum during the process, good things tend to happen. Conversely, negative momentum tends to feed on itself and diminish the viability of the deal.

Knowledge is power, especially when an owner decides to sell a business. For most owners, the business sale process is a mountain of uncertainty. As previously shown, the right advisor is critical for maximizing the selling price of your company. So how do you evaluate advisors and select the right one? The next section will help you identify what to look for in an intermediary and how to choose the best advisor to manage the sale of your company.

FINDING THE RIGHT INVESTMENT BANKER

Intermediaries take on many different forms but generally fall in three broad classes of professional advisors. There are *Main Street* (often referred to as business brokers), *middle-market*, and *large-transaction* intermediaries. Certainly, the three classes overlap, but firms tend to fall into one of these three groups. The primary differences among the groups are based on *deal size*, *methodology*, *type of buyer*, and *compensation*.

Methodology relates to the process and systems employed by the intermediary. *Main Street* firms work with a process more akin to real estate sales. They focus on acquiring a large inventory of listings, rely on business opportunity advertising, and cobroker deals with other Main Street brokerage firms. Additionally, Main Street firms tend to focus on local and community-based businesses, such as restaurants, dry cleaners, pet stores, auto body shops, lawn care companies, and convenience stores. Relative to the other segments, they spend a small amount of time on presales planning and packaging. Their informal marketing style is composed primarily of local mass advertising and contacts within their personal networks.

The *middle-market* mergers and acquisitions firms are characterized by heavy presales planning; broad, deep research; and wide marketing outreach. They spend significant time on the front end while developing a comprehensive deal book that outlines and discusses all of the key components of the business. Their methodology is heavily focused on researching the marketplace to identify strategic and private equity buyers and executing a comprehensive marketing campaign to attract their interest.

Large-transaction firms tend to employ a financial engineering methodology. They spend the greatest amount of time on presales planning and financial analysis. The universe of purchasers for large companies is much smaller, so less time is spent on actual marketing. Frequently, the ability to create financial synergy is the motivating factor behind large deals.

Deal size refers to the value of the transaction. Main Street intermediaries typically focus on transactions valued up to several million dollars. Middle-market firms generally focus on deals valued from $10 to $100 million, while large-transaction firms typically handle transactions more than $100 million.

The *type of buyer* involved in a Main Street transaction is typically an individual characterized by the following: he or she is usually looking to buy a job, has minimal cash flow, is reliant on seller financing, and has little or no experience as a business owner. In middle-market and large-transaction firms, buyers tend to be larger privately owned companies, private equity firms, or public companies. They normally have cash available for transactions or have bank financing in place, as well as experience in business acquisitions.

The *compensation* structure for a Main Street firm is usually 10%–12% of the transaction, paid at closing. Middle-market and large-transaction firms are typically paid in the form of a commitment fee, or retainer, paid in advance, credited against a performance fee paid upon closing. Commitment fees can range from $30,000 to $70,000 for middle-market deals and can reach the $100,000-plus range for larger transactions. Performance fees on middle-market and large-transaction deals frequently have a tiered structure depending on the deal size and often have additional performance bonuses based on the outcome.

As with any industry, you will find both quality firms and inferior firms. Main Street, middle-market, and large-transaction firms each have their own unique position in the marketplace. The question is not which type of firm is better but which one is best suited for your specific deal.

The Five Keys to Choosing a Firm to Represent You
After determining which type of firm offers the best fit for your company, you can turn your attention to the selection criteria for help in choosing a specific intermediary. While you should evaluate a number of factors when selecting your investment banker, five are key:

1. **P**assion

2. **P**romise

3. **P**rocess

4. **P**erseverance

5. **P**rofessionalism

Passion

Does the investment banker you are interviewing have a sense of passion for his or her work and, more importantly, for the sale of your business? Passion for the project will make all the difference in the sale of your business. Determine whether the banker works on high-quality engagements or whether you would become simply a number.

In other words, you do not want to work with an intermediary who will take any deal that comes along. A firm dedicated to high-quality deals will accept your project only if it senses a reasonable probability that the deal will close.

Promise

Does the banker keep promises? Integrity is the single most important factor in selecting the intermediary. Most of the time, you will not want anyone to know that you are contemplating selling your company. At the very least, you want to have control over who is aware of your plan. The firm you select must have tight control over how information is released to prospective buyers.

In addition, you need to know that your advisor will manage your expectations in accordance with reality. Is he or she simply telling you what you want to hear? Finally, you need a firm that maintains all requisite licensing.

Process

Does the banker have a proven process? Does the intermediary listen to your goals? Every deal is different, and every business owner has unique objectives. Especially during the presales planning phase, an intermediary should focus on your desires as opposed to a predetermined solution. A transaction is about more than closing the deal, and many intangibles need to be considered on the basis of the seller's objectives.

Perseverance

Because the process has so many uncontrollable variables, you will need to be certain that your investment banker will persevere, regardless of how long it takes. The deal life cycle is typically nine to 12 months, but it can take longer. Will your investment banker quit if the road gets tough?

Professionalism

A true professional generally seeks to further himself or herself through academics or credentials and demonstrates a commitment to continuing education. It is also helpful to find an intermediary who has had personal experience as a business owner or who has prior mergers and acquisitions experience in working for a larger entity. An intermediary who has bought and sold businesses for his or her personal portfolio or for an employer will have much greater empathy for the seller.

Of course, even when your selected mergers and acquisitions firm meets all of the criteria and the fit seems perfect, don't expect assurances that the deal will go through. Naturally, if you spend time evaluating your options and if you select wisely, your opportunity for success will increase.

Maximizing Your Value

The one thing that remains common among people wanting to exit their businesses is the desire to find the best deal for themselves and future leaders capable of taking the businesses to the next level. To find such a prospective buyer, you, the business owner, need to prepare in advance so others can see the value that your business offers and evaluate it accordingly.

Obviously, the best time to get out of a business is when performance is at a peak or is showing signs of continued growth. This gives the company maximum bragging rights as it touts such effective practices of an efficient team, a large and satisfied customer base, increasing profits, quality products, excellent goodwill, and other attributes associated with a successful business. Not surprisingly, buyers willingly pay top dollar to acquire such ventures.

Selling a business that is performing well is a win-win situation for both the seller and the buyer. While the seller gets a premium price promising a secure future, the buyer gets a well-organized unit to add to the existing core competencies of the acquiring business. With minimal adjustments, the buyer can hopefully expand his or her reach with the newly acquired business.

Importance of Preparation

A plethora of studies provides insight into what percentage of companies for sale actually sell within a reasonable time. I have seen percentages as low as 20% and some as high as 45%. Unfortunately, because accurate reporting typically does not occur for most nonpublic transactions, it is impossible to know for sure, but my best guess is somewhere in the 30% range. Clearly, something fails to click with the remaining 70%.

In most cases, sellers are inadequately prepared to sell their businesses. They simply do not put in the amount of time and effort required. A buyer has to find a venture valuable enough to accept the risk and receive the corresponding return. The owner has the responsibility to highlight positive features of the business. A well-prepared, carefully executed sale of a business can take anywhere from six months to a year—or even more.

Factors Affecting the Sale of a Business

Many factors add to the marketability of a business. Some of these drivers are external, while others are internal. External factors such as extent of competition (both foreign and domestic), barriers to entry, economic trends, market size, and industry growth are variables that are beyond your control. Everyone has the same constraints to work with.

The factors you can control—ones that influence the appeal of your business—are internal to the organization. Some of these value drivers include sales trends, gross margin trends, profit trends, unique selling proposition of the product or service provided, low customer concentration, sales and marketing, low vendor reliance, management team, recurring revenue, accurate standard operating procedures, business plan, information systems, reputation, ease of transfer, process advantages, and intellectual property. As a business owner, your ability to positively influence the internal value drivers will directly impact the value of your company when it is time to exit.

Work on internal value drivers to build the best possible organization so you as an owner are always ready to sell your company when the time is right. The following provides an overview of the mission-critical drivers that require your attention as you strive to maximize the value of your company.

Sales Trends

We all know that the main objective of a company is to generate an acceptable return to its shareholders. It may be an oversimplification, but you can't have any earnings without sales. Be it a small mom-and-pop shop, an online retailer, or a giant brick-and-mortar store, if it does not generate sales, it has no chance of making money. Not surprisingly, then, a business with steady annual increases in sales is considered more valuable than others.

Gross Margins

Gross profit margin, or gross margin, is one indicator associated with the well-being of an organization. A high gross margin indicates strong company performance. You need to be concerned about a low gross margin in your company, especially if you intend to sell it in the near future.

Gross margin is a gauge of the efficiency with which a business is running.

Though gross margin is an important indicator, business owners often fail to understand its significance and continue to operate ineffectively, resorting to lower selling prices and higher direct costs of their goods. In contrast, even a small increase in the gross margin significantly alters a company's efficiency.

Earnings

As a business owner, you already know that generating a profit is the final imperative for the business to keep running. Breaking even leaves you with insufficient funds to meet day-to-day expenditures or invest in expansion plans.

Real growth requires earnings. The ability to buy assets and new machinery, employ more people, invest in training, explore new markets, initiate novel research, contribute to charities, and indulge in product diversification takes capital.

Without profit, a business loses its sheen and quickly becomes an albatross. If your company does not show significant profits, the chance of receiving top dollar for it is greatly minimized. Identify the factors casting a negative impact on your profits. As a business owner, you must be in touch with everything that happens in your organization.

Unique Selling Proposition

Products and services offered by a company are its flag bearers. Consumers know the products they prefer, even when they may not be familiar with the actual company. Customers typically opt for goods with unique features, frequently referred to as the unique selling proposition (USP) of products.

Customer Concentration

Simply put, customer concentration refers to the degree in which a company has a substantial percentage of revenues generated by a small group of customers. High customer concentration points to a handful of customers contributing significantly to the total annual business of a company. The obvious disadvantage of this situation is the risk of incurring huge losses with the departure of any one of the top customers. In addition, these few customers tend to exert greater leverage against the business.

Low customer concentration, on the other hand, spreads sales across many customers so the business is never dependent on a handful of consumers. Needless to say, business buyers find a company with low customer concentration highly desirable.

Sales and Marketing

A good sales and marketing program is the driving force behind a successful company. Is yours well documented and consistently executed?

Vendor Reliance

Changes in business practices and outsourcing have increased the degree of vendor reliance. How will you manage if one of your key suppliers goes out of business tomorrow or is unable to meet your needs? What impact will it have? Do you have viable alternatives available? Have you considered that relying on only one or two key vendors will lessen the value of your business? Good business practice dictates that you should have a diverse number of suppliers to protect yourself in the event that your vendor experiences problems.

Management Team

As a businessperson, you already know that running a business alone is impossible; you need a strong team. Recruiting a management team that is effective and efficient is critical for an organization to be successful over the long term. The quality of your management team can have a significant impact on the value of your organization.

Standard Operating Procedures

How would you like your organization to be structured: people dependent or procedure dependent? In a people-dependent organization, daily business operations take place because the person responsible for performing them is actually there.

Successful businesses are people independent. Standard operating procedures (SOPs) make the company procedure dependent because they free the organization from dependence on people's subjectivity. Think of SOPs as building blocks of a quality system. Following a quality system gives the assurance of quality products.

Business Plan

The business plan is a document outlining the goals, the vision of a company, and the strategies to be used to achieve success. It is a blueprint of business events to happen in the future. Business plans empower management to make informed decisions.

One very important point: your company will never be perfect. In fact, buyers of companies enjoy seeing the opportunity for improvement in a company; it offers them a chance to bring additional value posttransaction. In light of this fact, you should always keep striving to improve, but when you are ready to sell, take action.

Oftentimes people don't have the energy or drive to continue working on their businesses even as they realize that numerous aspects of their businesses are underperforming. As a result, they continue to hold on to the businesses and watch them unmercifully decline. If you lack the will to continue investing and driving growth in your company, feel ill equipped to manage the future, or simply want to cash in some chips and diversify, then sell now—even if you feel that your company has room for improvement.

BUSINESS VALUE ENHANCEMENT: V-NUMBER

Historically, midsized businesses ($10–$100 million in revenue) tend to sell for three to six times EBITDA while smaller businesses fall in to the two to four times range. Depending on the type of business (generally, service), the value might be a multiple of revenue or gross profit. Again, this is due to the transfer of risk alleviation that is considered high when dealing with a personality-driven or creatively driven business.

We have compiled a list of 23 value drivers and have associated a rating system that will help to determine the company's strengths and weaknesses. We call this list a company assessment and label the outcome as your "V" number, or value number.

In the preparation to sell a company, these 23 points must be carefully considered. A good idea would be for you to rate your company and then have an investment banker rate it as well. Often, your perception is skewed on the basis of your perception of areas that you are directly involved with and the risk you associate with each one. For example, let's say that your business has a single client that comprises half of your total revenue. Let's also say that your company was built around this customer and the relationship is 10 years old. As the business owner, you have little fear of losing the client because of the great relationship you share. You sleep well every night, and everything is working just fine. However, the buyer sees it in a different light, and the risk is valid and measurable. It is valid in that buyer does not have the same relationship with the owner of the other business and measured by the profit generated by this customer. In some cases, it may take a bit of time to address these issues and make your company ready to go to market.

The following list contains the V-number categories that have been established as typical to most businesses in the middle-market range:

- ☐ Low customer concentration

- ☐ Low vendor reliance

- ☐ Low competition

- ☐ Uniqueness of your product

- ☐ High industry growth
- ☐ High barriers to entry
- ☐ Insulated from foreign threats
- ☐ Large market size
- ☐ High recurring revenue
- ☐ Positive sales trend
- ☐ Positive gross margin trend
- ☐ Positive profit trend
- ☐ High market share
- ☐ Strong management team
- ☐ Easy to transfer
- ☐ Technology/process advantages
- ☐ Intellectual property
- ☐ Distribution leverage
- ☐ Strong history/reputation
- ☐ Strong sales and marketing
- ☐ Strong infrastructure
- ☐ Strong information systems
- ☐ Accurate SOPs (standard operating procedures)/business plan

Understanding and correcting these issues may take some time and money. Remember that for every dollar of profit you add, and concentrating on high-risk dissipation, you will yield a multiple of that dollar paid, with more value added to the deal at closing. So an expense today is easily justified when you consider that it will be absorbed when the increased earnings are multiplied in purchase price. Please take a few moments and complete the V-number form for your company on the following page.

COMPANY ASSESSMENT

V-Number

A value driver measures systems, processes, and resources that create sustainable value. Rate your company for each of the following 23 value drivers by placing an "X" in the box that is most reflective. Use 1 for the lowest score and 5 for the highest. For drivers 24 and 25, place an "X" in the box that approximates your annual revenue and earnings numbers. Don't worry about an overall score. The goal is to get a picture of where your strengths and areas for improvements are.

Value Drivers	1	2	3	4	5
1. Positive sales trend					
2. Positive gross margin trend					
3. Positive profit trend					
4. High recurring revenue					
5. High market share					
6. Uniqueness of your product					
7. Low customer concentration					
8. Distribution leverage					
9. Low competition					
10. Low vendor reliance					
11. Strong management team					
12. Strong sales and marketing					
13. Strong infrastructure					
14. Strong information systems					
15. Strong history/reputation					
16. Easy to transfer					
17. Accurate SOPs/business plan					
18. Technology/process advantages					
19. Intellectual property					
20. Insulated from foreign threats					
21. Large market size					
22. High barriers to entry					
23. High industry growth					
24. Annual gross revenue	$0 to <$5M	$5M to <$10M	$10M to <$20M	$20M to <$50M	>$50M
25. Annual net income	$0 to <$500K	$500K to <$1M	$1M to <$5M	$5M to <$10M	>$10M

Courtesy of VERCOR Advisors

CONCLUSION

This book addresses what you know in your heart you need to do in order to take control of and defend your personal, family, and business wealth. It provides the strategies, tactics, and road map—but motivation to act must come from you.

As a successful entrepreneur, investor, and business leader, you represent the backbone of this country. You epitomize innovation and risk taking in the pursuit of excellence. You fuel our economy and build thriving business enterprises that, in turn, create jobs, capital, competition, financial security, and prosperity. You have overcome obstacles and met a myriad of daily challenges. However, achieving success often blocks you from satisfactorily addressing your long-range personal, family, and business objectives.

Stuart F. Smith was the architect of my firm's philosophy of "Serve First." Smith graduated from the Wharton School of the University of Pennsylvania in 1924 and went on to blaze a tremendous career as an advisor to many high-net-worth families. He addressed the paucity of proactive wealth preservation planning. Smith's "creed" says that many successful people, when it comes to addressing their personal planning needs and wealth stewardship, are "*in a mess.*" He went on to say: "*Their family and business ultimately suffer from that mess. It isn't their fault. They think they're alright. But someone strong is going to show them the light. I am going to be that person. I will be patient with them. I will inform them. I will concentrate on their problems. I will look them in the eye and quietly, gently, with dignity and singleness of purpose on their behalf and with a good-natured, courteous, persistent intelligence show them weaknesses in their current plans and help correct mistakes they have made. They will receive great personal financial security from my influence on their lives so their family can receive the legacy they have worked so hard to achieve. Armed with logical reasoning I will with every decent thing in me, persist, insist, persuade, until they put their financial house in order. I owe them that. I am strong enough to fight for that belief."*

I hope that the insights and wisdom in these pages will motivate many to put their financial house in order and defend their wealth.

—Dan Prisciotta

ABOUT THE
AUTHORS

Daniel A. Prisciotta—CFP, CPA/PFS, ChFC

Dan is a Prestige Advisor within Sagemark Private Wealth Services Group, helping high-net-worth families throughout the United States defend their wealth. He is also the founder and managing partner of Equity Strategies Group, whose mission is to develop and execute successful business exit strategies. With more than 25 years of wealth preservation experience, Dan delivers a superior level of commitment and expertise necessary to create unique situation-based financial strategies and translate them into immediate, actionable steps. He puts a premium on all of his relationships, and he believes that a successful outcome can be realized only through a shared vision.

By partnering with his clients, Dan is able to help them put their financial houses in order. Having worked on more than 2,000 cases, his knowledge of the steps required throughout the planning process enables him to explore multiple design scenarios before presenting the appropriate client-tailored options—no cookie-cutter solutions!

Dan understands your desire to defend your wealth and reach financial independence with certainty and tax efficiency. He recognizes your need to build your business and plan for your future exit. Dan shares your passion for leaving a legacy to your loved ones.

As an active member of the financial, business exit and estate preservation community, Dan is always on the cutting edge of industry and legislastive changes. He holds the designations, certifications, and affiliations listed below:

- ◆ Certified Financial Planner (CFP)

- Certified Public Accountant (CPA)*

- Personal Financial Specialist (PFS) designation

- Chartered Financial Consultant (ChFC)

- Member of the American Institute of CPAs (AICPA)

- Member of the NJ Society of CPAs

- Member of the Alliance of Mergers and Acquisitions Advisors

- Member of the Society of Financial Service Professionals (SFSP)

- Member of the Financial Planning Association (FPA)

- Registered Securities Principal and Representative

- Member of Sagemark Consulting's Private Wealth Services and Resource Groups

- Certified Continuing-Education Instructor

Dan is a much sought after speaker on the topics of Business Exit Strategies and Financial and Estate Planning and has presented at numerous industry and association events. He has been interviewed by CNN Business News, WFAS Financial Radio and quoted in the *LA Times, The Record* and *Journal New Business* columns.

Dan is a magna cum laude graduate of Fairleigh Dickinson University, with a BS degree in accounting. He resides in Ramsey, New Jersey with his wife, Teresa, and their two children, Michelle and Danny.

* Licensed, not practicing public accounting

Russ Jones—Executive Director, Private Wealth Services Group of Sagemark Consulting/Lincoln Financial Advisors
Russ's primary area of expertise lies within the high-net-worth market, where he is responsible for the development of key concepts and strategies that will have a significant impact on the financial lives of these individuals and their families.

Prior to assuming his role as executive director, Russ was the regional chief executive officer of Sagemark Consulting in Denver for 12 years. He led and supported a team of 100 financial planners and management personnel who provided sophisticated estate, business, and investment strategies to affluent business owners and individuals, whose net worths were typically seven to 10 figures. Russ has been a main platform speaker at the annual conference of the International Association of Financial Planning, the Allied Jewish Federation's Annual Estate Preservation Forum, GAMA International's LAMP meeting, and numerous technical and business management sessions for Sagemark's Managing Directors and senior financial advisors.

Mark Jordan has a unique, multidisciplined background composed of advanced tax strategies and estate and financial markets knowledge. He also holds an MBA, a BS in business administration, and various professional designations. He has been involved in numerous transactions both personally and as an advisor. He is also founder and managing partner of VERCOR, a middle-market mergers and acquisitions firm. Mark has authored and coauthored six books.

Mark Gould has been actively involved in the mergers and acquisitions industry for more than 20 years. Mark holds numerous professional designations, including certified business intermediary (CBI), which, together with his broad depth of transaction experience, brings a practical application and perspective to his clients. He has been president of six business entities and has had ownership in more than 10 businesses. He is also cofounder of VERCOR.